Technical Design Solutions for Theatre
The Technical Brief Collection
Volume 3

Technical Design Solutions for Theatre
The Technical Brief Collection
Volume 3

Edited by

Bronislaw J Sammler, Don Harvey

Focal Press
Taylor & Francis Group

NEW YORK AND LONDON

First published 2013
by Focal Press
70 Blanchard Rd Suite 402
Burlington, MA 01803

Simultaneously published in the UK
by Focal Press
2 Park Square, Milton Park, Abingdon, Oxon OX14 4RN

Focal Press is an imprint of the Taylor & Francis Group, an informa business

Notices
Knowledge and best practice in this field are constantly changing. As new research and experience broaden our understanding, changes in research methods, professional practices, or medical treatment may become necessary.

Practitioners and researchers must always rely on their own experience and knowledge in evaluating and using any information, methods, compounds, or experiments described herein. In using such information or methods they should be mindful of their own safety and the safety of others, including parties for whom they have a professional responsibility.

Product or corporate names may be trademarks or registered trademarks, and are used only for identification and explanation without intent to infringe.

Library of Congress Cataloging in Publication Data
Sammler, Bronislaw J. and Don Harvey
Technical design solutions for theatre: the technical brief collection / Bronislaw J. Sammler and Don Harvey.
3 v. : ill. ; 28 cm.
Reprint of articles from Technical brief
Includes index.
ISBN 0240804902 (v. 1)   0240804929 (v. 2)
        0415824309 (v. 3)
1. Stage machinery. 2. Theaters—Stage-setting and scenery. 3. Theaters—Lighting 4. Theatres—Sound effects
PN2091.M3 T43 2002
792.02/5

ISBN: 978-0-415-82430-9 (pbk)
ISBN: 978-0-203-54913-1 (ebk)
ISBN: 978-0-415-82429-3 (hbk)

Typeset in ITC Bookman by Don Harvey
Drawings by Don Harvey

Printed in China

Table of Contents

COSTUMES

Taking a Pattern from an 18th-Century Clothing Piece — *Linda Kelley-Dodd* — 2

Deriving a Pattern for 18th-Century American Men's Fall-Front Breeches — *Linda Kelley-Dodd* — 5

LIGHTING

Calculating LED Circuit Requirements — *Daniel T. Lisowski* — 10

Magnetic Color Flipper for a Source Four® 10° Follow Spot — *Kathryn Krier* — 13

Focus Track and Chair — *Jonathan A. Reed* — 15

The Panhandler: Pillow-Block Assist for ERS Panning — *Brian Swanson* — 17

Modular Stor-Mor Solution — *Joel Furmanek* — 18

The Cadillac of Rolling Booms — *Matt Welander* — 20

Dimmable Fluorescents — *Alan Hendrickson* — 22

Guidelines for Using Neon on Steel Structures — *Chris Swetcky* — 25

Using Black Screening Material As Inexpensive "Black Scrim" Panels — *Barbara Tan-Tiongco* — 27

LIGHTING EFFECTS

A Motion-Controlled Practical — *Pablo Souki* — 30

Overlooking-the-Town Light Box — *Christopher Jensen* — 32

A Light-Beam Box — *Michael Kraczek* — 34

Safe Chimney Smoke Generators — *Maura LaRiviere* — 36

An Inexpensive Fog Chiller — *Steven Hood* — 39

Constructing a Battery-Powered Candle — *Eric Lin* — 41

Simulating Neon with Rope Light — *Chris Russo* — 42

A Liquid Lamp — *Karen Walcott* — 43

PAINTING

A Durable Plaster Texture Revisited — *Owen M. Collins* — 46

An Affordable Gold Leaf Finish — *Ben Stark* — 47

A More User-Friendly Lining Stick — *Don Harvey* — 49

Large-Scale Crackle Paint Effect — *Ben Stark* — 52

A Clean Solution for Colored Dirt — *Nora Hyland* — 53

Using Alum to De-Wrinkle Drops — *Nicole L. Bromley* — 55

PROJECTIONS

Melded Technologies: Video Projections and Moving Mirrors — *M. Barrett Cleveland* — 58

Low-Memory, High-Quality Digital Images for the Stage — *David B. Carter* — 61

A Servo-Controlled Projector Dowser — *Lung-Kuei Lin* — 64

Low-Cost RP Screens for the Stage — *Daniel J. Anteau* — 66

A Stock Batten-Mounted Projector Bracket — *Pierre-André Salim* — 68

PROPS

Making a Severed Head	*Michael Banta*	72
Replicating Bones, Part I: Molds	*Julia Powell*	75
Replicating Bones, Part II: Casting	*Julia Powell*	78
Realistic Stage Stun Gun	*Mike Vandercook and Joe Huppert*	80
CO$_2$ Gunshot Wound	*Brian Smallwood*	82
Three Favorite Blood Recipies	*Jennifer McClure*	85
Three Techniques for Applying Stage Blood	*Sandra Jervey and Jennifer McClure*	87
Urinal Head Wax Mold Casting Process	*Andrew Hagan*	90
A Device to Simulate Urination Onstage	*Ryan C. Hales*	93
Bas-Relief Sculptures in Durham's Rock Hard Water Putty®	*Greg Blakey and Samantha Porter*	94
A Cremora®-Fueled Pyrotechnic Alternative	*Adam J. Dahl*	96
A Remotely Extinguished Cremora®-Fueled Flame Effect	*Chris Peterson*	99
A Mechanism for a Battery-Operated Torch	*Katherine Gloria Tharp*	102
A Safe Glass Mirror Breaking Effect	*John McCullough*	104
1970s' Period Pull-Tab Beverage Cans	*Jeff Smejdir*	105
An Affordable Chair for *Sweeney Todd*	*Colin Buckhurst*	108
Using a Trolling Reel to Move Small Furniture and Props	*Steve Schmidt*	110
Hand-Held Dancing Fireflies	*Andrew V. Wallace*	111

RIGGING HARDWARE

An Adjustable Flat Hanger	*Moshe H. Peterson*	114
A Versatile Flat-and-Track System	*Rich Desilets*	115
A Convenient Shop-Built Mini-Arbor	*Joe Hamlin*	116
A Sleeve for Increasing Arbor Capacity	*Drew Becker*	118
Positioning Catches for Traveler Track	*Justin Elie*	119
Plans for a Double Kabuki Drop	*Kate Wicker*	120
An Inexpensive Quiet Shop-Built Track System	*Shaminda Amarakoon*	122
A Simple Drop Rig for Small Payloads	*Andrew V. Wallace*	124

RIGGING TECHNIQUES

Flying an Actor with a Ghost-Load Rig	*Mark Prey*	126
Hardware for a Ghost-Load Rig	*Michael Madravazakis*	128
An Inexpensive Controllable Drip System	*Stuart Little*	131
Fabric Swag Scene Changes Made Easy	*Aaron Bollinger*	133
Tilting a Wall	*Greg Winkler*	135
Pick Length Calculator: A Quick Reference	*Andrew James Gitchel*	137
Rocking a Batten for *Pirates of Penzance*	*Brian Frank*	139

A Tricking Batten System for Stretched Panels	*Aaron Verdery*	141
Falling Leaves Effect for the Stage	*Kellen C. McNally*	143
A Temporary Lineset for Lightweight Objects	*Amanda J. Haley*	145
Automating a Snow Bag	*Ryan Retartha*	146
Soaker-Hose Rain Effect	*Thomas R. Delgado*	147
A Fan Powered Confetti Drop	*Alex Bergeron*	148
A Device for Dropping Sand from Above	*Mike Backhaus*	150
Four Continuous-Beam Formulas for Stage Battens	*Dan Perez*	151

SAFETY

An LED and SPST Safety Feedback	*Jim Siebels*	154
Introducing a Live Animal to the Stage	*Kristan Falkowski*	155
Comparison of Safety Wrap Techniques for Counterweight Linesets	*John Starmer*	157

SCENERY

Pneumatically Actuated Caster Planks	*Drew Monahan*	162
Making Oversized Cove Moulding on the Table Saw	*Nick Bria*	165
Using 18-Gauge $1\frac{1}{2}$"-Square Tube Steel to Build Taller and Longer	*Annie Jacobs*	167
Compound Miters Simplified	*Peter Malbuisson*	169
Kerfing Steel for Larger Arcs	*Andrew Farrow*	172
"Pacing" Groundrow Elements	*Kevin Hines*	174
Building Stairs from Scrap Plywood	*David A. Griffith and Gerald Kawaoka*	176
Isolating Door Vibration in Flats	*Sam Michael*	177
Changing Portraits with Ganged Sunroofs	*Andrew F. Southard and Don Harvey*	179
Eleven Quick Tips	*Craig Martin*	181
Flexi-Pitch Handrail	*Dorian James Robison*	182
Fauxberglass: An Inexpensive Alternative to Fiberglass	*Kalen Larsen*	184
Setting Up an X-Ref Master File	*Ted Griffith*	186
Providing a Column Shaft with Entasis	*Dan Perez*	189

SCENERY DECKS

Doors on Rakes: Avoiding Gaps and Wedging	*Nathan Tomsheck*	192
The Flip Floor: A Two-Sided Deck Surface	*Bradley Powers*	194
A Tracking System for Tricsuit Decks	*Gegg Carlson*	197
An Interchangeable Lift-Lid System	*David Calica*	200
A Low-Profile Sprung Floor	*Erich Bolton*	201
Two Methods for Planking Floors Quickly	*James Zwicky*	202
A Sandwich-Style Flip Floor	*Don Harvey*	205

Comparing Four Standard Stock Platforms: Part I - Weight, Cost, and Strength	*Sean Culligan*	207
Comparing Four Standard Stock Platforms: Part II - Structural Calculations	*Sean Culligan*	210
A Simple and Durable Touring Deck	*Joe Stoltman*	213
A Fast and Inexpensive Grooved Floor	*Hannah Shafran*	216

SCENERY HARDWARE

Actor-Friendly Pneumatic Brakes	*Josh Prues*	220
A Simple Hydraulic Caster Lift System	*SteveBeatty*	222
A Floating Knife for Tracking Scenery	*Guerry Hood*	225
A Locking Mechanism for Telescoping Tubing	*Chris Brown*	227
A Caster Grid	*Justin McDaniel*	229
Opera-Scale Rotating Walls	*Timothy D. McCormick*	231
Tracked Scenery Using PVC Glides	*John D. Ervin*	234
Compact Toggled Tip-Jacks	*Stephen Henson*	236
Electromagnets as Scenic Connectors	*Mikey Rohrer*	238
Black Carpeting as a Glide for Narrow Scenic Units	*Don Harvey*	239

SCENERY MECHANICS

Guiding Scenery with Linear Bearings	*HaeWon Yang*	242
A Curved Track and V-Groove Caster Guide	*Nathan Wells*	244
Tripping Casters with Pneumatics: System Basics	*Kimberly Corbett*	246
Stabilizing Pneumatic Lift Jacks	*Steven Green*	249
Building Portable Pneumatic Systems: An Overview	*Lily Twining*	251
Using an Endless-Loop Winch as a One-Way Drive	*Jonathan Pellow*	254

SCENERY TOOLS

Two Useful Shop Tools	*F. Chase Rozelle III*	256
An Affordable Steel Roller	*Chris Brown*	257
Handy Tip Carts	*Steven Neuenschwander*	260
A Shop-Built Ladder Standoff	*Rich Desilets*	261
A Shop-Built Rotisserie for Welding Large Units	*Brian Dambacher*	262
A Winch-Driven Bench-Mount Panel Saw	*Jeff Smejdir*	264
A Shop-Built Sliding-Head Hold Down	*Eric Casanova*	267

With this book, *Technical Design Solutions for the Stage, Volume 3*, we literally and figuratively close the cover on a 30-year project aimed at keeping ourselves and technical theatre colleagues throughout the world from having to reinvent the wheel in the face of each unfamiliar technical challenge.

We know that no one could ever fully meet that objective completely, but we've kept our eye on that target and we're confident that we've succeeded reasonably well. We are proud to have made the attempt and we are even more proud to offer you the results.

In preparing this particular set of articles we've come to recognize how radically technology has changed over the last three decades. We routinely use tools and approaches today that weren't available to us 10 or even 5 years ago – CNC routing, for instance. But reworking this set of articles has also brought us to recognize with satisfaction how many of the good ideas we've had the good fortune to publish have withstood the test of time and technological change.

It's also brought us to recognize something even more significant: that those same individuals who demonstrated drive and commitment in sharing their solutions to technical problems by writing these articles have developed careers characterized by exactly that same drive and commitment. Many of those who wrote *Technical Briefs* have since become recognized leaders in theatre technology throughout the world.

Bronislaw J. Sammler ● Donald A. Harvey

To make this book and its two companion volumes as useful as possible we suggest you read through each article in each volume at least once and at a leisurely pace – to put the ideas in the back of your head, in effect – before shelving the books for future reference.

Once you've done that, you should remember roughly where you read about that particularly clever approach and, to help you find it quickly, we've included a great search tool as the last eleven pages of this volume...

The Combined Topical Index to Volumes I through III.

TECHNICAL BRIEF

Costumes

Taking a Pattern from an 18th-Century Clothing Piece — *Linda Kelley-Dodd*

Deriving a Pattern for 18th-Century American Men's Fall-Front Breeches — *Linda Kelley-Dodd*

Taking a Pattern from an 18th-Century Clothing Piece

Linda Kelley-Dodd

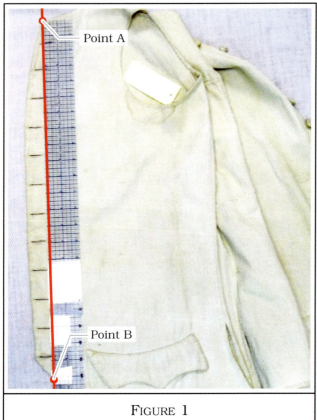

FIGURE 1

This article describes a method for deriving an "as-built" pattern from an existing garment: an 18th century waistcoat. This method, which, though simple, requires careful observation and meticulous documentation, can help you manage your time well, and will give you the best pattern possible.

BACKGROUND: GETTING STARTED

Most of the few remaining 18th-century garments are held by museums. Finding the right museum for your purposes and getting and keeping the willing cooperation of museum staff requires that you treat holdings reverently and use your time and theirs efficiently.

You begin by building a professional working relationship with a textile or clothing curator. Once you've learned which nearby repository has the piece that you want to study, meet with the curator to describe your objective. The curator may be able to share unexpected advance information that other researchers have gathered, and will certainly be instrumental in providing you with the necessary access. In your meeting, describe what you'll need and what you'll be doing to the garment itself. Set up a time to work, realizing that the "work date" may be a month or more away: the garment may need to be pulled from storage, a work space will have to be set up, and the curator will probably want to be on hand while you work.

Pack the following materials for your work: $\frac{1}{8}$" graph paper, mechanical pencils, lead (*F*, *HB*, red and blue), magnifying glass, camera, grid ruler, and a 60" measuring tape. A note about graph paper: most graph paper has a black or non-reproducing blue grid of lines of uniform weight. I prefer sheets of my own design: a letter-sized piece of white paper with a dark grey 1" grid overlaid on a light-grey $\frac{1}{8}$" grid. This paper, which can easily be generated in either AutoCAD® or Adobe Illustrator®, is easier to read and xerox.

DERIVING THE PATTERN

In general, museums document only a garment's overall size for their records so, on your appointment date, begin by assessing the garment's structure and taking a more nearly complete set of measurements. On a waistcoat, for example, you would note the length of the center-back, or CB, the hem, the side seams, the armscye (front and back), the front panel chest width, the back panel chest width, etc. Having documented those measurements, follow the steps below.

Step 1. Like many other garments, the waistcoat consists of a number of flat fabric panels sewn together. Figure 1 shows the waistcoat's back and front right panels folded back so that the front left panel can be laid flat and its shape clearly revealed. With the panel laid out, establish the direction of the panel's grain and use a ruler to establish a grainline (GL) on which two distinctive points can be used as landmarks. In Figure 1, the ruler is laid along the GL and landmark points A and B, and intersections with GL are identified.

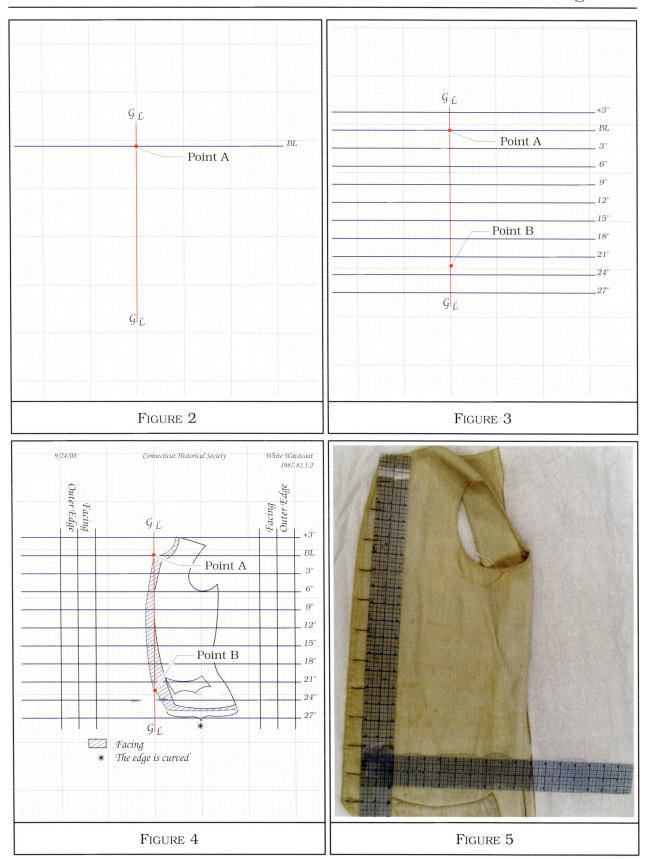

FIGURE 2

FIGURE 3

9/24/08   *Connecticut Historical Society*   *White Waistcoat*
1987.82.1.2

Facing
Outer Edge

Facing
Outer Edge

+3″
BL
3″
6″
9″
12″
15″
18″
21″
24″
27″

Point A

Point B

▨ Facing
✳ The edge is curved

FIGURE 4

FIGURE 5

Step 2. In a convenient place near the center of your graph paper, draw a heavy red line and label it "GL". Along a convenient gridline, draw a heavy blue line through and perpendicular to GL. Label the blue line "BL". Decide which landmark point – A or B – will be easier to measure from (A, in this case) and mark that point at the intersection of GL and BL (see Figure 2).

Step 3. Next, treating every $\frac{1}{8}$" gridline on the graph paper as 1" on the garment, locate the other landmark point (B, in this case) correctly on GL. Follow this by laying out, on every third gridline, as many more heavy blue lines perpendicular to GL as you'll need to extend beyond the garment in both directions. Label these lines as shown in Figure 3.

Step 4. Now, using an *F* lead and working from GL, sketch a reasonable facsimile of the panel you're studying. The sketch doesn't have to be exact since it only has to serve as a map on which you'll document the garment's true measurements. Make sure, however, that the outline of the sketch passes through points A and B where it should. On the sketch, draw in and label the panel's distinctive features – in this case, a pocket, a facing and a curved edge that appears straight. Finally, mark off columns for the measurements of the distinctive features as shown in Figure 4.

Step 5. Making sure that your GL ruler stays precisely in place on the garment, use a second ruler as shown to measure the distances between GL and the distinctive features at points corresponding to the blue lines on your sketch. Figure 5 shows the second ruler in position to measure the corners of the pocket. Enter these numbers in the columns on the graph paper. (Note that, for clarity in Figure 5, a piece of white cloth has been used to hide all panels except the front left panel.)

SOME LAST NOTES

You may be able to use entomologist's pins to mark points on the garment if the museum allows it. The pins can be eased between the woven garment threads and should be removed shortly after use. Whether to measure in English or metric units is up to the user and, for that matter, so is the choice of measuring and sketching on a 3" grid, a 2" grid, or something else. A 3" grid works well enough for most purposes, but many closer-spaced points may have to be used around armscyes, pockets, and other details.

ACKNOWLEDGMENTS AND BIBLIOGRAPHY

The author extends special thanks to the staff of the Connecticut Historical Society for so generously sharing their time, space, and expertise in documenting this particular 18th-century waistcoat, which was a gift of Mrs. Nancy Burdge.

Arnold, Janet. *A Handbook of Costume.* Reprint. Hong Kong: Macmillian London Limited, 1978.

Baumgarten, Linda, John Watson, and Florine Carr. *Costume Close-Up, Clothing Construction and Pattern, 1750–1790.* Williamsburg, VA: The Colonial Williamsburg Foundation in association with Quite Specific Media Group LTD., 1999.

Waugh, Nora. *Cut of Men's Clothes.* New York: Theatre Arts Book, 1987

This article documents the construction of a pair of 18th century American men's fall-front breeches and publishes the derived pattern.

THE BREECHES' BACKGROUND AND HISTORICAL CONTEXT

These breeches are part of a three-piece suit worn by Henry Thompson Curtiss (1751–1814) at his December, 1778 wedding to Phebe Sherman (1759–1826). Curtiss and his family lived in Stratford, Connecticut, and the garment is now held by the Connecticut Historical Society.

The garment reflects its times. 1778 was a promising year for the American Revolution and, to some degree, for the Curtisses. In that year, France became the first country to recognize the Declaration of Independence, and by the end of the year the British forces were focusing their attention farther south. Nevertheless, most colonists, probably including the Curtisses, were far from well-to-do or even financially comfortable.

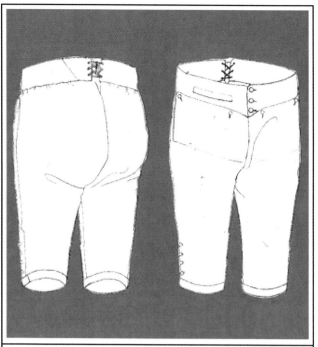

FIGURE 1: MR. CURTISS' FALL-FRONT WEDDING BREECHES

THE BREECHES' MEASUREMENTS AND DESCRIPTION

The tailor is unknown and the construction is fairly crude. The garment is unlined except for the waistband and knee bands, and the linen on the left front panel of the leg shows signs of staining. Mr. Curtiss was not a large man. The breeches waist measures 31" (78.7 cm); its inseam, $16\frac{3}{4}$" (42.5 cm); its outseam, $23\frac{1}{2}$" (59.7 cm); its girth front, 6" (15.2 cm); and its girth back, $14\frac{1}{2}$" (36.8 cm). The outer (fashion) fabric is a white woven-twill linen and the fall is edged with irregular pieces of a plain-weave linen that may have been scraps. Lining is present on the interior of the waistband and the knee bands. It is the same plain weave linen at both locations.

The facings are cut in various shapes from both the white woven–twill linen and the plain-weave linen. The fall and front side pockets have been combined to create a long fall front and closes with four covered buttons. The fall is sewn across the front of the breeches 3" (7.6 cm) down from the waistband creating a visible stitch line. The waistband closes center front with three large, domed buttons of the linen woven-twill. Three sets of overcast thread eyelets and a braided-cotton cord are located at the back of the waistband for adjustment. The hand-stitching is done in linen thread.

A watch pocket with a welt opening is set into the right side of the waistband. The welt is made of the white-woven twill linen and is $5\frac{3}{8}$" (13.7 cm) in length. The knee band is $1\frac{1}{2}$" (3.8 cm) wide and $8\frac{1}{2}$" (21.6 cm) long. The knee bands appear to have been shortened at a later date and a 19th century white glass button added in place of the presumed original knee buckles. The knee slit has a four-button placket of domed buttons covered in the linen woven twill.

For an overview of the instructions on deriving a pattern from existing historical garments, consult the preceding article, "Taking a Pattern From an 18th-Century Clothing Piece." Understanding the procedure for deriving a pattern from these breeches relies on concepts, terms, and abbreviations introduced in the earlier article.

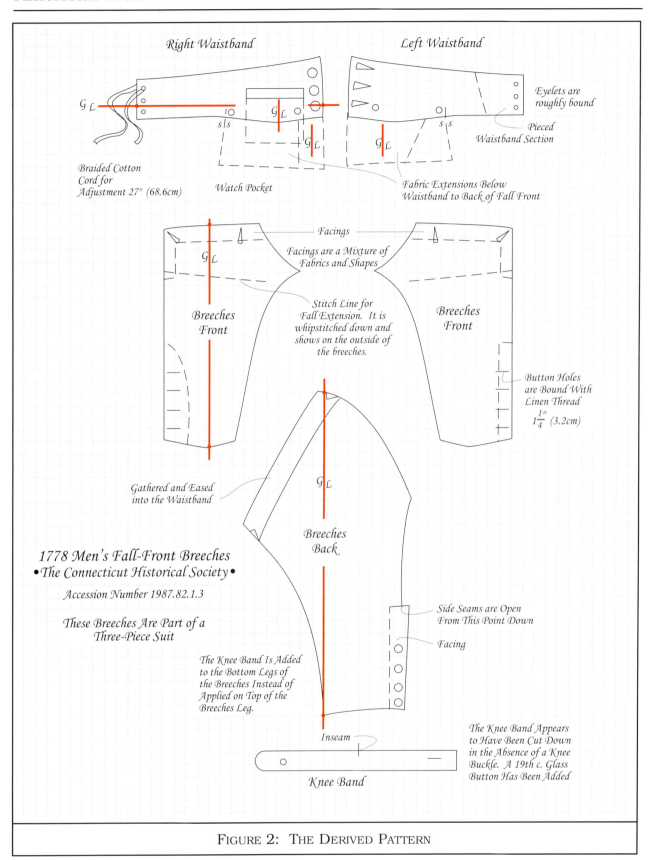

Right Waistband

Left Waistband

G L

Eyelets are
roughly bound

Pieced
Waistband Section

s s

s s

G L

G L

G L

Braided Cotton
Cord for
Adjustment 27" (68.6cm)

Watch Pocket

Fabric Extensions Below
Waistband to Back of Fall Front

Facings

Facings are a Mixture of
Fabrics and Shapes

G L

Breeches
Front

Breeches
Front

Stitch Line for
Fall Extension. It is
whipstitched down and
shows on the outside of
the breeches.

Button Holes
are Bound With
Linen Thread
$1\frac{1}{4}"$ (3.2cm)

Gathered and Eased
into the Waistband

G L

Breeches
Back

1778 Men's Fall-Front Breeches
•The Connecticut Historical Society•

Accession Number 1987.82.1.3

These Breeches Are Part of a
Three-Piece Suit

Side Seams are Open
From This Point Down

Facing

The Knee Band Is Added
to the Bottom Legs of
the Breeches Instead of
Applied on Top of the
Breeches Leg.

Inseam

Knee Band

The Knee Band Appears
to Have Been Cut Down
in the Absence of a Knee
Buckle. A 19th c. Glass
Button Has Been Added

FIGURE 2: THE DERIVED PATTERN

These breeches are visualized as 8 separate parts – 2 waistband pieces; 2 fronts, 2 backs, and 2 knee bands – all of which are shown as scaled patterns in Figure 2. Note the location of the GL and all other references on each of the parts.

ACKNOWLEDGMENTS AND BIBLIOGRAPHY

The author extends special thanks to the trustees of the Society of Antiquaries of London's Janet Arnold Award for research funding and to the staff of the Connecticut Historical Society for so generously sharing their time, space, and expertise.

Baumgarten, Linda, John Watson, and Florine Carr. *Costume Close-Up,Clothing Construction and Pattern,1750-1790.* Williamsburg, VA: The Colonial Williamsburg Foundation in association with Quite Specific Media Group LTD., 1999.

Chenoune, Farid,Deke Dusinberre. *A History of Men's Fashion.* Paris, NewYork, Flammarion,1993.

Kornhauser, Elizabeth Mankin. *Ralph Earl: The Face of the Young Republic.* New Haven: Yale University Press, 1991.

Waugh, Nora. *Cut of Men's Clothes.* New York: Theatre Arts Book, 1987.

ᶓ▲ᶓ▲ᶓ▲

TECHNICAL BRIEF

Lighting

Calculating LED Circuit Requirements — *Daniel T. Lisowski*

Magnetic Color Flipper for a
  Source Four® 10° Follow Spot — *Kathryn Krier*

Focus Track and Chair — *Jonathan A. Reed*

The Panhandler: Pillow-Block Assist for
  ERS Panning — *Brian Swanson*

Modular Stor-Mor Solution — *Joel Furmanek*

The Cadillac of Rolling Booms — *Matt Welander*

Dimmable Fluorescents — *Alan Hendrickson*

Guidelines for Using Neon on Steel
  Structures — *Chris Swetcky*

Using Black Screening Material as
  Inexpensive "Black Scrim" Panels — *Barbara Tan-Tiongco*

Several productions at the Yale Repertory Theatre have required battery power illuminated objects. The illuminating device most frequently used in these effects is the LED. LEDs have a high intensity-to-power-dissipated ratio and are inexpensive. This article addresses a method for properly sizing the components required to operate a battery powered LED effect.

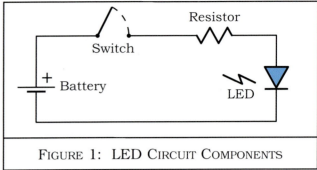

FIGURE 1: LED CIRCUIT COMPONENTS

CIRCUIT BASICS

LED circuits have four components: Switch, Power Supply, Resistors, and LEDs. Figure 1 shows the simplest arrangement of these components, a series circuit that is the basis for all battery-powered LED circuits. Two equations dictate the size and number of components required for proper operation. Following these equations is a discussion of how each variable is determined for a given circuit.

Equation 1: $R = (m(V_{Battery})-n(V_{FV}))/I$ Equation 2: $m = int(n(V_{FV})/V_{Battery})+1$

where...
$V_{Battery}$ = Nominal Voltage of Battery, Volts

V_{FV} = LED Forward Voltage, Volts

R = Resistance Required, Ohms, Ω

I = Current Required for Desired Intensity, milliamperes, mA

n = Number of LEDs in Series

m = Number of Batteries

int = Integer Value Function

LEDS

Identifying the minimum voltage and current required is the first step in designing an LED circuit. The minimum or *forward voltage* (V_{FW}) ranges from $1.5V_{FW}$ to $3.8V_{FW}$, and is determined by the color of the LED. Yellow LEDs, which are the most common and inexpensive, have a forward voltage of $2.1V_{FW}$ and, like nearly all LEDs, reach full intensity at 20mA.

When LEDs are wired in series, the sum of their V_{FW} values is the circuit's total V_{FW}. If all the LEDs have the same V_{FW} the circuit's total V_{FW} can be found by multiplying the number (*n*) of LEDs by their individual V_{FW} values. Thus, a series-wired circuit of four yellow LEDs, each with V_{FW} = 2.1V, has a total V_{FW} of $n(V_{FV})$ = 4(2.1V) = 8.4V. When LEDs with different V_{FW} values are wired in series, their individual V_{FW} values must be added to find a circuit's total forward voltage. The total V_{FW} of a series circuit of a yellow LED and an "ultra blue" LED is 2.1V + 3.8V = 5.9V.

BATTERIES

The supply voltage in any LED circuit must be greater than the LEDs' total V_{FW}, and when batteries are wired in series, the total voltage they supply is the sum of their individual voltages. AA batteries have proven to be an excellent power source for LED circuits. They last longer than the smaller AAA batteries but are nevertheless small enough to fit into confined spaces. Each AA battery supplies 1.5V. Fitted into battery holders, which are available at electrical suppliers, a number of series-connected AA batteries can offer a total supply voltage equalling a multiple of 1.5V.

CURRENT AND RESISTANCE

All LEDs' specifications state a luminous intensity value at a specific current, usually 20mA, the current at which most LEDs reach full intensity. Using a resistor that limits the current to 15mA instead of 20mA produces a slightly less intense but much steadier LED output. Once an LED's V_{FW} has been met, current passes through it unchecked, and adding a resistor in series is often necessary to balance the total voltage drop with the voltage offered by the supply.

DESIGN CONSIDERATIONS AND EXAMPLES

For circuits that require more power than a single battery holder can handle, multiple series components can be connected in parallel. Each leg of a parallel circuit receives or sends the same voltage. Adding combination LED-and-resistor legs can increase the number of LEDs that can be powered by a given source, but the increased current draw will decrease battery life. Conversely, additional battery legs reduce the current draw on each leg, thereby increasing battery life.

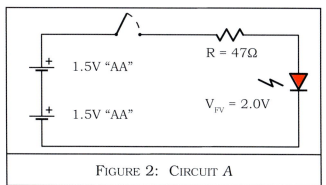

FIGURE 2: CIRCUIT A

Circuit A: One Red LED (Refer to Figure 2)

Givens: $V_{FV} = 2.0V$ $n = 1$
$I = 15mA$ $V_{Battery} = 1.5V$

Solution: $m = int(n(V_{FV})/V_{Battery})+1$
$= int(1(2.0V)/1.5V)+1 = 1 + 1 = 2$

$R = (m(V_{Battery})-n(V_{FV}))/I$
$= (2(1.5V)-1(2.0V))/0.02A$
$= 1V/0.02A = 50\Omega$

Circuit A requires 2 AA batteries and a resistor of $\approx 50\Omega$ to operate properly.

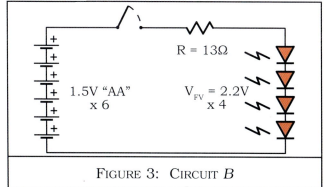

FIGURE 3: CIRCUIT B

Circuit B: Four Orange LEDs (Refer to Figure 3)

Givens: $V_{FV} = 2.2V$ $n = 4$
$I = 20mA$ $V_{Battery} = 1.5V$

Solution: $m = int(n(V_{FV})/V_{Battery})+1$
$= int(4(2.2V)/1.5V)+1 = 5 + 1 = 6$

$R = (m(V_{Battery})-n(V_{FV}))/I$
$= (6(1.5V)-4(2.2V))/0.015A$
$= 1.2V/0.015A = 13\Omega$

Circuit B requires 6 AA batteries and a resistor of $\approx 13\Omega$ to operate properly.

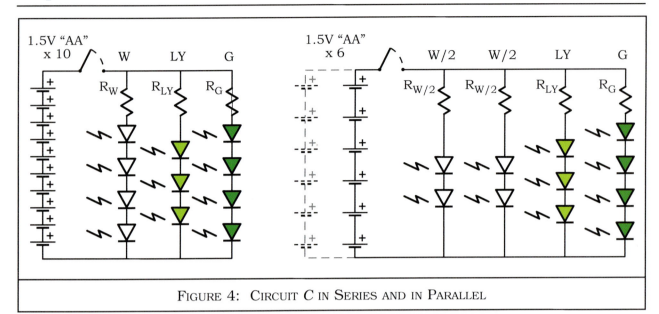

FIGURE 4: CIRCUIT *C* IN SERIES AND IN PARALLEL

Circuit C: Three Lime Yellow, Four Green, and Four White LEDs (Refer to Figure 4)

Givens: $V_{Battery} = 1.5V$ $I = 15mA$ $V_{FV-LY} = 2.4V$ $V_{FV-G} = 2.1V$ $V_{FV-W} = 3.6V$
$n_{LY} = 3$ $n_G = 4$ $n_W = 4$

Solution: $m = int(n(V_{FV})/ V_{Battery})+1$

$m_{LY} = int(3(2.4V)/1.5V)+1 = 4+1 = 5$
$m_G = int(4(2.1V)/1.5V)+1 = 5+1 = 6$
$m_W = int(4(3.6V)/1.5V)+1 = 9+1 = 10$

Wired in series as shown at the left in Figure 4, the white LEDs would need 10 batteries – many more than either of the other two colors would need. If the white LEDs were wired in parallel as shown at the right in Figure 4, the entire circuit would need only 6 batteries – the number required to power the green LEDs. Adding the parallel branch of 6 batteries represented by the broken lines, though not necessary to power the circuit, would prolong battery life.

$m = 6$
$R = (m(V_{Battery})–n(V_{FV}))/ I$
$R_{LY} = (6(1.5V)–3(2.4V))/0.015A = 120\Omega$
$R_G = (6(1.5V)–4(2.1V))/0.015A = 40\Omega$
$R_{W/2} = (6(1.5V)–2(3.6V))/0.015A = 120\Omega$

Wired optimally as at the right in Figure 4, Circuit *C* needs 6 AA batteries (though using 12 would prolong battery life), two ≈120Ω resistors, and one ≈40Ω resistor.

RESOURCES

http://www.theledlight.com
http://www.duracell.com/procell
Neville, Tom. "Two Simple LED Circuits", *Technical Design Solutions for Theatre, Vol. I* ed. Bronislaw J. Sammler and Don Harvey. Boston: Focal Press, 2002.

Usually, quick color changes in a follow spot are accomplished with the industry-made Boomerang. However, no such device is available for the Source Four® 10° ERS which is often used as a follow spot. This alternative is simple, affordable, and safe. As pictured below, the color can be added and removed with a one-handed motion that involves no loose parts.

FIGURE 1: FLIPPER DOWN

FIGURE 2: FLIPPER UP

MATERIALS FOR ONE FLIPPER

Blacktak® (approximately 4')
Paper brads
Small adhesive-backed magnets (available from 3M)

ASSEMBLY

1. Prepare a standard 12" square 10° cut of color.

2. Frame the color with $\frac{1}{2}$" to $\frac{3}{4}$" of Blacktak® on both faces of each edge.

3. Wrap an additional strip of Blacktak® around the bottom edge of both the color and the frame, creating a hinge.

4. To reinforce the attachment, brad through the frame holes at each bottom corner.

5. Attach one or two adhesive-backed magnets to the top of the color on the side facing the frame.

6. Insert the frame into the Source Four® 10° frame slot, with Blacktak® framed color facing out and hanging below lens. The solid frame may hold diffusion or any other gel to be used in additive mixing. Other color changes may be made between this frame and the lens if necessary.

7. To engage the color, flip up. To disengage it, flip down as shown in Figures 1 and 2.

FIGURE 3: ASSEMBLED FRAME OPEN

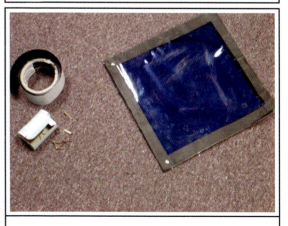

FIGURE 4: ASSEMBLED FRAME CLOSED

APPLICATION AND LIMITATIONS

This device is designed to solve a very specific problem. The Boomerang can accommodate several colors which can be added and removed to the beam of light in any combination with a single, one handed motion. The Blacktak® frame, however, can only accomplish one color change. Most 10° color changes will still need to be achieved by removing or adding an entire framed cut of color. This operation is easily executed if the instrument is off at the time. The Blacktak® frame becomes valuable when the color change is called for while the follow spot is in use.

THANKS

To Abigail Trarbach and the Glimmerglass Opera's 2005 Electrics Crew.

❧❧❧

For a 2005 Yale Repertory Theatre production of *Comedy of Errors*, large scenic units made it impossible to reach portions of the over-stage electrics from the deck. After high costs ruled out renting a focus track package, we decided to purchase a load-rated track system and build a focus chair. Not only would the focus chair be available to future productions, but the track would be on hand for other overhead scenic uses. This article explains the process we followed to build a focus chair, and purchase and assemble the track system.

THE TRACK

The track we used was developed by Knight Industries, Inc., of Auburn Hills, Michigan (http://www.knight-ind.com/). It is primarily used in auto assembly plants, and is designed to support overhead point loads in excess of 1000 lbs. While available in a number of sizes, the 5300 series 4" Steel Rail System, which has a rating of 500 lbs. per carrier when spanning 8' between hangers, seemed our best choice (see Figure 1). The track is shipped in 20' sections, but splice kits are available to create longer lengths. With added end caps, load trolleys, and track hangers as shown in Figure 2, we reached a total quote of $2,453.00 for a 60' track package, not including freight. Assembling the track is simple: the sections bolt together with the splice kits, the redundant end caps attach to each end, and the track hangers clamp onto the top of the rail.

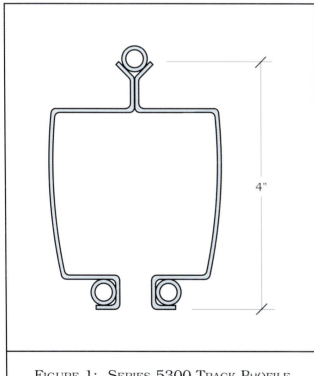

FIGURE 1: SERIES 5300 TRACK PROFILE

FIGURE 2: ASSEMBLED TRACK WITH TRACK HANGER, END CAP AND LOAD TROLLEY

THE HANGERS

There are many ways to attach the track hangers to a batten. We attached them to Clancy Full Pipe Clamps (J.R. Clancy #026-22x1.5) with $\frac{1}{2}$" x $1\frac{1}{2}$" grade-8 hex bolts and grade-8 nylon-insert nuts. The manufacturer allows for virtually any spacing between the track hangers, the maximum span is 9'-0" for the safe working load of 500 lbs. per carrier. Since our lift lines are 10'-0" apart, we used more than the 8 track hangers required to transfer the loads as directly as possible.

THE CHAIR

Our focus chair was built from 1" x 1" x $\frac{3}{16}$" steel angle, with the exception of the two top rails, which were made from 2" x 2" x $\frac{3}{16}$" angle and through-bolted to the track carriers. The outside dimensions of the base were 2'-2" x 1'-3", allowing the seat to easily fly out of sightlines when not in use, while still providing the electrician with an adequate perch. To make the chair as comfortable as possible, the plywood seat bottom was covered with 3" upholstery foam and wrapped with black fabric. Also, two short pieces of rope were strung between the vertical members to provide a backrest.

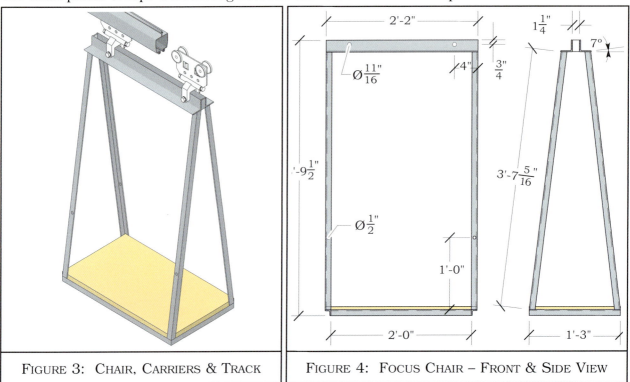

| FIGURE 3: CHAIR, CARRIERS & TRACK | FIGURE 4: FOCUS CHAIR – FRONT & SIDE VIEW |

THE CARRIERS

Knight Industries offers a number of carrier options that are compatible with their track systems. We found that the most practical option was the Load Trolley with Yoke (Knight MRTA5309) because it provides a through-bolt that is easily passed through the pre-drilled holes in the top rails of the chair. They also allow the chair to pivot upstage/downstage, which can be useful when you are maneuvering along the electric. Three trolleys are required; two suspend the chair and the third (not shown above) acts as an attachment point for the technician's safety harness lanyard.

SAFE USE

When a crew member climbs into the chair, the system can become dangerously imbalanced. We dealt with this issue by attaching the arbor to the lockrail with aircraft cable and chain, sized to let the pipe fly out of sight, but no farther in than necessary to reach the electric. We also kept a drop line that reached to the deck whenever an operator was in the chair. This provided a way to send gel and patterns to the electrician and would have allowed the focus chair to be pulled to either end of the track in an emergency.

Many theatres are purchasing newer-style, load rated C-Clamps like the Mega-Clamp®. For theatres used to loosening the collars on C-Clamps to use ERS instruments as followspots, these one-piece units have an inconvenient drawback: they offer no means of panning control. Hybrid yokes that overcome this limitation are available, but can be prohibitively expensive. In response the Aspen Opera Theatre Center's Master Electrician, Derek Easton, devised the panhandler, which solves the problem in a cost-effective way.

As shown in Figure 1 the panhandler is functionally simple. A piece of $1\frac{1}{2}$" x $1\frac{1}{2}$" x $\frac{1}{8}$" angle iron is bolted to both a pillow block and a C-Clamp. A section of $\frac{3}{4}$" rod, tapped on the lower end to receive the yoke bolt, is inserted in the pillow block. The upper end of the rod is through-bolted so the rod cannot slide out of the bearing. Though not shown, a traditional safety cable, is still looped through the instrument's yoke.

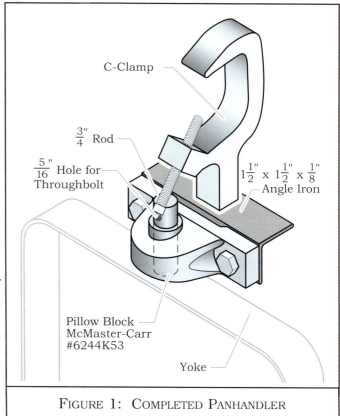

C-Clamp

$\frac{3}{4}$" Rod

$\frac{5}{16}$" Hole for Throughbolt

$1\frac{1}{2}$" x $1\frac{1}{2}$" x $\frac{1}{8}$"
Angle Iron

Pillow Block
McMaster-Carr
#6244K53

Yoke

FIGURE 1: COMPLETED PANHANDLER

CONSTRUCTION

Cut a piece of $1\frac{1}{2}$" x $1\frac{1}{2}$" x $\frac{1}{8}$" angle iron to a length of $5\frac{1}{2}$". In the center of one leg of the angle iron, drill a $\frac{9}{16}$" hole for the C-Clamp attachment. In the other face drill two $\frac{7}{16}$" holes, each $1\frac{7}{8}$" from center for attachment of the pillow block. Cut a piece of $\frac{3}{4}$" rod to a length of $2\frac{1}{2}$". From one end of the rod measure $\frac{1}{2}$" down and drill a $\frac{5}{16}$" hole. Centered in the opposite end drill and tap a hole for a standard $\frac{1}{2}$" x 1"–13 yoke bolt. Assemble the components as shown in Figure 1.

NOTES

The pillow block specified here (McMaster-Carr 6244K53) is self-aligning and worked wonderfully for Aspen's circumstances. Using a rigid-bearing pillow block would most likely produce even better results, especially if the unit is overhung. The panhandler can also work with traditional C-Clamps.

Efficiency of any shop begins with the organization of materials and tools. The previous storage solution for the electrics department at Glimmerglass Opera consisted of road boxes crammed into the end of a tractor trailer. If greater efficiency were to be achieved, something needed to be done that would better use the available space and that could be loaded into rented trailers at the close of each season. With these considerations in mind the following design took shape.

GENERAL DESIGN CONCEPTS

A modular design was determined to be the most practical approach to reconfiguring the layout as needed and to make the components manageable. The modules consist of 5'-0"-long sections that can function independently or with other modules. The trailers are rented, but by using horizontal spacer bars on top and small feet on the bottom and by making the modules fit tightly inside the trailers, Glimmerglass avoided having to make connections to the floor or walls of the trailers. To make the most of the space available, each module utilizes space all the way up to the top of the trailer. Since the modules are 9'-0" tall, a dedicated ladder is needed to get to the less frequently used items on the top shelves and racks, but the increased storage space is well worth the trouble. Figure 1, below, depicts how a group of ten modules might be arranged to fill 25' of a 53' trailer.

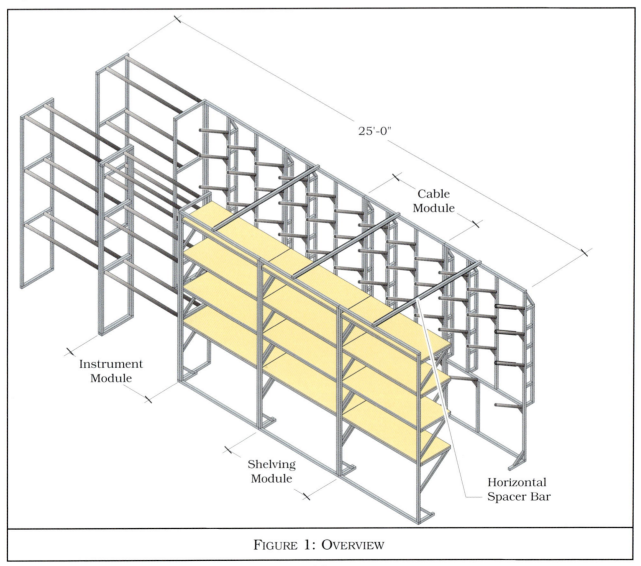

FIGURE 1: OVERVIEW

MODULES

For ease of construction, only three different types of modules were built (see Figure 2). The first is a Cable Storage Module that includes places for larger cables on the bottom and smaller ones on the top. The back of this module serves as a pipe rack. The Instrument Storage Module, in the center, provides storage for approximately 50 standard-size instruments. The Shelf Module, on the right, is a straight-forward shelving unit comprising 4 shelves and leaving space below for bins or road boxes.

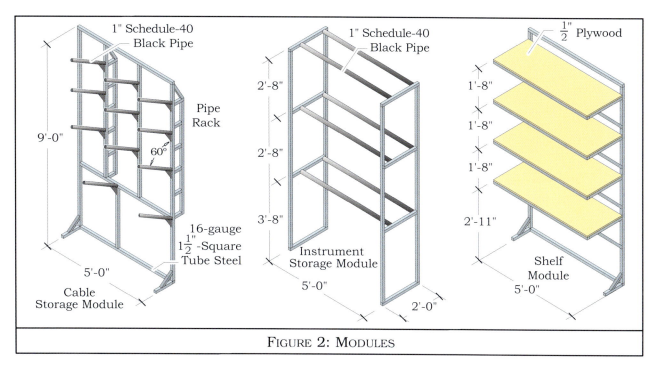

FIGURE 2: MODULES

CONNECTIONS

Connection of adjacent modules is accomplished with 3 bolts through each of the uprights and, for this reason, the location of bolt holes must be the same from one module to the next. One other hole drilled in the top of each module receives the horizontal spacer bars as shown in Figure 1.

CLOSING

This article is intended to provide a jumping-off point for your new modular storage system. Detailed construction drawings and cut lists are not included because every situation and shop has its own particular needs and will need to customize this design accordingly.

❧❧❧❧❧

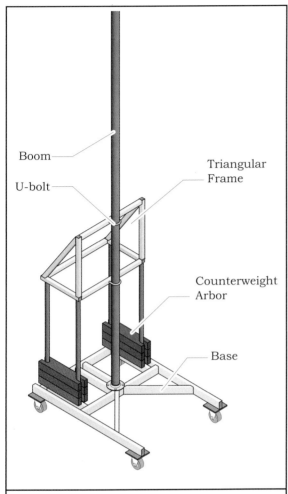

FIGURE 1: THE CADILLAC BOOM

Lighting booms pose a consistent challenge for repertory theater and opera companies. At Glimmerglass Opera, Technical Director Abby Rodd and Lighting Supervisor Jeff Harris developed a rolling boom that accommodates tall lighting pipes and allows you to hang a shinbuster at floor level. Its compact frame is stable enough to be moved by one stagehand and allows multiple booms to nest together for storage. They roll so smoothly when fully loaded that the crew refers to them as "Cadillac booms".

DESCRIPTION

The boom is essentially a length of $1\frac{1}{2}$" schedule-40 black pipe and two custom-built counterweight arbors attached to a sturdy rolling base. The pipe is inserted vertically into a Kee Klamp® pipe flange welded to the base and attached with 2 U-bolts to a triangular frame on top of the arbors. Because of the pipe flange, the boom height is easily adjustable: simply swap the pipe out for whatever length of pipe you need, usually 6' to 16' (you could use a longer pipe, but they tend to sway significantly over that height). Calculate the weight of the lighting fixtures and cable on the boom, add a corresponding amount of weight to the counterweight arbors, and you are good to go.

THE ROLLING BASE

The rolling base is made of 16-gauge 1" x 2" tube steel. As shown in Figure 2, it is U-shaped with the counterweight arbors and pipe flange attached to the base of the U. Four 4"-square caster plates cut from $\frac{1}{4}$"-flat bar are welded to the base for easy attachment and replacement of 3" swivel casters. The open space between the legs allows a lighting fixture to be hung as a shinbuster close to the floor. The open U shape also allows the booms to be nested together face to face when they are being stored. Cane bolt keepers or stage screw tabs can be attached to the rolling base as needed to allow them to be consistently placed on spike.

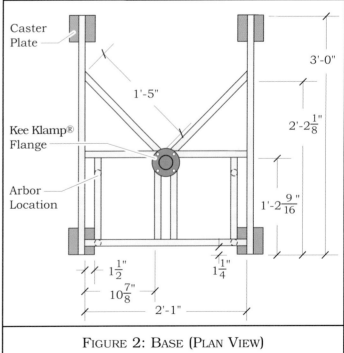

FIGURE 2: BASE (PLAN VIEW)

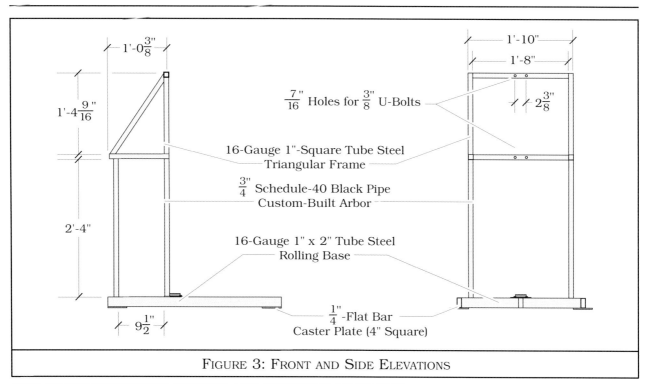

FIGURE 3: FRONT AND SIDE ELEVATIONS

THE COUNTERWEIGHT ARBORS AND TRIANGULAR FRAME

The counterweight arbors are made of $\frac{3}{4}$" schedule-40 black pipe. They are 2'-4" tall and are capped by a triangular frame made of 16-gauge 1"-square tube steel. The triangular frame connects and stabilizes the arbors and also provides two horizontal framing members where the lighting pipe is attached with $\frac{3}{8}$" U-bolts. Dimensions and layout of the counterweight arbors and the triangular frame are given in Figure 3.

The booms are so stable and center of gravity so well balanced that you need only a minimal amount of counterweight in the arbors when the boom is stationary. When you roll the booms, however, you need to be sure there is enough counterweight in the arbors to offset the sway of the boom and its tendency to tip. There is plenty of arbor space to allow adequate counterweight for those situations.

SUMMARY

These rolling booms are an excellent design solution to a common problem. They can be built in-house, are easy to move when fully loaded, and take up a relatively small footprint when in storage.

❧❧❧

Fluorescent lamps offer unique lighting possibilities to both set and lighting designers. The look of a fluorescent fixture may suit the set designer's concept for office or industrial lighting, while a lighting designer may be seeking a soft wash or a certain color temperature of light. Regardless of the application, fluorescent lamps in theatre usually need to be dimmable, and this unfortunately accentuates their somewhat quirky behavior. This article discusses two types of dimmable fixtures using commonly available 4'-long tubes, and provides troubleshooting hints for some of the more common problems they and others like them may have.

Fluorescent lamp operation is complex in comparison to the relative simplicity of conventional incandescent lamps. To provide a detailed description of fluorescent lamp operation would itself occupy many pages (look at www.howstuffworks.com/fluorescent-lamp.htm if you are interested in the details), so here in brief are the key points. Fluorescent tubes contain a drop of mercury and an inert gas (typically argon) in a phosphor-coated glass tube, sealed in at a very low pressure, and capped with a pair of electrodes at each end. The electrodes, powered by a device called a ballast, enable the argon/mercury gas mix to ionize, passing current through the tube. The gas emits ultraviolet light when excited by this current, and that light in turn causes the phosphor coating to fluoresce, which is the visible light we see coming from the lamp.

A ballast is essential with these lamps. Its two main functions are to provide a high enough voltage to start current flow through the tube and to limit that flow once it has begun because the gas offers little resistance once conduction begins. Ballasts come in two types: magnetic and electronic. The magnetic ballast is the older style and it combines copper wire wrapped around an iron structure to provide power to warm the electrodes at the ends of the tube, and inductance to limit current flow. The electronic ballast, not surprisingly, contains electronics that control the starting and running of a lamp. All ballasts are designed to work only with certain models and numbers of lamps, and to dim a fluorescent lamp, the ballast, regardless of the type, must be designated specifically as dimmable.

For an example of a dimmable magnetic ballast setup, see Figure 1. Here an Advance DIM-240-H-TP magnetic ballast runs two F40T12 lamps. The ballast has two wires to each end of the lamps which provide power to heat the electrodes, enabling them to emit electrons easily into the gas. The electrode power must be on continuously, fed by the wire labeled "constant hot". A connection is made to a standard theatre dimmer through the "dimmed hot" lead. Both the constant and dimmed

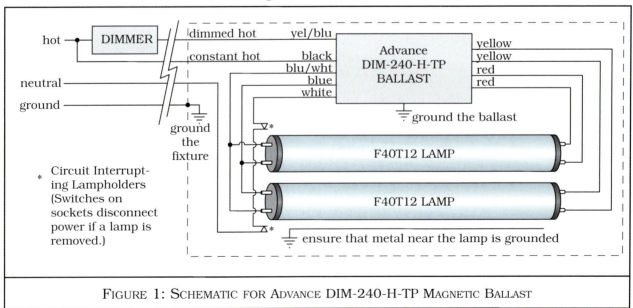

FIGURE 1: SCHEMATIC FOR ADVANCE DIM-240-H-TP MAGNETIC BALLAST

hot leads must be on the same electrical phase else the lamp will not work Finding two dimmers on the same phase (with one set up as a non-dim for the "constant hot") may take some trial-and-error testing of circuits until a working combination is found. While this setup has worked well in a number of productions there are two issues of note. First, the constant power to the electrodes causes both ends of each lamp to visibly glow, and a gradual fade up from black can involve the tube ends glowing in the darkness before the stage lights become visible. Delaying turning the non-dims on until some light is established onstage can help, but the glow is inevitable with this type of ballast. Second, government energy efficiency legislation has required the phasing out of the F40T12 cool-white and warm-white lamps these ballasts were originally designed to run, and these ballasts, like all ballasts, will only work with a very narrow range of lamps. Some equivalent lamps are still available, but the lesson here is to ask electrical supply houses about the future status of a product in light of the evolution of green regulations before you invest in equipment that may soon be obsolete.

Figure 2 shows the schematic for a dimmable setup using an Advance REZ-132-SC electronic ballast. This ballast runs one F32T8 lamp (different models will run 2 or 3 lamps), and it only needs to be connected to a dimmer, no constant hot is needed. This means that not only is circuiting easier, but there is no lamp end glow. While these points are both good, there are some negatives as well. The electronics keep the lamp from lighting for about two full seconds after power is applied, and this will certainly affect its cueing. Also, the lamp is a T8, or "eight eighths" or 1" in diameter, a full $\frac{1}{2}$" less than the older T12. If the lamp is visible, savvy audience members will know it is not in period if it is used in an older style fixture.

POTENTIAL PROBLEMS IN ANY DIMMABLE FLUORESCENT

The dynamics of an electric current flowing through a low pressure gas is complex and subject to effects that never affect incandescent lamps. The relatively low currents in dimmed fluorescent lamps do not always flow evenly through the lamp tube, and moving swirls or a bright and dark pattern can appear as a result. These do not harm the lamps, but they are visually distracting. Setting dimmer levels higher can help, as can using seasoned and warmer lamps, as discussed below.

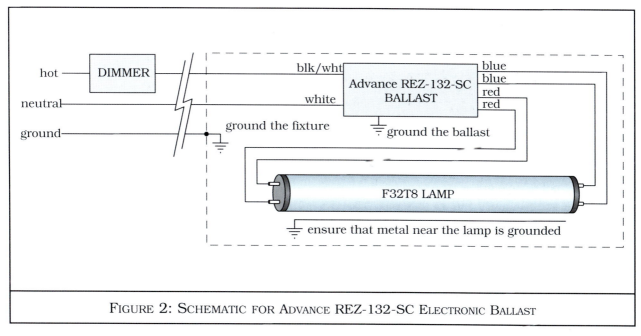

FIGURE 2: SCHEMATIC FOR ADVANCE REZ-132-SC ELECTRONIC BALLAST

Lamp temperature – which depends on the ambient temperature, airflow across the lamps, how long a lamp has been on at a given dimmer setting, and whether there is a protective or colored sleeve that acts as insulation around a tube – influences whether a lamp starts, swirls, or is very dim. Temperatures cooler than 60°F (and hotter than 100°F, though this is rarer) will often cause these troubles, so outdoor summer theatre air temperatures, the location of HVAC air vents relative to a lighting fixture, and even the lack of a warm-up pre-show can cause problems.

The relatively low voltage available from a dimmer set to a low level may not be enough to start a fluorescent lamp, although a lamp started at a higher setting may continue to run as the dimmer level is moved to that same low level. This effect results in lamps that appear to just pop on at some level rather than fade up from black as an incandescent will do. The ballast used influences this, and most manufacturers state a percentage of full on brightness at lamp turn on as their specification. Ballasts are available with 1%, 5%, and 10% specs, and for theatre the lower the number the better. This is most often an important issue if the audience can see the lamps, rather than just the light from the lamps bounced off an illuminated surface.

New lamps often dim at different levels than used lamps, and the fix may be to replace all lamps if any one burns out. You can try burning-in or seasoning new lamps by leaving them on at full for some number of hours, but opinions differ as to whether this is beneficial. Sylvania, for instance, recommends a 12-hour burn-in; Crestron, 100 hours; and Advanced, none at all.

Fluorescent light fixtures require excellent grounding, and this is for reasons beyond the necessary grounding for electrical safety purposes. The ionization of the gases inside the lamp progresses across the tube in part due to capacitive coupling through the glass tube to the close presence of the grounded metal housing. A missing or high resistance ground usually prevents a fixture from working, and a marginal ground can cause poor low level dimming performance. Gelled or protective sleeves over the tubes, dirt on the tubes, and even high humidity can also cause grounding problems. A partly disassembled fixture will probably not work either. A grounded metal plate just under the lamp is absolutely necessary for proper operation.

The dimmers running fluorescents may be a cause of problems too since they are designed to run large incandescent lamp loads. One fluorescent fixture may run its whole dimmable range between the lamps off at 25% and full on at 80%, while another fixture with a different ballast may do something quite different. Also, magnetic ballasts are inductive loads that some dimmers cannot operate. A ghost load, often a 100-watt incandescent lamp hidden somewhere out of the audience's sight and two-ferred in with the fluorescent, will provide the dimmer with enough of a resistive load to work well. If the ghost load ever burns out, replace it with one of identical wattage or the dimming curves may be radically altered.

And one last curious thing. Because mercury is heavier than the other inert gases in a lamp, vertical tubes may become brighter at the bottom than at the top as the mercury settles.

CREDITS

The author extends thanks to Yale Repertory Theatre Lighting Supervisor Donald W. Titus for his contributions to this article.

In a production of *The Evildoers* at the Yale Repertory Theatre, the primary scenic elements in the production were 2 large steel structures covered in Plexiglas® and outlined with roughly 120 feet of 12mm white neon. Each element had 6 transformers that operated on 6 independent channels. This posed three distinct problems. First, multiple neon wires were running together causing interference between the pieces of neon. Second, the transformers were located up to 15 feet away from their corresponding neon tubes in a confined space. Third, the pathways for the neon wire required that the wire come in contact with the steel structure. These three problems posed some significant side effects that needed to be addressed such as randomly flickering neon, and abnormally short transformer life. From these problems, three guidelines were developed. The three guidelines provide invaluable information as to the installation of the neon wire and the location of the transformers allowing for the use of neon in a less than ideal environment.

A STANDARD NEON SYSTEM

Neon lamps are very simple devices. They use a transformer to generate a high voltage alternating current within a neon-gas-filled tube. The transformer is connected to both ends of the tube and when power is applied the tube lights up. Typically, two 100-watt incandescent lamps wired in parallel are added to the circuit to provide a linear dimming curve as shown below.

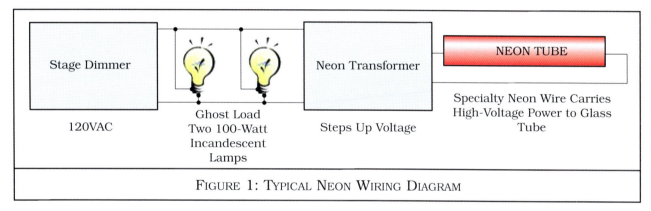

FIGURE 1: TYPICAL NEON WIRING DIAGRAM

THE CORONA EFFECT

The thickness of the insulation in the wire used to connect neon to its transformer is important to a neon system. This is especially true in steel structures and when neon transformers are not located adjacent to the neon lamp. If a neon wire is located too close to a piece of steel or another neon wire, an interesting phenomenon called the corona effect occurs. The corona effect is caused by a high-potential source (*e.g.*, the high-voltage line of the neon wire) generating an invisible inductive current into the air, ionizing it. When the air becomes sufficiently charged, it transforms into plasma. The current generated is passed through this plasma to a lower-potential conductive material (*e.g.*, steel framing or other neon wires). This can prove to be problematic when running a neon system on a scenic element built out of steel. The corona effect literally uses the steel as a low-potential device that generates a large amount of power that passes through the air (Cool! wireless power! – not quite....) to nearby neon wires, sending power to other pieces of neon, causing them to glow and flicker randomly. The corona effect also sends power to the transformer, overloading the current-limiting devices of some transformers, effectively destroying them. Another by-product of the corona effect is that it dries out insulation on neon wires after a while, causing them to crack and break.

GUIDELINES FOR NEON SUCCESS

No two situations are the same when it comes to scenery construction and what worked in *The Evildoers* may not necessarily work in other situations but the guidelines should provide a starting off point for troubleshooting a malfunctioning system.

- The first rule of thumb is to install neon wires of separate neon channels a MINIMUM of 4 inches away from each other. Voltages in the 10,000 volt range have a minimal corona effect range and 4 inches should provide enough room to limit its effects.

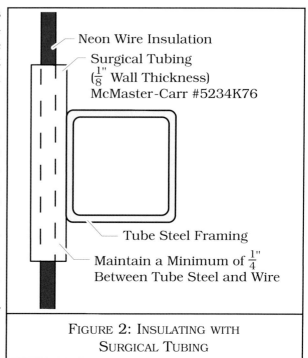

Neon Wire Insulation

Surgical Tubing ($\frac{1}{8}$" Wall Thickness) McMaster-Carr #5234K76

Tube Steel Framing

Maintain a Minimum of $\frac{1}{4}$ Between Tube Steel and Wire

FIGURE 2: INSULATING WITH SURGICAL TUBING

- The second guideline is to keep all neon wires a MINIMUM of $\frac{1}{4}$" inch away from steel. The insulation already enclosing the neon wire is NOT enough. One simple way to maintain this distance is to enclose the neon wire in PVC conduit. When conduit is not a possibility, enclosing the neon wire in surgical tubing as shown in Figure 2 provides adequate insulation near steel. Fully enclosing the wires in PVC conduit or surgical tubing is good practice even if only one channel is being used because by limiting the corona effect the lifetime of neon wire will increase.

- The final guideline is that, when a system contains multiple transformers, a MINIMUM distance of 6" to 12" should be maintained between them. This will lessen the chance of burning out a transformer.

Even though these guidelines were proven on an all steel structure, they also apply to other metals as well. Neon systems are very temperamental but by taking the right steps, Neon can be a successful and awesome effect.

❧❧❧❧❧

A 2008 production of David Henry Hwang's *Golden Child* at the Cultural Center of the Philippines required a number of 21' tall x 3' wide scrims to be used as dividers to isolate simultaneous actions in a scene. For most of the play, actors walked between the scrims from one area to another. The stage blocking was done in such a way that actors did not block each other's side light.

Sharkstooth Scrim is neither affordable nor readily available in the Philippines. However, we found a black fiberglass window/door screening material an appropriate substitute. Locally available in 3' wide rolls, the screening material cost much less than the scrim and, once we had mastered its one drawback, it produced the desired effect as shown in Figures 1 and 2. The drawback was that the material's relatively high reflectivity, best illustrated in Figure 3, limited its ability to be transparent. We used side lighting with shutters cut to about 2" off the window screening as the key source of light, and we kept the actors' movements and maneuvers precisely along the shafts of side light.

CONSTRUCTION AND HANDLING

Since wrinkles would make the screening more reflective and force even narrower shutter cuts, care must be taken in giving the material just the right amount of tension. We found that stapling the screening to 2x2 wood strips, top and bottom, and hanging the panels from battens was sufficient: there was no need to fasten the panels to the floor. We did face the bottom edge of each panel with a strip of $\frac{1}{4}$" lauan, but only to give the bottom edge a "clean" finish. We did not weight the bottoms at all. That meant that, not being stretched too tightly, the screening material had little tendency to hourglass.

FIGURE 1: TRANSPARENCY OF THE SCREENING MATERIAL

FIGURE 2: ACTORS PASSING ALONG THE SIDE-LIGHT SHAFTS

FIGURE 3. REFLECTIVITY OF THE SCREENING MATERIAL

TECHNICAL BRIEF

Lighting Effects

A Motion-Controlled Practical — Pablo Souki

Overlooking-the-Town Light Box — Christopher Jensen

A Light-Beam Box — Michael Kraczek

Safe Chimney-Smoke Generators — Maura LaRiviere

An Inexpensive Fog Chiller — Steven Hood

Constructing a Battery-Powered Candle — Eric Lin

Simulating Neon With Rope Light — Chris Russo

A Liquid Lamp — Karen Walcott

For a 1999 dramatization of selections from Pablo Neruda's poetry in Caracas, Venezuela, the creative team requested a curious practical: a flashlight that, while in the hands of an actor, had to "appear to be running out of batteries." The flashlight should work properly at first, then stop working in mid-scene, then turn on and off repeatedly while the actor shook it violently trying to "make it work", and finally stop working completely. The creative team made it very clear that, for a number of reasons, the actor that held the practical could not be constantly pressing and releasing a button to turn the flashlight on and off. As a solution, one of the members of the technical team suggested the use of a mercury switch, having previously used one of them as a motion detector.

DESCRIPTION OF TILT SWITCHES

A typical tilt switch is an extremely simple device. It consists of a small tube that contains a free-moving piece of a conductive material, and two leads. These leads extend to the outside of the tube, where they become the contacts that attach the switch to the rest of the circuit.

Figure 1 depicts the basic working principle of tilt switches, using as an example a mercury-based tilt switch. The switch is designed to be installed horizontally; when tilted down the conductive material (mercury, in this case) moves to the bottom of the tube, touching both leads and closing the circuit. When the switch is returned to its original position, the material moves away from the leads, breaking the circuit. The dimensions of a common tilt switch tube are approximately $\frac{3}{16}$" in diameter and $\frac{7}{8}$" in length, including the leads.

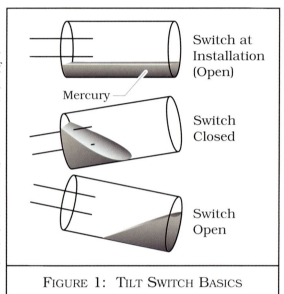

Switch at Installation (Open)

Mercury

Switch Closed

Switch Open

FIGURE 1: TILT SWITCH BASICS

Because of availability, we used a mercury-based tilt switch for this particular application. However, due to the concerns surrounding the toxicity of mercury, this is not the most popular kind of tilt switch. The most common tilt switch is the rolling-ball switch, which contains a conductive ball that rolls inside the tube as the switch is moved, opening and closing the circuit.

BASIC WORKING PRINCIPLE

For the purposes of this practical we wired the tilt switch into the flashlight circuit in series with the existing flashlight switch. The actor walked in with the flashlight turned on while holding the flashlight in a position that kept the mercury switch closed. Then, as the actor moved his hand and made the mercury move up and down inside the tilt switch, the flashlight repeatedly turned on and off.

MATERIALS

Flashlight	$8.00
Tilt Switch - www.elexp.com N1700TLRB	$0.70
20AWG Wire	(stock)
$\frac{1}{2}$" x $\frac{1}{2}$" Cardboard	(stock)
$\frac{1}{2}$" x $\frac{1}{2}$" Tinfoil	(stock)
Hot-Melt Glue	(stock)

- The construction of the flashlight made it impossible to place the tilt switch inside. The creative team agreed to mounting the switch to the outside of the flashlight as long as the switch could be discreetly hidden.

- The electrical circuit inside the flashlight needs to be broken so that the mercury switch can be spliced in. We found that the easiest way to accomplish this would be by inserting a piece of cardboard with tinfoil glued to one side between the batteries and the lamp, as shown in Figure 2.

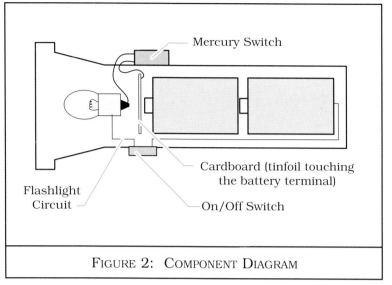

FIGURE 2: COMPONENT DIAGRAM

ASSEMBLY STEPS

1. Solder a piece of 20 AWG wire to each lead of the mercury switch. Each piece should be long enough to make it from the switch to the lamp.

2. Drill a hole through the flashlight body, about $\frac{1}{4}$" from the place where the tilt switch will be attached. The hole should be wide enough to let the 20 AWG wires into the flashlight body. Be careful not to drill through any part of the flashlight's electric circuit.

3. Open the flashlight and remove the batteries. Feed the soldered wires through the drilled hole.

4. Solder one of the wires to the contact on the flashlight's lamp.

5. Glue the $\frac{1}{2}$" x $\frac{1}{2}$" piece of tin foil to one side of the $\frac{1}{2}$" x $\frac{1}{2}$" piece of cardboard.

6. Strip the end of the unattached lead wire and lay it on the tin foil, so that it makes electrical contact. Using hot glue, affix the wire to the foil maintaining the electrical contact. Test this connection using a continuity meter.

7. Insert the batteries in the flashlight and place the cardboard on top of the batteries with the tin foil facing down and making contact with the battery (our flashlight opened between the lamp and the body; invert the order of the instructions in this step if the flashlight opens only at the end).

8. Close the flashlight, and attach and cover the tilt switch. In our particular case, the designer liked the idea of the flashlight's handle being covered with electrical tape, so that became our attachment technique.

༄༅༄༅༄

Overlooking-the-Town Light Box

Christopher Jensen

The director of our production of *The Laramie Project* asked me to recreate in light the last moment that the actors describe: the town of Laramie sparkling at night as viewed from a nearby mountain. I decided early on to build the upstage mountain-range groundrow as a light box to accomplish that objective.

CONSTRUCTION NOTES

Upstage of the playing space, my students and I built a 2x4 frame 24'-0" long, 5'-0" tall, and 4'-0" deep as shown in Figure 1. Leaving the offstage ends open for access, we covered the top with lauan and the back with two layers of fabric: a bounce of unbleached muslin on the inside and a black-out of duvetyne on the outside. The sheets of lauan we screwed to the front of the box were cut to a maximum height of 6'-0" to simulate the profile of the mountain range.

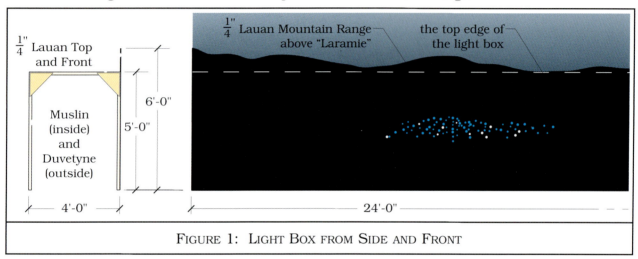

FIGURE 1: LIGHT BOX FROM SIDE AND FRONT

After building the mountain range, we had to "settle" the town. I drew a forced-perspective grid to represent the streets of the town and drilled a series of $\frac{3}{8}$" holes along the grid for street lights. Among those holes I interspersed a random set of $\frac{1}{4}$" holes to represent house lights, as shown in Figure 1, and then painted the entire groundrow black.

LIGHTING NOTES

Four clip lights fitted with 25w blue-colored "party" bulbs and spaced evenly on the floor as shown in Figure 2 cast a uniform field of blue light throughout the box To give the street and house lights some individuality, I cut the blue swatches out of old gel sample booklets, discarded the heavy saturated hues, and from inside the box taped the remaining blues at random over the holes. This made the light glow rather than glare through the holes – something we referred to as "the Lite-brite® effect". Though now lit, the town seemed lifeless: it lacked the sparkle that would be caused by humidity, heat, and distance.

To give the town some life, I hung an 8" mirror ball in the center of the light box and directed two lekos at it as shown in Figure 2. When lit from either side, the mirror ball's constantly spinning dance of lights passed over the holes and gave the front view a random flicker. To help break up the constant glow from the holes, I hung reflective silver, holographic, white, and blue streamers between the mirror ball and the front of the box. Oscillating fans directed at the streamers from either end of the box blew them in a wave-like pattern, and as they increased or decreased the amount of light shining through the holes they produced the desired impression.

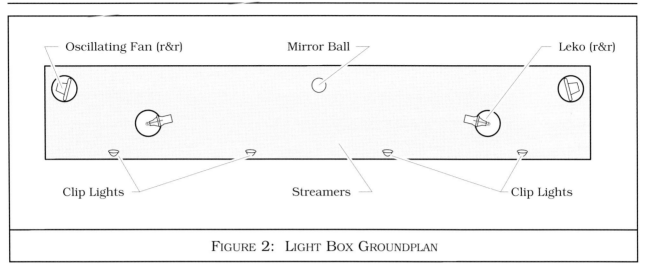

Oscillating Fan (r&r)   Mirror Ball   Leko (r&r)

Clip Lights   Streamers   Clip Lights

FIGURE 2: LIGHT BOX GROUNDPLAN

The last thing that was needed was a faint blue light shining onto the town itself, and once we had gelled the strips hanging in front of the light box, the total effect was stunning. The town could not have turned out better and was the perfect end to this emotional play.

ୡ୶ୡ୶

Pilobolus Dance Theatre's 2001 *Monkey and the Bone Demon* called for a thin, variable-color beam of light that, playing as a backdrop behind the dancers, would span the 40' dance space and change elevation. The production photo in Figure 1 suggests how effectively Lighting Designer Steven Strawbridge and Director of Production Daniel Feith met their objectives.

FIGURE 1: PILOBOLUS' *MONKEY AND THE BONE DEMON*, 2001

Judging that the best way to simplify color changing would be to minimize the number of light sources, Strawbridge and Feith mounted one PAR 64 equipped with a 600-watt 28 volt Aircraft Landing Light (ACL) and CXI color scroller on either end of their 46'-long light-beam box. To be tourable, the box was made of bolt-together sections. At each load-in the sections were assembled and hung from a batten 1'-6" to 3'-0" upstage of a black scrim. A single piece of seamless fire-retardant muslin stretched across the front of the assembled sections smoothed out any inconsistencies in the light beam.

CONSTRUCTION

Figure 2 offers an overview of Pilobolus' light-beam box, and Figure 3 provides construction details of a typical middle section. As illustrated, each section of the light-beam box consisted of a top and bottom frame of 16-gauge 1"-square tube steel faced with $\frac{1}{4}$" MDF painted white on the inside and black on the outside. Similarly faced square tube steel verticals welded between the top and bottom frames formed the back of the box. Between sections, tapered $\frac{3}{4}$"-diameter steel bar pins welded into the ends of the top and bottom frames insured alignment of the sections. Pre-drilling $\frac{5}{16}$" holes for the $\frac{1}{4}$" hardware that joined the sections speeded load-in.

Spaced 4'-0" apart along the top frame, pairs of $1\frac{1}{2}$" angle iron tabs with $\frac{3}{8}$" holes provided the necessary pick points. The boom bases for the PARs consisted of $13\frac{1}{2}$"-long pieces of $1\frac{1}{2}$" schedule-40 black pipe welded to 6" x 6" pieces of $\frac{1}{4}$" flat bar held back $2\frac{1}{2}$" from the ends of the end sections to provide access to the section-joining bolts. The seamless muslin for the face of the light-beam box was cut to a 9" width and grommetted every 18" along its top and bottom edges. Bungy cords looped through the grommets and wrapped around the back of the box stretched the muslin taut.

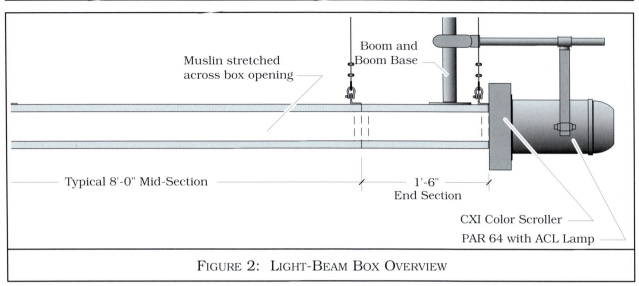

Muslin stretched
across box opening

Boom and
Boom Base

Typical 8'-0" Mid-Section

1'-6"
End Section

CXI Color Scroller

PAR 64 with ACL Lamp

FIGURE 2: LIGHT-BEAM BOX OVERVIEW

SYSTEM DESIGN CONSIDERATIONS

Pilobolus' design requirements dictated the 46' overall length and 6" height of this particular box, and its 6" depth was based on an educated guess.   Other proportions would probably work, but testing any new combination's effectiveness with a mock up is recommended. Other boxes might also be built either in sections or as continuous pieces, but with either approach, the box must be built long enough to hide the PARs behind legs or other masking.

In performance, the line of light created by this light-beam box was only about half as bright in the middle as on the ends.   Shorter boxes would suffer less from such light drop off, but any box's performance might be improved through two yet untested design modifications: shimming out the verticals progressively to make the box shallower towards the middle, and painting the interior with a graded wash, darker towards the ends, rather than painting it evenly white.

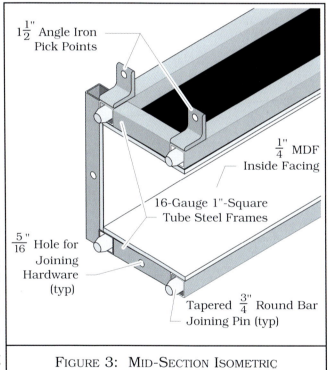

$1\frac{1}{2}$" Angle Iron
Pick Points

$\frac{1}{4}$" MDF
Inside Facing

16-Gauge 1"-Square
Tube Steel Frames

$\frac{5}{16}$" Hole for
Joining
Hardware
(typ)

Tapered $\frac{3}{4}$" Round Bar
Joining Pin (typ)

FIGURE 3: MID-SECTION ISOMETRIC

Period shows often call for chimneys or wood stoves that have small curls of smoke rising from their pipes. After experimenting for years with dry ice, sal ammoniac, and glycol-based foggers, the Electrics Department at the Santa Fe Opera has come up with a convenient and safe alternative method for generating such chimney effects. Their smoke generator of choice – an ultrasonic humidifier. The effect is shown below in Figure 1 as it was used in the 2006 production of *Cendrillion*. Each of the two tall chimney pipes (called out in circles) is being supplied by its own humidifier.

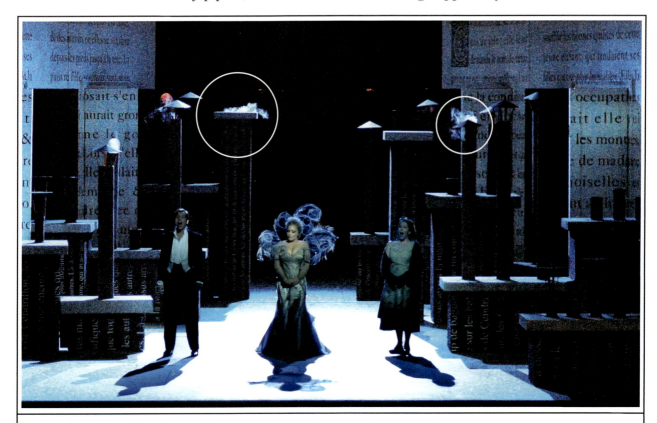

FIGURE 1: SMOKING CHIMNEYS IN THE 2006 SANTA FE OPERA PRODUCTION OF *CENDRILLION*

Ultrasonic humidifiers work by passing water over a small circle of metal called the ionic disk. This disk is similar in construction to the diaphragm in a high-frequency speaker. The sides are fixed to the bottom of the humidifier reservoir, and the center is free to move up and down. When the reservoir is filled with water and the humidifier is powered on, the ionic disk is driven to vibrate at an ultrasonic frequency. This throws water droplets into the air, creating wispy curls of smoke. Water is heavier than air, so the smoke has a tendency to settle downward as it disperses. The effect is visible almost instantly upon energizing the humidifier. Since the effect is pure water, it does not present any of the chemical hazards found in other types of smoke.

PICKING A HUMIDIFIER

Ultrasonic humidifiers sold by Sunbeam and by Walgreens have been used with great success at the Santa Fe Opera. These humidifiers are approximately 14" tall by 12" wide by 8" deep. Both cost approximately $30.00. Many other companies distrubute products based on the same technology that have different body designs and therefore different dimensions. When building a fog system to fit inside a scenic piece with tight tolerances, it may be well worth the effort to investigate several different brands to find the one with the best fit.

PLUMBING THE EFFECT

Figure 2 shows a system developed to direct smoke within a scenic unit. Most humidifiers have an exhaust port at the top of the ionic disk chamber; on the Sunbeam and Walgreens models, this port is $1\frac{3}{8}$" in diameter. A piece of $1\frac{1}{4}$" PVC tubing wrapped with a few layers of foil tape makes a tight seal in this port. More foil tape can then be used to connect $1\frac{1}{2}$" diameter pool hose to the other end of the PVC tubing. The pool hose will carry the smoke to the opening on the scenic unit, for instance up to the tops of the chimney pipes. Pool hoses up to 8' long have been used without any noticeable loss of smoke volume. The only factor to consider is that a longer hose may result in a slight delay between activating the unit and the first release of the smoke.

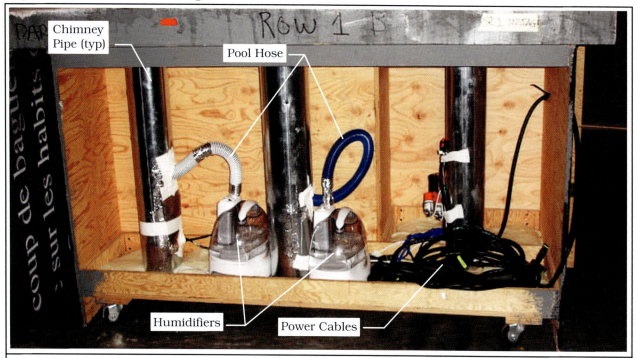

FIGURE 2: Two Ultrasonic Humidifiers Installed in a *Cendrillion* Chimney Unit

The direction of the smoke can easily be influenced by mounting a small fan near the exhaust end of the pool hose. The color can be changed by mounting gelled birdies or MR-16s near the exhaust end of the pool hose. When fitting the pool hose into the ultrasonic humidifier, be sure to leave a way to access and refill the water reservoir. Also, some humidifiers will have a slotted diffuser cap over the exhaust port, which should be removed prior to installation of the PVC tubing.

POWERING THE EFFECT

The humidifier units are designed to operate on 120v AC (wall power) but they could be connected to a power inverter and powered by a 12V car battery. The inverter costs $35.00 at an auto parts store, and the battery another $60.00 or so. This arrangement was used, in conjunction with a remote trigger, for a 20 minute long smoke effect intended for the 2007 Santa Fe Opera's production of *La Boheme*. During tests, this configuration ran for more than 6 hours, with the limiting factor being the amount of water contained in the reservoir.

CONCERNS AND COMPLICATIONS

The humidifiers are designed to fill a small room with water vapor, not to fill an 800-square-foot stage with an atmospheric effect. The smoke cloud produced by the humidifier will vary between 2' and 3' in diameter – a convincing amount for a stove or chimney, but not practical for a larger effect.

If the reservoir tank is not properly seated, the unit may produce intermittent output. It is important to know that the flow of water from the bottom reservoir over the ionic disk is driven by internal reservoir tank pressure. Any past attempts to alter the reservoir tank in order to enlarge the exhaust port or add a second port have met with failure. If the reservoir body is punctured, the pressure balance inside the tank is altered and the unit stops generating the visible smoke.

ACKNOWLEDGEMENTS

This system was developed by the Santa Fe Opera Electrics Department. Credit is due especially to Dave Hult, Erika Kissam, Travis Shupe, and the Santa Fe Opera's 2006 Electrics Apprentices.

꿍꿍꿍꿍

One of our goals for a production of *A Midsummer Night's Dream* was to make the fog generated by our LeMaitre G150 fog machines cold enough to hug the floor like a dry-ice fog. We wanted to avoid buying any expendables other than the fog fluid we always purchase. To reach that goal, we used an inexpensive window air conditioner as the heart of a fog chiller.

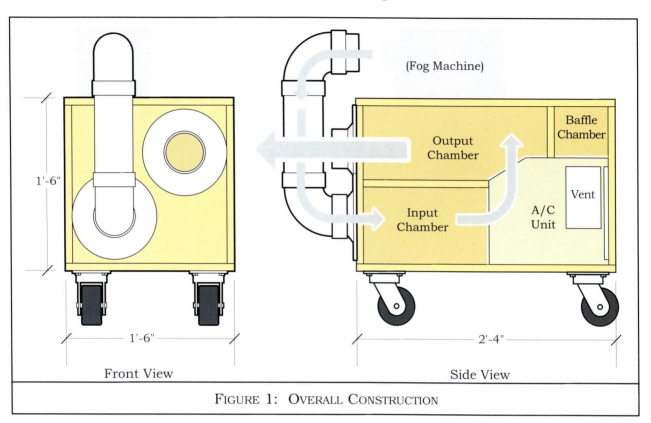

FIGURE 1: OVERALL CONSTRUCTION

CONSTRUCTION

We built the chiller as a three-chambered box as shown in Figure 1. The air conditioner pulled the fog into the box's input chamber and pushed it out through the output chamber, from which a number of hoses distributed it around the stage. The baffle chamber collected the air that the air conditioner would normally vent to the atmosphere.

We built the box out of $\frac{3}{4}$" plywood and fitted it with 4" PVC pipe and fittings as shown. To isolate the chambers from each another, we secured strips of polystyrene foam to both the box and the A/C unit with Liquid Nails Paneling/Molding adhesive.

Not included in the drawing but visible in the photo in Figure 2 is the electrical quad box with two receptacles. Since we had sealed the air conditioner's power switch inside the box, we needed a switched receptacle to control the air conditioner. The non-switched outlet powered the fogger.

OPERATION

We set the machine to maximum cooling and high fan speed before sealing it into the box. We ran the fog machine at about 75% of its output strength to avoid pushing more fog into the air conditioner than it could turn around. We found that if we tried to push too much fog through the box, some of the fog would be exhausted through the vents on the side of the box.

SPECIAL MODIFICATIONS

The air conditioner we used, a Haier HWF05XC6, has no condensate drain. In a normal window installation, atmospheric heat outside evaporates the condensate, but in this application, we discovered that the condensate quickly formed a pool of liquid in the bottom of the baffle chamber. When the cooling fan touched the pool, it created an annoying splashing sound.

Being careful not to drill into the heat exchanger or the fan, we drilled a 1" hole through the air conditioner's housing and the bottom of the baffle chamber to get rid of the condensate and the noise. For a drain pan, we used an ordinary cookie sheet, which the crew emptied each night.

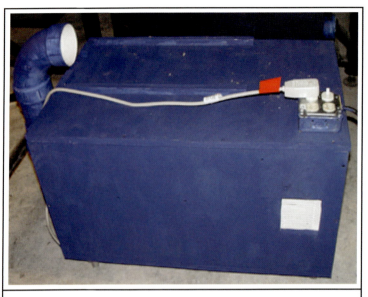

FIGURE 2: SIDE VIEW OF THE CHILLER

For the 2010 production of *We Have Always Lived in the Castle* at Yale Repertory Theatre, Master Electrician Kate Wicker needed to provide battery-powered non-flickering candles for use in a three-candle candelabra. The vigorous and even rough handling that the candelabra was predicted to receive suggested that commercially available products might not last. Wicker responded to the need by building the candles described here.

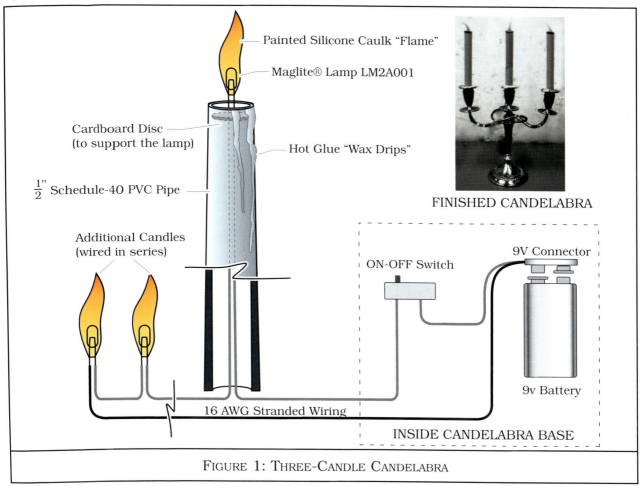

Painted Silicone Caulk "Flame"

Maglite® Lamp LM2A001

Cardboard Disc
(to support the lamp)

Hot Glue "Wax Drips"

$\frac{1}{2}$" Schedule-40 PVC Pipe

Additional Candles
(wired in series)

FINISHED CANDELABRA

ON-OFF Switch

9V Connector

9v Battery

16 AWG Stranded Wiring

INSIDE CANDELABRA BASE

FIGURE 1: THREE-CANDLE CANDELABRA

The candle shaft consists of a suitable length of $\frac{1}{2}$" schedule-40 PVC pipe dressed with durable "wax drips" of hot glue before being painted. A cardboard disc glued into the top end of the candle shaft supports the light source – a MagLite® LM2A001 lamp. To make the lamps look more like flames, each is inserted into the end of a caulk gun loaded with clear silicone caulk, the trigger is pressed briefly, and the lamp is pulled away and left hanging upside down while the caulk sets, at which time the caulked lamp is painted to resemble a flame. Wiring the 3 lamps in series and connecting them to a 9V battery provided each lamp with the required 3 volts. The circuit is controlled by an ON-OFF switch hidden inside the candelabra base.

❧❧❧

FIGURE 1: THE *FAR AWAY* NEON FRAME

For a summer 2008 production of *Far Away* at Barnard College's Minor Latham Playhouse, a neon window frame was to fly in during a bedroom scene. To reduce costs, Shaina Graboyes built the inexpensive but workable representation illustrated in Figure 1 out of ordinary rope light, which she then laid in a shop built frame and covered with Rosco #80 (Primary Blue) and #104 (Tough Silk).

CONSTRUCTION

The frame is essentially a channel. As shown in Figure 2, the base of the channel consists of a $\frac{1}{2}$"-wide strip of $\frac{1}{2}$" or thicker plywood cut in the desired shape. In this case, that shape was a simple rectangle, but any other shape that rope light can assume would work just as well. The channel's sides are strips of $\frac{1}{4}$" lauan or MDF stapled to the base. The strips are cut wide enough to extend $\frac{1}{2}$" above the base. Painting the inside of the channel white as shown in Figure 2 gives the channel a more reflective surface.

$\frac{1}{4}$" Lauan or MDF Sides

Plywood Base

Note that using two layers of Tough Silk (Rx 104) decreases transmission but provides a more continuous neon-like glow. The Tough Silk is applied with its grain perpendicular to the rope light.

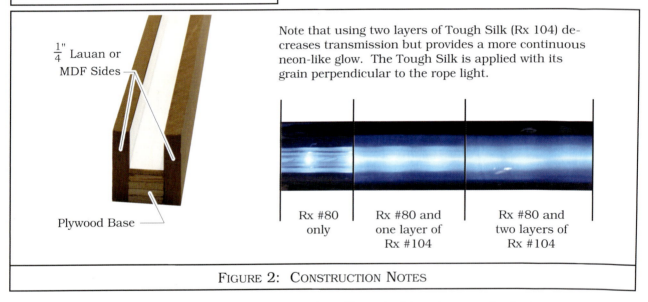

| Rx #80 only | Rx #80 and one layer of Rx #104 | Rx #80 and two layers of Rx #104 |

FIGURE 2: CONSTRUCTION NOTES

The illustration at the right in Figure 2 shows the effect of adding layers of gel. Experimentation under working conditions will determine which combination works best. Obviously, the rope light's plug, power cord and end connectors must be hidden or masked in some way. A hole drilled into an upper corner of the frame allows the rope light's power to be fed through from behind the frame.

For the premiere of *Fluke* at The Collapsable Hole in New York City, Radiohole's Eric Dyer and Maggie Hoffman developed a simple, tourable bubbling light effect using a common vapor-proof outdoor pendant light and a fish tank air pump.

MATERIALS

Vapor-Proof Pendant Light
25 Watt Colored "A" Lamp
$\frac{1}{4}$" Clear PVC Tubing
Light Viscosity Mineral Oil
Dual-Outlet Fish Tank Air Pump with Flow Control (not shown)

DESCRIPTION

Dyer and Hoffman originally used a wall-mount fixture in the effect, but switched to a more tourable, weather-proof light (the VP100PW pendant light from RAB Lighting). Inside the fixture, a 25-watt colored "A" lamp submerged about halfway in mineral oil gave the light an "aquatic" look that could be easily read from an audience. $\frac{1}{4}$" clear PVC tubing ran from the mineral oil to a fish tank air pump in the grid above. During construction and installation, care was taken to avoid submerging electrical components in the oil, and it was determined that a GFCI was unnecessary, as mineral oil is a non-conductive material.

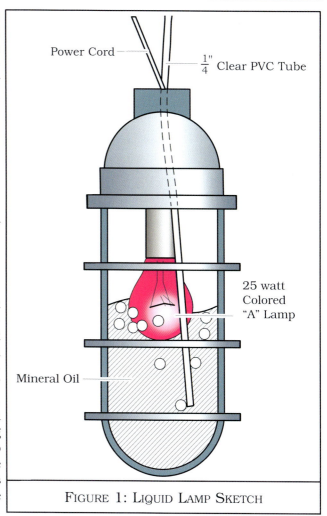

FIGURE 1: LIQUID LAMP SKETCH

A dual-outlet air pump with flow control proved key to the project; a dual-outlet is a bit noisier than a single-outlet model, but allows for the control of two fixtures from the same pump, and for adjustment of air flow to achieve the desired aquatic effect. In multiple-fixture installations, the bubbling sound can overcome the pump noise.

To muffle the noise of the air pumps, Dyer housed them in foam-lined box-mounts, attaching them to the $1\frac{1}{2}$" schedule-40 black pipe grid with U-bolts. Lamp and air pump power were run from a conventional lighting console. Higher wattages have not been tested, but with a 25-watt lamp, this fixture can run for over 24 hours with no mineral oil-heating issues.

See "LiquidLamp" (http://www.youtube.com/watch?v=mH7Xmu8u0Ls) for an online video of this effect.

TECHNICAL BRIEF

Painting

A Durable Plaster Texture Revisited — *Owen M. Collins*

An Affordable Gold-Leaf Finish — *Ben Stark*

A More User-Friendly Lining Stick — *Don Harvey*

Large-Scale Crackle Paint Effect — *Ben Stark*

A Clean Solution for Colored Dirt — *Nora Hyland*

Using Alum to De-Wrinkle Drops — *Nicole L. Bromley*

Designers love to use plaster on walls for texture. The trick is how to get it to stay on scenery that is shifted night after night, week after week. Plaster by itself does not adhere well to a typical hard cover flat. Since it is so rigid when it dries, it can flake off when the unit is flexed. So what is needed is to increase the adhesion properties of the plaster and give it enough flexibility not to crack. While I was at the Flat Rock Playhouse we developed a formula for a plaster coating that was incredibly tough, flexible, and long-lasting.

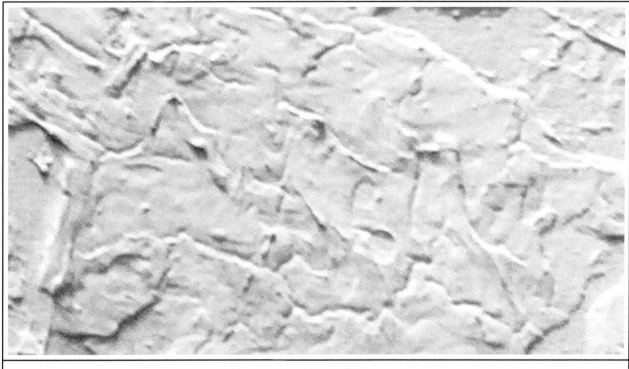

FIGURE 1: SCULPT OR COAT ® PLASTER TEXTURE

We started with Sculpt or Coat®, made by Sculptural Arts Coatings in North Carolina. Sculpt or Coat® is a thick paste made as a coating for Styrofoam. Mixing one part Sculpt or Coat® and three parts joint compound produced a mixture with the right combination of stickiness and flexibility to keep the joint compound on the flat with minimal chipping. We also added some universal tint, changing the color of the mixture to that of the base coat. Consequently, the audience didn't notice places where something had bumped into the wall and chipped the plaster; and few touch-ups were needed throughout the run. As a further refinement, the next time we did rustic plaster walls we put a coat of Clear Flat Acrylic over the texture before base coating, and the plaster lasted the whole run without any marring of the surface.

RESOURCES

Sculptural Arts Coating, Inc: http://www.sculpturalarts.com

The richness of gold leaf is usually only accomplished with equally rich budgets; however, a similar and more affordable finish can be achieved by using gold colored confectioner's foil instead of expensive gold leaf.

MATERIALS

• Gloss Clear Acrylic Sealer (e.g., Minwax Polycrylic®)
• 0.00045" Gold Colored Confectioner's Foil

PROCESS

Tear confectioner's foil into appropriately sized pieces to cover the object. The area and shape of the object should inform the size of the applied foil pieces (i.e., larger pieces for larger areas and smaller pieces for greater detail). Next, if desired, crinkle the foil for texture. Using gloss acrylic sealer as an adhesive, coat both the surface of the object and the back (non-gold side) of the confectioner's foil. Apply the foil to the object, smoothing it out as desired. Finally, recoat the gold foil to seal the foil to the object. Repeat foil application overlapping pieces for additional texture and strength. After the sealer has dried, the object can be painted for additional aging or color as shown below.

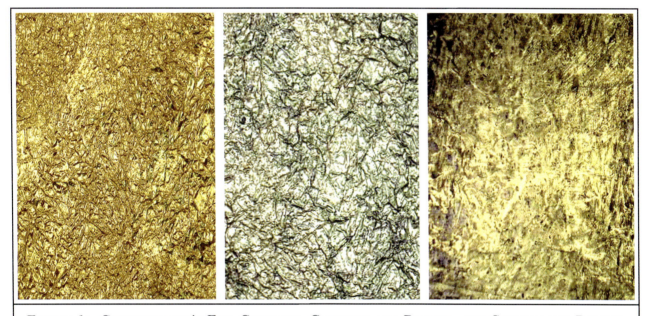

FIGURE 1: CONFECTIONER'S FOIL CRINKLED, CRINKLED AND PAINTED, AND SMOOTH AND PAINTED

COST

This simple technique yields a stunning finish at a fraction of the cost of gold leaf. The most affordable gold leaf costs more than $13.00 psf. Other gold foil systems cost about $1.50 psf. One roll of confectioner's foil (20"x 50') covers over 80 sq.ft. at a cost of $.08 psf. These gold leaf and gold foil prices do not include the cost of sealers and adhesives which can cost $80.00 per quart. Acrylic sealer for confectioner's foil costs about $15.00 per quart. The cost accumulates quickly when using gold leaf or foil systems, especially if undertaking a large project. Using confectioner's foil, a large project (around 75 sq.ft.) should cost under $25.00 including acrylic sealer. At the Yale School of Drama, we covered an ornate 6 ft. chandelier using only half a roll of confectioner's foil.
In terms of labor, the time necessary to complete each finish ranges from over two hours for gold

foil to minutes with confectioner's foil. The difference is in the drying time for a sealing base coat, a paint base coat, then an adhesive for gold foil or gold leaf. The confectioner's foil technique uses sealer as both a sealing base coat on most surfaces (wood, metal, foam) and as an adhesive. Also, because confectioner's foil is opaque, there is no need to paint the object as a preliminary step.

FIGURE 2: GOLD PAINT, GOLD LEAF, GOLD FOIL, AND CONFECTIONER'S FOIL

Additionally, confectioner's foil is more durable than gold leaf. The material is less fragile and easier to handle and does not require the use of messy contact adhesives. Given these differences and the aesthetic result compared to paint, gold leaf, and gold foil in Figure 2, confectioner's foil offers a comparable and affordable finish.

NOTES

• When covering detailed moulding or profiles, it may be necessary to use white glue instead of acrylic sealer to adhere smaller foil pieces. Seal over the foil with gloss acrylic sealer.

• Gold confectioner's foil may be substituted with aluminum gold foil sheets (commonly used to wrap sandwiches and hot dogs) available from most food service distributors.

• Alufoil Products Co., Inc offers over 15 colors of confectioner's foil, including red gold, green gold, silver, copper, and various other non-metallic colors.

ACKNOWLEDGEMENTS

Will Ingham
Alufoil Products Co., Inc

Figure 1 illustrates two types of lining sticks. The traditional lining stick, shown in the background, is simple, reliable, and easily made from scraps of 1x lumber. It is also somewhat heavier than its purpose requires, and the rigid connection between the handle and the painting edge makes it awkward to manipulate and carry in the trunk of a car. The improved lining stick, shown in the foreground in Figure 1 and described here, was developed to address those disadvantages.

DESIGN DETAILS: THE BASE

To reduce weight while still offering a straight line guide, this lining stick uses two 6'-0" pieces of square-edged $\frac{1}{16}$" x 1" x 1" 6063-T52 aluminum angle spaced 3" apart as shown in Figure 2. Oriented as show in Figure 2, the angles provide two, parallel lining edges that are held 1" above the work, avoiding any paint seepage or bleeding. The base's end spacers – two pieces of $\frac{3}{4}$" plywood cut 3" wide and 10" long – let the user pin one end of the lining stick to the floor with a foot while swinging the other end into a desired position. The lining stick's intermediate spacers (see Figure 2) are pairs of $\frac{5}{16}$" x $1\frac{1}{2}$" tension pins (slotted spring pins) sleeved over 10-24 x $3\frac{1}{2}$" round head machine screws capped with lock washers and nuts.

DESIGN DETAILS: THE HANDLE

The handle adapted for use here is an inexpensive, commercially available handle that is designed to clamp onto a wire dust mop frame (see Figure 3). The handle's clamp cannot open wide enough to fit over $\frac{5}{16}$"-diameter tension pins like those used in the intermediate spacers. It can, however, clamp onto the $\frac{1}{4}$" x $3\frac{1}{2}$" machine screw that is double-

FIGURE 1: TWO TYPES OF LINING STICKS

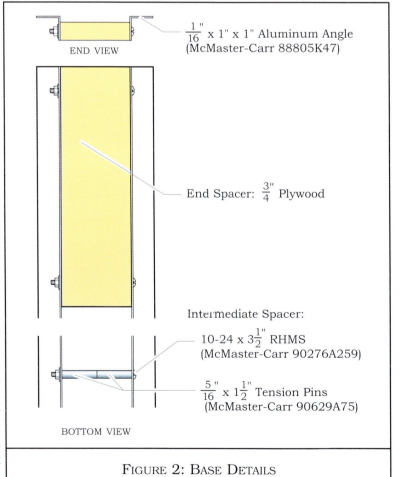

END VIEW

$\frac{1}{16}$" x 1" x 1" Aluminum Angle (McMaster-Carr 88805K47)

End Spacer: $\frac{3}{4}$" Plywood

Intermediate Spacer:

10-24 x $3\frac{1}{2}$" RHMS (McMaster-Carr 90276A259)

$\frac{5}{16}$" x $1\frac{1}{2}$" Tension Pins (McMaster-Carr 90629A75)

BOTTOM VIEW

FIGURE 2: BASE DETAILS

nutted at the center of this lining stick in place of a spacer. After the sides of the clamp have been ground to slightly less than 3" the handle provides its own spacer.

| FIGURE 3: THE PIVOTING HANDLE | FIGURE 4: TIPPING THE STICK |

The white plastic band visible in Figure 3 is a handle lock. Left unlocked, the handle can be swung into any position above the painting edges as Figure 3 implies. Sliding the band all the way down locks the handle and, as in Figure 4, lets one painting edge be lifted farther off the work as is sometimes needed. Whether used locked or unlocked, this "pivotable" handle permits the user greater freedom of movement and positioning above the work, promoting control and reducing fatigue. Dust mop handles of this type are available from a number of suppliers, such as Parish Maintenance Supply in Syracuse, New York.

THE MINI-BUNGIES

Whenever the handle is locked, one or more mini-bungies can be attached to the intermediate spacers as shown in Figure 1 to return the handle to a neutral, upright position. More commonly, however, they are left dangling while the stick is being used. When the stick is folded or disassembled to fit in the trunk of a car, the bungies can be re-attached to keep the parts together as shown in Figure 5.

NOTES

• The key dimension in this lining stick is the width of the handle clamp. Spacers and hardware should be sized to that dimension.

- Either square or rounded edge aluminum angle could be used in this lining stick, but the square edge stock is the less expensive of the two.
- McMaster-Carr and Parish Maintenance are cited only to provide a base of reference, and are not the exclusive sources of the hardware and materials used in this lining stick.

ช่อช่อช่อ

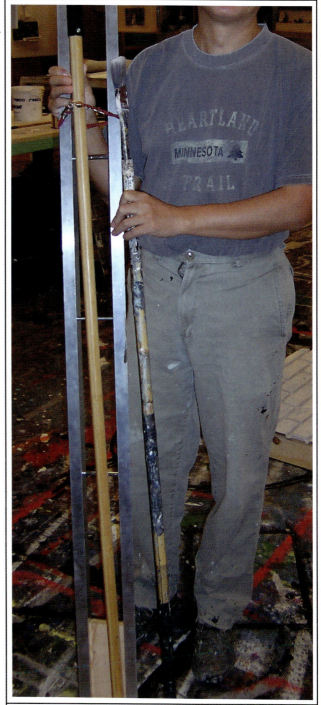

FIGURE 5: DISASSEMBLED FOR TRAVEL

A Yale Repertory Theatre production of *The Cherry Orchard* required furniture distressed with a crackle paint treatment. I began experimenting with commercially available crackle mediums, however, they did not produce crackle texture that would read from the audience. As a result, I explored other methods; specifically, shellac and white glue as crackle mediums. Once cured with a heat gun, I found that white glue worked the best in producing a large scale crackle paint effect.

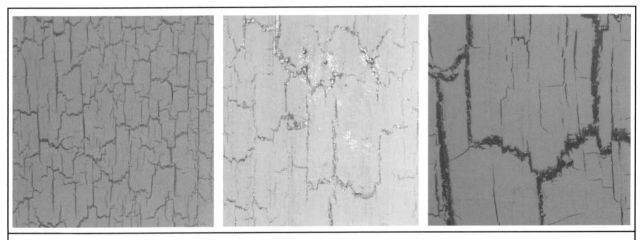

FIGURE 1 (FULL SCALE): BEHR CRACKLE MEDIUM, SHELLAC, AND WHITE GLUE

MATERIALS AND TOOLS

Latex Paint - contrasting base color and top color
White Glue thinned with water
Three (3) cheap brushes - one for each paint color and one for thinned glue
Heat Gun

PROCESS

Begin by applying the darker base coat to the entire piece and allow this layer to dry thoroughly. Second, thin white glue with water to aid in application. Apply a generous amount of glue to a workable area of the piece; typically no more than 4 to 6 sq. ft. to avoid the glue drying before applying paint. Next, brush the top color lightly onto the glue. The paint should float on the glue, but if more paint is needed, reload the brush and gently begin applying again. Do not go back over an area without reloading the brush with paint; to do so will mix the wet glue and paint into a marbled mess. Once the area is covered with glue and paint, use a heat gun to dry the surface. The heat gun also allows the user to control the crackle treatment with more or less heat (more heat speeds the drying time and creates larger cracks). Long cracks will form in the direction the paint and glue were applied with fewer lateral cracks joining them. Continue the process until the desired area is covered. Once complete, allow at least an hour to cure. The end result is a durable and dramatic weathered finish.

❧❧❧❧❧

The design for Yale Repertory Theatre's 2010 production of *Battle of Black and Dogs* called for a large stream of red dirt to fall from the sky onto a Plexiglas™ deck. Since real dirt would have generated too much dust and raised health concerns, and sand would have left scratches in the deck, the decision was made to use finely ground cork, which was only available in natural cork color. Therefore, the scenic charge had to come up with a reasonably cost- and time-effective way to dye it.

MATERIALS AND TOOLS

Granulated cork (Available from the Maryland Cork Company – 14/30 size)
Rosco Supersaturated® paint
Clear flat acrylic sealer
Water
5-gallon bucket
5-gallon paint strainer
Gloves (nitrile, latex, etc.)
Synthetic mesh fabric with fine weave
Sawhorses
Adjustable electric floor fan

FIGURE 1: TREATED SAMPLES

SETTING UP YOUR DRYING SURFACE

1. Pick an area of your workspace that can get messy; despite your best efforts, cork will end up everywhere.

2. Stretch mesh fabric between two sawhorses and attach it securely. In this instance, the edges were folded over and stapled to the sawhorses; be aware of staple placement as added weight can cause your staples to pull through the fabric.

3. Position fan so that air flows gently under the fabric, but does not cause significant movement.

4. Place trays or buckets underneath sawhorses to help catch loose cork and minimize clean-up.

PAINTING PROCESS

1. Mix paint, sealer, and water in 5-gallon bucket. Specific ratios will vary depending on desired color and saturation.

2. Place the paint strainer in your bucket, using its elastic top to hold it in place.

3. Add cork slowly, stirring to achieve maximum saturation. Continue until bucket is filled to capacity.

4. Lift strainer out of bucket, and wring out until little to no liquid is dripping out. Be careful to keep the top closed, so as not to lose any cork. You will probably want to be wearing gloves for this step (see Figure 2).

5. Spread wet cork on mesh fabric set-up. Keep the layer relatively thin for quickest dry time (see Figure 3). Turn on fan, and adjust positioning as needed.

6. As the cork dries, it will tend to congeal, sticking both to itself and to the fabric. Leave the cork to dry for approximately half an hour, then spread the cork around, taking care to break up any clumps (see Figure 4). Let the cork dry again, then return and repeat the process. As the cork becomes drier, you can allow more time in between each redistribution. You will get a

FIGURE 2: WRING OUT THE PAINT STRAINER

FIGURE 3: SPREAD CORK ON MESH FABRIC

sense of how often you need to check on it based on how easy it is to unstick the cork from the fabric.

7. When you can run your hand through the cork without color coming off, it is completely dry. Scoop it off the fabric and into a storage receptacle.

8. Repeat Steps 3 through 7 as often as necessary. You should be able to get several batches of cork done before needing to mix more paint.

FIGURE 4: BREAK UP CORK CLUSTERS

FIGURE 5: FINISHED CORK

Although it may at first not seem so, this process provides plenty of down-time for working on other projects. One final note: due to Connecticut's stringent fire codes, all scenic materials must pass a basic flame test. After painting, the cork did not live up to the required test standards and had to be spread out again, sprayed with a liquid flame retardant, and left to dry. Adding flame retardant to the original paint mixture could have eliminated this redundancy.

❧❧❧❧❧

Over the centuries, scenic artists have developed a number of mostly undocumented techniques to remove unsightly wrinkles and creases from stage drops.   One of the oldest and most reliable techniques is still used by Technical Director Albert "Stub" Allison at Theatre Aspen. It involves using alum, a chemical commonly described as "a pickling spice" and found in grocery stores.

WHAT IS ALUM

Alum is potassium alum, the hydrated form of potassium aluminum sulfate. It has long been used to make pickles crispier and is the key ingredient in many if not most styptic pencils, which are used to stop the bleeding from shaving nicks and cuts. Its astringent character makes it a perfect choice for removing wrinkles from scenic materials.

STEPS IN DE-WRINKLING

The first step is to load in the drop and hang it in its proper location, typically with a bottom pipe and clever-blocks or other clamps along the sides to eliminate the worst of the wrinkles. If time allows, the drop should be left to relax for a day or two, with the clever blocks adjusted to account for any new large wrinkles that develop as the fabric settles under its own weight.

Once the drop has relaxed sufficiently, the remaining smaller wrinkles are treated with an alum solution applied with a Hudson sprayer. A good ratio for the solution is one tablespoon of alum per gallon of very hot water. The solution is sprayed liberally on the back of the drop and allowed to dry fully.

TIPS

It is smart to spray-test a small sample or corner of the drop first to make sure that there will be no discoloration and to discover how much spraying will be required. Further, it is best to spray the back of the drop rather than the front to avoid all possible damage to the paint treatment. Finally, while it is completely nonflammable and can be bought in grocery stores for less than $10.00 a pound, alum is a chemical astringent. Users should wear gloves and avoid prolonged or extensive contact with the solution, and should take care not to inhale it in its dry state.

⁊❦⁊❦⁊❦

TECHNICAL BRIEF

Projections

Melded Technologies: Video Projections
   and Moving Mirrors

M. Barrett Cleveland

Low-Memory, Higy-Quality Digital
   Images for the Stage

David B. Carter

A Servo-Controlled Projector Dowser

Lung-Kuei Lin

Low-Cost RP Screens for the Stage

Daniel J. Anteau

A Stock Batten-Mounted Projector Bracket

Pierre-André Salim

Choreographer Jill Tarkett-Jackson wanted to expand the parameters of her contemporary dance piece *Sly* by incorporating video projections that would play on different areas of the cyclorama. We owned equipment that could accomplish separate parts of her objective: our Toshiba TLP57® LCD projector and multimedia laptop could certainly generate images – but not move them to different areas; and our Rosco I-Cue Intelligent Mirrors® could move beams of light – but not video images – around a cyc. This article describes the system we developed to combine the two technologies.

OVERVIEW OF THE MOUNT

Designed to be slid into a gel-frame holder, the I-Cue® enables an ETC Source 4® or Altman Shakespeare® ellipsoidal spotlight to be remotely aimed at a variety of positions via DMX 512 control. The I-Cue's gel-frame mount is visible in Figure 1.

Since Tarkett wanted *Sly's* video images to be as large as possible, the projector image would need to fill the moving mirror without spilling beyond its edges. Consequently, we built a mount that would allow us to change the distance between the I-Cue® and the projector without damaging either device.

I-CUE® MODIFICATIONS

For this use, the I-Cue® is fastened to a $\frac{3}{4}$"-square tube shaft sleeved into a length of 1"-square tube that is built into the mount. Figure 2 details Scene Shop Supervisor Stan Werne's hardware for fastening the I-Cue® to the $\frac{3}{4}$"-square tube shaft. Once the shaft's position has been set for optimal image size, a knurled knob (visible at the upper left) fixes the shaft in place.

The corner irons shown are attached to the I-Cue® with sheet metal screws driven through factory-drilled holes. The corner irons, along with a mending-plate hook on the front of the shaft, easily support the I-Cue®. At strike, we removed the two bolts to free the I-Cue®, leaving the corner irons on the I-Cue® since they do not interfere with its operation.

FIGURE 1: MODIFIED I-CUE® ON A PROJECTOR MOUNT

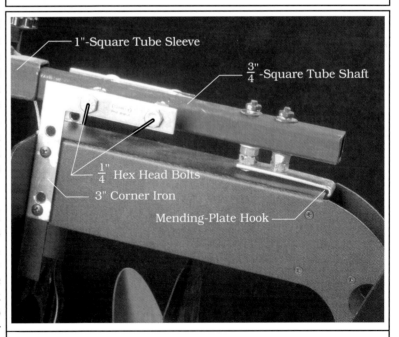

FIGURE 2: I-CUE® HARDWARE

THE I-CUE®/PROJECTOR MOUNT

As Figure 3 illustrates, expanded metal welded to a square-tube frame forms the base of the mount, and a second square-tube frame surrounds the bottom of the projector. Two U-shaped flat-bar brackets encase the projector and hold the 1"-square-tube sleeve directly above the center of its lens. Two pieces of flat bar connect the U-brackets to a custom flat-bar hanging yoke, and a third piece, welded across the top of the brackets, accommodates the projector hold-down: a length of all-thread rod welded to a flat-bar hold-down plate.

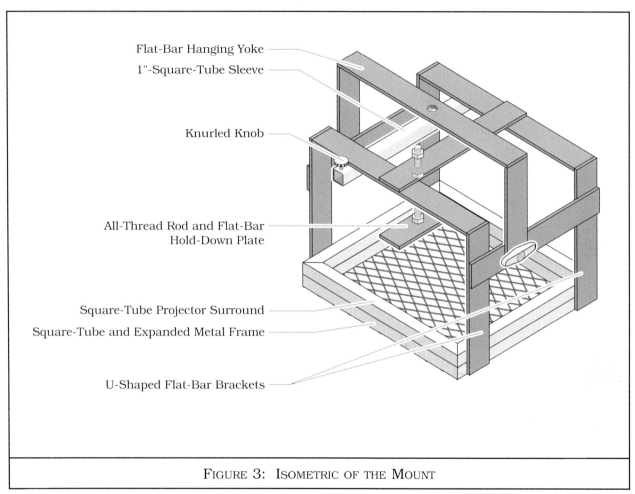

FIGURE 3: ISOMETRIC OF THE MOUNT

PUTTING IT ALL TOGETHER

Since the I-Cue® reverses a projected image, it is necessary to reconfigure the projector menu settings for rear-screen operation. Although these settings can be programmed by infrared remote, the I-Cue® may block the sensor, forcing users to change the settings manually from a ladder — as it did for us. Programming cues for the positioning and movement of the video images was done outside of technical rehearsals. Two backstage laptops controlled the projections and movement. One was dedicated to the PowerPoint® file projecting the video and the audio track, and the second played the Horizon file controlling the I-Cue®. On cue, the backstage operator simultaneously started both playback files, and all of the subsequent video and moving mirror cues executed automatically.

IMMEDIATE RESULTS AND SUBSEQUENT IMPROVEMENTS

The results of the *Sly* project were generally encouraging, but we were not completely satisfied. We addressed several remaining issues in producing *This Speaking Body*, an original dance/theatre piece by Judy Bejarano at Colorado State University in April 2002 in association with Impact Dance:

> Image Brightness — Although the images produced by the 1000-lumen Toshiba TLP57® were intense enough for *Sly*, we needed more punch for the more brightly lit *This Speaking Body*. The images generated by the $12,000.00, 2800-lumen Proxima DP6860® projectors used for *Body* were stunning. Fortunately, new Toshiba models offering outputs of up to 2000 lumens are now available for about $4,500.00.

> Complete Dowsing — For *Sly*, this proved to be the most frustrating problem. When the projector was "blacked out," a good deal of light still leaked from the unit: a gray rectangle remained on the cyc even when we were not projecting. The work-around, programming extra cues to direct the I-Cue® out of sightlines when not needed, was only somewhat effective, and still the images never "magically" appeared. We had better success in producing *Body*, for which we used a Wybron Eclipse II® DMX Dowser. The Eclipse II® works by irising down like a camera, leaving nothing to interfere with the projection. Driven by a Coloram II® power supply, it required only 1 lighting channel for operation. *Body's* LD, John McKellar, patched two dowsers into his rig and programmed their opening and closing in the lighting desk, a Whole Hog II®. The Eclipse IIs worked flawlessly, completely solving the dowsing problem.

> Image Size — Since *Sly* was only one of 15 pieces in an evening, our choices for I-Cue® placement were limited. Ideally, we would have preferred a longer throw and a larger image than were possible. Image size, especially in rear projecting, was again an issue with *This Speaking Body* — and, here too, the solution remained beyond reach: Proxima offers a wide angle conversion lens, but it carries a list price of $2,200 and one was not available for the project.

Significant product support from the following sources contributed to the design and production elements for *This Speaking Body*. The Colorado State University Office of Instructional Services supplied 2 Proximas®. Barbizon, Light of the Rockies, let us test their newest automated fixtures. And Wybron, Inc., loaned us the Eclipse IIs® and the Coloram® Power Supply.

RESOURCES

Rosco IQ: http://www.rosco.com/main.html (Follow path: Products/Motion Effects/IQ)
Toshiba LCD Projectors: http://www.Toshiba.com (Follow path: Products/Data Projectors)
Proxima LCD Projectors: http://www.proxima.com/projectors/projector_detail.asp?pid=dp6860
Wybron Eclipse II DMX Dowser: http://www.wybron.com/Entertainment/EclipseII/eclipseII.pdf
Wybron Coloram II Power Supply: http://www.wybron.com/Entertainment/Coloram/index.html

❧❧❧❧❧

Coupled with large-format printers, Adobe Photoshop offers a quick and relatively painless method for creating scenic images of excellent quality. But resampling drawings or photographs only a few inches square to a size that is useful for the stage often distorts the quality of the artwork, at times making it almost unrecognizable. Enhancing the resolution of the larger image takes such enormous amounts of memory that it is often prohibitively wasteful in terms of time. Further, if the original artwork and the final image have different aspect rations (height-to-width proportions), fitting the artwork into the scenic frame can be time-consuming and extremely trying.

Designs for a production of *On the Verge* required 22 panels ranging in size from 24" x 36" to 44" x 60". The original artwork consisted of pencil sketches, each one only a few inches across, that were "aged" and "sweetened" in Photoshop 7 and overlaid with text. Given time constraints, digital resampling seemed the best path to take, despite the anticipated obstacles of memory, distortion, and proportional differences. Fortunately, by integrating the use of Photoshop and Illustrator, I discovered a process for creating stunning images with a minimum of fuss.

Illustrator produces very compact files with high-resolution. A 150-dpi image filling 140 mb of storage space in Photoshop takes up only 14 mb of storage as an Illustrator file – and Illustrator's default resolution is 800 dpi. With this 10:1 advantage, I was able to store all 22 of my images on a single CD with superb quality control. Further, because Illustrator reads images as whole objects instead of a myriad of individual pixels, it exports quickly to large format printers. On a high setting, a 36" x 63" image prints out in 20 to 30 minutes. This article describes a step-by-step process for transferring an image from Photoshop to Illustrator, quickly resizing it, and setting it up for output on a large-format printer. The scenic images were created using Adobe® Photoshop 7 and Adobe® Illustrator 10 on a Windows platform. The printer used was an Epson® 9000 Large-Format printer on a Mac platform.

SETTING UP AND IMPORTING

After launching Illustrator, go to the *File* menu and click on *New*. In the *Artboard Setup* section of the New Document window as shown in Figure 1, make the *Size* "Custom", the *Units* "Inches", and set the height, width, and orientation to the dimensions of your final image. Set the *Color Mode* to match the color mode of the Photoshop source image – usually *RGB* – and click "OK".

The black rectangle you see represents a full screen view of your page, and the dotted rectangle (probably much smaller) represents the printable area of the assigned printer, a setting we will change later. Next, go to *View>Smart Guides* and make sure there is a checkmark next to *Smart Guides*. Smart Guides give visual prompts when you are close to an anchor point, much like Object Snap in AutoCAD. Now, click on Illustrator's Selection Tool, the black arrow on the top left of the Toolbox, as shown in Figure 2.

Next, launch Photoshop and open the source image: in this example, a sketch of a baboon, aged in Photoshop and overlaid with handwriting.

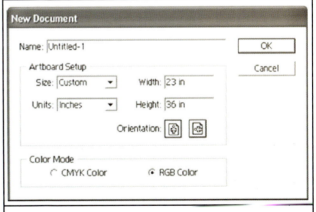

FIGURE 1: THE NEW DOCUMENT WINDOW

FIGURE 2: ILLUSTRATOR'S SELECTION TOOL

FIGURE 3: THE WINDOWS SIDE BY SIDE

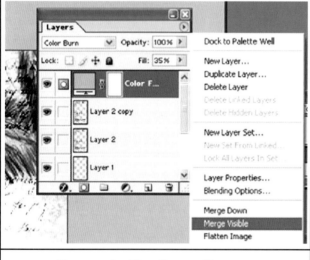

FIGURE 4: THE LAYER PALETTE

Arrange your Photoshop and Illustrator windows so that they are side by side on your monitor, as shown in Figure 3, and click on the Photoshop window to activate it. If the source image has multiple layers, you want to merge them so you can move them as one. The quickest way to do this is to use the *Window>Layers* menu to activate the Layer Palette. Clicking on the arrow in the upper right corner of the Layer Palette will open the pop-up menu shown in Figure 4. Scroll down and click on *Merge Visible* to put all the elements on a single layer. Then select the "Move" Tool from the Photoshop toolbox, put your cursor in the middle of the image, and click and drag the image into the Illustrator window. After you've released the mouse button, the image will appear in your Illustrator window, surrounded by a colored "bounding box" with several small, white, rectangular, anchor points on its perimeter. You can now close Photoshop.

In Illustrator, click on empty space to deselect the image. If you've done this correctly, the bounding box has disappeared. Zoom out as necessary until you have a complete view of both the image and the page it needs to fill. Now move the cursor near a top corner of the image until you get a "Smart Guide" prompt labeled "anchor". Click on the anchor and drag the image to the corresponding corner of the Illustrator page. When you see another prompt labeled "Intersect", release the mouse button. Move your cursor over the diagonally opposite corner of the image's bounding box until you again see an "anchor" prompt and the cursor transforms into a double-headed diagonal arrow. Click on the anchor and drag it to the corresponding corner of the Illustrator page. When you see the "intersect" prompt, release the mouse button. The image is quickly and accurately resized.

PRINTING

While images can be resized on any desktop, you will need access to a Large-Format Printer (LFP), such as an HP DesignJet or Epson 9000 in order to set the printable area. For these settings, I generally add 2" to the image size, for example setting a printable area of 38" x 65" for a 36" x 63" image. If you are working on a Windows platform, click on *File>Print Setup*. When the "Print Setup" box opens, click on "Properties". Click on the arrow next to the "Paper Size" window to open a pop-up menu. Scrolling to the bottom, choose the option labeled "User Defined" to open another box that will let you customize the printable area. (Someone will no doubt point out how much easier this is on a Mac: click on *File>Page Setup>Customize* and enter your dimensions and margins when the box pops up.) Though the steps listed here are for Epson printers, the procedure is similar for HP printers. If you can find a "paper size" category and a "customize" option, you can do no wrong. Once you've defined your printable area, turn Smart Guides off. Illustrator has a nifty little tool for making sure your image is inside the page. In the toolbox, you'll see a tool button marked with a hand icon. Click on this tool and hold the mouse button down until a fly-out menu appears, making the "Page Tool" available as shown in Figure 5. With the "Page Tool" selected, move your cursor to the lower left edge of the image. Clicking and holding down the mouse button will reveal a double dotted rectangle of the dimensions of your custom paper size. Position that rectangle around the image, and release the mouse button. Once all this is done, you are ready to print.

A NOTE OF CAUTION AND A FINAL TIP

Before dragging a Photoshop image into an Illustrator drawing, make sure that they are both in the same *Color Mode* — either *RGB* or *CMYK*. For both programs, the active mode can be found on the title bar above the image next to the file name and the zoom level. To change the mode, use *Image>Mode* in Photoshop or *File>Document Color Mode* in Illustrator. If that is done, the image should print out in acceptable colors. Nevertheless, I recommend that you do smaller test prints and tweak the color profile in the printer's custom properties window. Although I am somewhat biased, I find that, for most desktop printing, Epson printer drivers are excellent at matching screen colors.

I also recommend that if a source image is letter-size or smaller, the resolution should be set at a minimum of 300 dpi for best results. You can change the resolution by typing "300" in the "Resolution" box of the *Image>Image Size* menu.

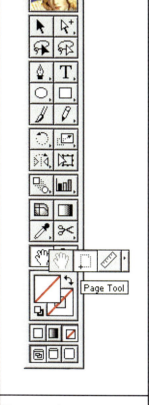

FIGURE 5: PAGE TOOL

Like many other projectors, the three video projectors available to Yale Repertory Theatre's 2003 production of *The Black Dahlia* lacked true fade-in/fade out capability. Though entirely suitable for our purposes in all other ways, they could not provide acceptably smooth cross-fades with each other or with general stage lighting. To address this problem, we fitted each projector with a shop-built dowser like that shown in Figure 1 – a shutter-like device controlled by a DMX signal from the light board.

DOWSER DESIGN

The dowser consists of a set of pivoting metal shutters mounted parallel to each other in a 7" x 7" frame and ganged together at a servo-driven operating arm. The dowser works like a motor driven Venetian blind mounted sideways. Figure 2 shows that the counter-clockwise rotation of a disc mounted on a servo pulls the shutters closed, and clockwise rotation pushes them open.

Maintaining close tolerances in machining the parts is essential. Shutters (see Figure 3) must be parallel and must overlap completely when closed.

FIGURE 1: THE SERVO-CONTROLLED DOWSER

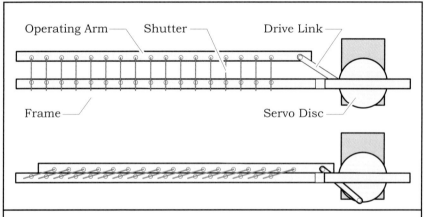

FIGURE 2: TOP VIEW – THE DOWSER OPEN AND CLOSED

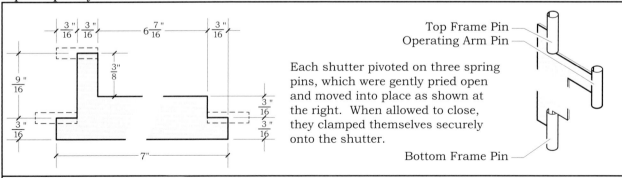

Each shutter pivoted on three spring pins, which were gently pried open and moved into place as shown at the right. When allowed to close, they clamped themselves securely onto the shutter.

FIGURE 3: SHUTTER DIMENSIONS AND SHUTTER/PIN ASSEMBLY

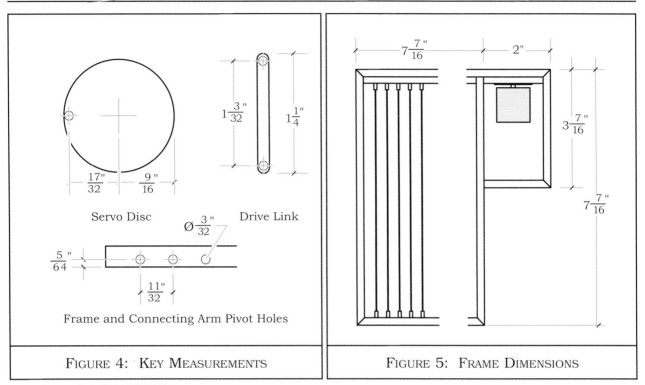

FIGURE 4: KEY MEASUREMENTS   FIGURE 5: FRAME DIMENSIONS

CONSTRUCTION NOTES

Dimensions are given as guidelines only. The shutters in this dowser were sized to work with a 5"-diameter projector lens, and the servo this frame was designed to accommodate is now discontinued. Other builders must modify the dimensions given to suit their own lenses and servos.

PARTS AND PRICE LIST

Item	Model	Price	Qty	Total
Type 420 Stainless Steel Spring Pins $\frac{3}{32}$" Diameter, $\frac{3}{8}$" Length (pkg / 100)	92383A202	$2.25	2	$4.50
Type 316 Stainless Steel Sheet with #2B Finish .024" Thick, 24" x 24"	88885K31	$26.17	1	$26.17
Miniature Brass Shapes Alloy 260, Square Tube,	8859K45	$10.13	2	$20.26
Flat Black Spray Paint		$3.34	1	$3.34
9V DC 1000mA Power Supply		$15.00	1	$15.00
Servo (this model now discontinued)	HS-306 (Hi-Tec)		2	Stock
Male XLR Plugs	SC1010-ND	$3.51	10	$31.10
			Total	$104.37

A recent production at the University of Hawaii at Manoa required a round 12'-0" diameter projection screen designed to display front and rear projections. Purchasing an RP screen in a shape that would see limited, if any, later use was not an affordable option. Our attempts at making a screen by sanding clear plastic sheeting proved far too labor intensive and produced unsatisfactory results. After considerable research and experimentation, I discovered that standard white industrial shrink-wrap can be used to make efficient, cost effective, and disposable screens of various sizes.

Available in rolls 14' to 30' wide and up to 300' long, industrial shrink-wrap is typically used for protecting boats and other large objects from snow, wind, and rain. Readily available, this material can be purchased in thicknesses of 6 to 9 mm directly from distributors online. The 9-mm shrink-wrap has the additional advantage of being flame retardant (FR). A 14'-wide length of 9-mm FR shrink wrap costs about $.30 a square foot. By comparison, commercially available screen material comes in 55", 96" and 110" widths at costs ranging from $1.14 to $3.50 a square foot.

TWO VIEWS ON LUMINOSITY

I compared two 12' x 16' shrink-wrap RP screens in an objective side-by-side luminosity test using Rose Brand's Twin White as a control. One of my test screens was made of FR 9-mil shrink wrap; the other, of NFR 6-mil shrink-wrap. Figure 1 illustrates the results of that test, in which the Twin White screen far out performed the shrink-wrap screens.

	RoseBrand Twin White	9-mil FR Shrink Wrap	6-mil NFR Shrink Wrap
Luminescence at Front of Screen	1.30 fc	0.66 fc	0.66 fc
Luminescence at Rear of Screen	1.90 fc	2.50 fc	2.50 fc
Projector located 20'-0" from front of screen. Readings taken at 1'-0" from screen surface.			

FIGURE 1: THE OBJECTIVE COMPARISON — WHAT THE METER MEASURED

In a subjective visual comparison, however, the difference was negligible. Figure 2, photos of a test pattern as it was projected onto each material, suggests how similar the projected images looked to the casual viewer.

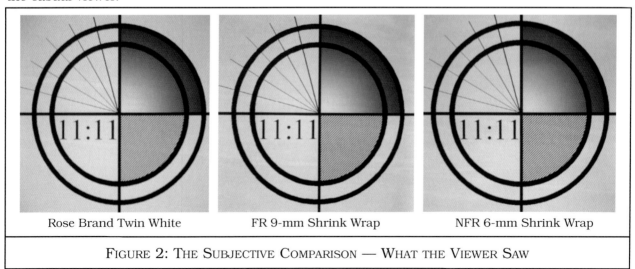

Rose Brand Twin White   FR 9-mm Shrink Wrap   NFR 6-mm Shrink Wrap

FIGURE 2: THE SUBJECTIVE COMPARISON — WHAT THE VIEWER SAW

MAKING A SHRINK WRAP SCREEN

Construct a sturdy frame for the plastic. Whether you use wood or metal, the frame needs to be sturdy enough to resist the plastic's tendency to cause the sides to bow in as it shrinks. The plastic can be attached to the frame with staples, glue, or a special heat-shrink tape. In attaching the plastic to the frame, be sure to pull the plastic evenly taut so that it will shrink evenly. If you choose to staple the plastic, make sure to wrap it around the edge of the frame and staple as if you were building a soft-covered flat. If the material is not wrapped in this fashion, the shrinking action can pull the plastic out of the staples.

After the plastic has been secured to the frame, stand the screen up and provide vertical support for the shrinking process. To ensure safety, wear long-cuff safety gloves, eye protection, and make sure the area is well ventilated. Have an assistant with a fire extinguisher stand by as "fire watch".

Begin by lightly warming the center of the screen using a propane fired torch. Then, working from a bottom corner and proceeding around the perimeter, heat the plastic until it becomes taut. Once the perimeter is taut, continue warming the center of the screen until all the wrinkles are gone. Be careful not to overwork the plastic, which causes weak spots and can reduce the image quality, causing a cloudy projection. Properly shrunk, a screen cools to a durable, drum-tight surface.

THE CONS – AND THE PROS – OF INDUSTRIAL SHRINK-WRAP

Shrink-wrap has two downsides. The material picks up ambient light more readily than true RP screen material does and perfecting the shrinking technique does take some practice. On the other hand, industrial shrink-wrap is very durable and, if necessary, can be patched by cutting away holes and shrink-taping a new section into the screen. It can also be painted with brushed-on or sprayed-on latex paint. Finally, it can be used to cover traditional scenic pieces to provide a glossy surface.

In the past year, I have used industrial shrink-wrap to produce the 12'-diameter projection screen mentioned above, a 12' x 16' RP screen used for PowerPoint presentations, a 15' x 30' shadow screen, and a full-stage, bright white cyclorama. Most recently, I used the material in a Jingju Chinese Opera set, whose walls needed to glow softly, conveying the serenity of Chinese lanterns.

In my experience, you will not find a less expensive or more efficient RP screen alternative than shrink-wrap. Its low cost provides the freedom to build show-specific screens of unique shapes and sizes, which can be destroyed or recycled at the end of the production.

❧❧❧❧

One of the key objectives in using projection technology is to place the projector at a specific distance from and angle to the screen. Too often, the projector ends up on a custom built stand that wastes valuable space when moved into the wings between uses. In stagehouses with rigging systems, however, projectors can be flown in and out as needed on batten-mounted projector brackets like that shown in Figure 1.

The original version of this device was used for a production at Esplanade Theatre (Singapore). A video segment was introduced towards the end of Act 2 on a flown-in RP screen. A projector mounted on the bracket was flown in behind the RP screen for the video segment and then flown out again afterwards – without taking up any ground space.

THE COMPONENTS

The bracket, made mostly of typically stocked materials, consists of three main components: the Batten Mount Frame, the Extensions, and the Projector Carriage, shown in an overview in Figure 1. The components are designed to optimize storage space and to offer ease of adaptability.

THE BATTEN MOUNT FRAME

This piece is a rectangle of 1"-square tube steel, corner-braced to prevent racking. The two standard C-clamps at the top provide quick connection to the batten. Four 4"-long tabs of $\frac{3}{16}$" x $\frac{3}{4}$" flat bar with $\frac{7}{16}$" holes drilled as shown in Figure 2 are welded to the uprights for through-bolt connections to the Extensions.

THE EXTENSIONS

The Extensions are lengths of 1"-square tube steel cut long enough to keep the batten above sightlines and place the projector in its desired location.

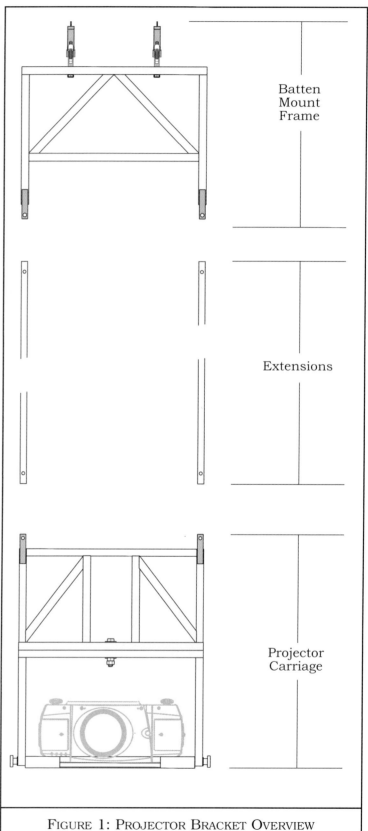

Batten
Mount
Frame

Extensions

Projector
Carriage

FIGURE 1: PROJECTOR BRACKET OVERVIEW

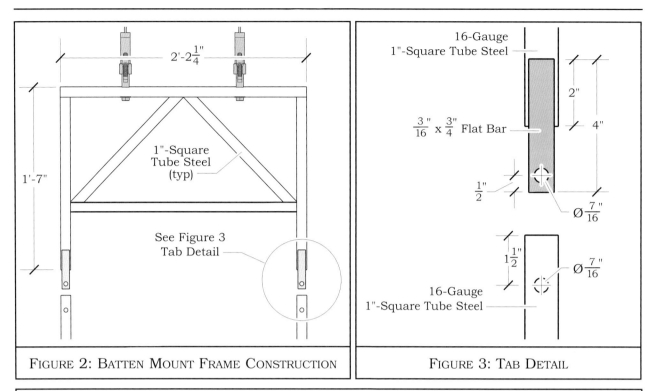

FIGURE 2: BATTEN MOUNT FRAME CONSTRUCTION

FIGURE 3: TAB DETAIL

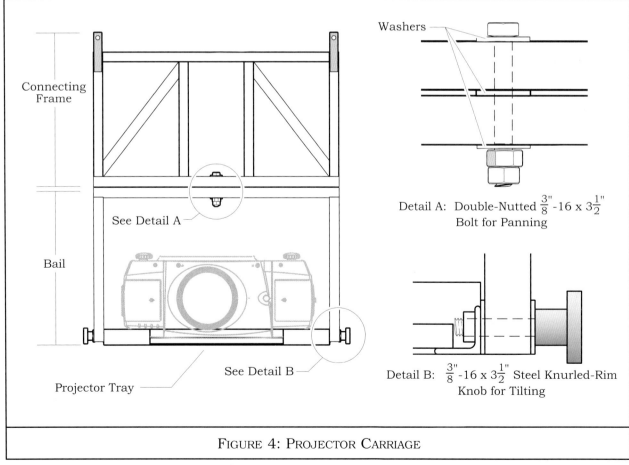

FIGURE 4: PROJECTOR CARRIAGE

THE PROJECTOR CARRIAGE

Projectors cannot always be placed squarely behind the center of an RP screen. For that reason, the Projector Carriage is built as three separate parts – the Connecting Frame, the Bail, and the Projector Tray – which are joined to each other as shown in Figure 4 to allow panning and tilting.

The top-most part of the Projector Carriage, the Connecting Frame, is a cross-braced assembly of 1"-square tube steel with four 4"-long tabs of $\frac{3}{16}$" x $\frac{3}{4}$" flat bar welded to the uprights for connection to the extensions. A single grade-5 $\frac{3}{8}$"-16 x $3\frac{1}{2}$" bolt centered in the bottom of the Connecting Frame allows panning at the connection to the Bail.

The Bail, the second part of the Projector Carriage, is a simple, inverted-U made of 1"-square tube steel with three $\frac{7}{16}$" holes drilled through it. The hole through the center of the Bail's top receives the double-nutted panning bolt from the Connecting Frame. The other two holes, drilled near the bottom of the Bail's legs, allow connection to the third part of the Base – the Projector Tray.

The Projector Tray is a rectangle of $\frac{1}{2}$" plywood framed in $\frac{1}{8}$" x $\frac{1}{8}$" x $1\frac{1}{2}$" angle iron. The legs of the angle iron are wide enough to provide a toe rail for the projector, and part of the vertical leg of the front of the frame is cut away to provide clearance for the projector lens. Two $\frac{7}{16}$" holes centered on the sides of the frame are capped with $\frac{3}{8}$"-16 round-base weld nuts. These weld nuts receive the two steel knurled-rim knobs (McMaster-Carr 6079K22), which give the unit its tilt adjustment.

FINAL NOTES

In addition to permitting the focus to be fine-tuned through panning and tilting, this projector bracket disassembles into separate, compact pieces for easy storage.

❧▲❧▲❧

TECHNICAL BRIEF

Props

Making a Severed Head — Michael Banta

Replicating Bones, Part I: Molds — Julia Powell

Replicating Bones, Part II: Casting — Julia Powell

Realistic Stage Stun Gun — Mike Vandercook and Joe Huppert

CO_2 Gunshot Wound — Brian Smallwood

Three Favorite Blood Recipes — Jennifer McClure

Three Techniques for Applying Stage Blood — Sandra Jervey and Jennifer McClure

Urinal Head Wax Mold Casting Process — Andrew Hagan

A Device to Simulate Urination Onstage — Ryan C. Hales

Bas-Relief Sculptures in Durham's Rock Hard Water Putty® — Greg Blakey and Samantha Porter

A Cremora®-Fueled Pyrotechnic Alternative — Adam J. Dahl

A Remotely Extinguished Cremora®-Fueled Flame Effect — Chris Peterson

A Mechanism for a Battery-Operated Torch — Katherine Gloria Tharp

A Safe Glass Mirror Breaking Effect — John McCullough

1970s' Period Pull-Tab Beverage Cans — Jeff Smejdir

An Affordable Chair for Sweeney Todd — Colin Buckhurst

Using a Trolling Reel to Move Small Furniture and Props — Steven Schmidt

Hand-Held Dancing Fireflies — Andrew V. Wallace

Many scripts call for the display of a severed head to the audience, but all too often the technical difficulty in creating believable skin results in either a painfully fake-looking head or the old "head-in-a-bag" trick. In one scene of the Yale School of Drama's 2001 production of *The Master and Margarita* a character's head was ripped off, displayed to the audience (seated mere feet away), and restored to his body. In this case, neither of the aforementioned alternatives seemed acceptable, so we researched materials that would create a more realistic look. We settled on the design described here: a skin of silicone rubber with a core of poured urethane. Silicone rubber can be tinted to a skin tone and fine-tuned with stage makeup, which makes matching the head's coloring to the actor's skin tone fairly easy. The urethane core is durable and believably weighty and provides the skin's yellowish undertone through the translucent silicone.

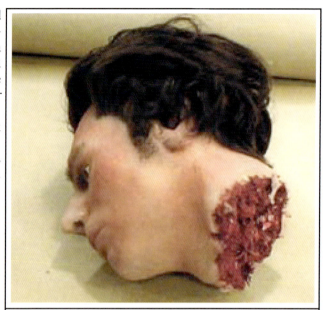

FIGURE 1: A BELIEVABLE SEVERED HEAD

Several molds are required to reach this finished product:

> an alginate negative taken from the actor's face
>
> the full-head form, a plaster positive taken from the alginate negative built out with clay
>
> the casque, a silicone and fiberglass negative taken from the full-head form
>
> the finished product, a silicone and urethane positive taken from the casque.

Maskmaker Thurston James describes the construction of the first two molds in *The Prop Builder's Molding and Casting Handbook* and *The Prop Builder's Mask-Making Handbook*. This article describes the refinement of the full-head form and the construction of the casque and finished product.

REFINING THE FULL-HEAD FORM

The finished plaster positive can be carved to correct errors caused by air bubbles in the alginate and to make other alterations such as opening the eyes. The back of the positive is then built out with clay into a full-head form — about five pounds will be enough; less if the inside is packed with newspaper. The clay must not be a high-sulfur compound like plasticine, since sulfur interferes with silicone rubber's curing. Finally the plaster portions of the form are sprayed with a clear lacquer primer to help release the silicone.

BUILDING THE CASQUE

The next step is to make a casque in two halves, one containing the face and ears and the other the back of the head. For the front of our casque we chose PlatSil 71-20, a two-part silicone rubber made by Polytek, for its relatively short demold time of 4 hours and ease of mixing.

Propped up by blocks or wads of clay to elevate the base of the neck, the full-head form is laid face up on a sheet of glass. A dam of clay about an inch in height is built from the top of one ear, over the crown of the head, and down to the top of the other ear. Half of the PlatSil 71-20 is mixed and poured in small amounts over the face. The silicone needs no mold release but will be quite runny, so to provide even coverage it must be constantly scooped up with a spatula and reapplied until it starts to set. Once the silicone has started to thicken, it can be applied to the underside of the neck up to the hairline. For this part of the process two sets of hands are definitely best.

Fiberglass-reinforced body filler is mixed and poured over the silicone and down to the dam to a thickness of about half an inch. When this has set, the clay dam is removed, the form is turned over, and the surfaces where the front and back parts will meet are painted with petroleum jelly as a release. Body filler is then poured over the back of the form to complete the two-piece casque. Care must be taken that the back does not overlap the front by too much, since the halves will be pulled apart to free the form and later the finished head. When the back half has set, the casque is opened and the form is removed, leaving a silicone negative in the face side of the casque as shown in Figure 2.

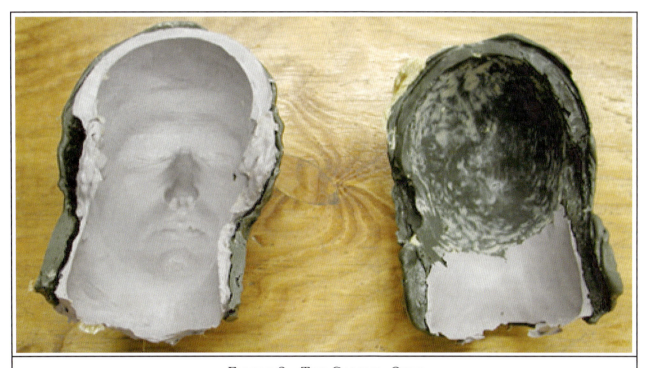

FIGURE 2: THE CASQUE, OPEN

BUILDING THE FINISHED PRODUCT

PlatSil Gel-10, also made by Polytek, forms the final silicone skin, ideal because it is translucent and colors easily with artist's oils or commercial pigments available from Dispersion Technologies. This is a good point to experiment with small quantities of PlatSil Gel-10 silicone and coloring to achieve the desired skin tone. The silicone is fast-setting and this part of the process need not take long. Once the ratios of coloring have been determined, the entire batch is mixed and poured into the re-assembled casque. The silicone is swirled around in the casque to coat the face area. A spatula is used to push silicone into the ears and other hard-to-fill areas and to pull it up to cover the back of the neck.

The final step in casting is to fill the mold with pourable urethane foam. This foam expands greatly upon mixing, so it's a good idea to add it gradually to the mold so that it doesn't overflow. The halves of the casque must be restrained to resist the expansion of the foam.

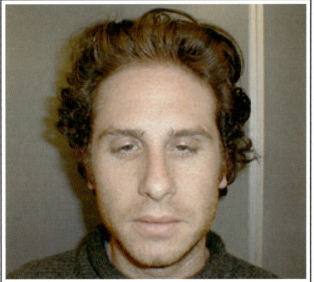

FIGURE 3: THE ACTOR

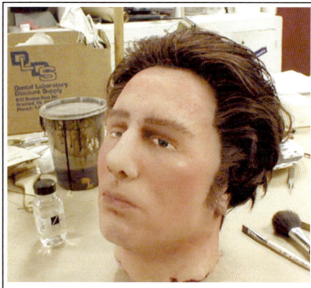

FIGURE 4: THE FINISHED PRODUCT

After the head is removed from the mold, a wig is affixed with long hatpins. For added realism, the eye of a sewing needle clipped at an angle can be used to push individual hairs along the hairline into the silicone. The eyes present the greatest challenge in making a realistic head. To achieve their characteristic glossy quality we painted the eyes' features with ordinary scene paint and coated the result with a glossy clear acrylic. The base of the neck is easily textured and painted. The skin can be colored with stage makeup and powdered. Figures 3 and 4 illustrate the close resemblance between the actor and the finished product.

NOTES

In all, these steps represent a considerable time investment, but the result is worth the effort. The mold should be usable for years, and the resulting casting is convincing and durable. The same steps are also applicable to any number of other flesh effects.

RESOURCES

James, Thurston. *The Prop Builder's Mask-Making Handbook.* Whitehall (VA): Betterway, 1990.

James, Thurston. *The Prop Builder's Molding and Casting Handbook.* Whitehall (VA): Betterway, 1989.

PlatSil 71-20, PlatSil Gel-10, and PolyFoam R-8 (urethane): Polytek Development Corp. http://www.polytek.com; (610) 559-8620.

Silicone pigments: Dispersion Technologies (732) 364-4488.

FIGURE 1: MILWAUKEE REPERTORY THEATRE'S BONES FOR *A SKULL IN CONNEMARA*

For each performance of the Milwaukee Repertory Theatre's 2002 production of *A Skull in Connemara*, 21 recognizably human bones and 3 skulls needed to be dug up and smashed onstage. Casting the nearly 1000 bones needed for technical rehearsals and performances took careful organization and a lot of hard work, but the techniques and materials described here made the job manageable.

The shop bought a disarticulated, plastic half-skeleton from the Anatomical Chart Company and, working with the production's director, chose a number of bones that could be cast relatively easily and would read well in performance. Skulls, of course, were specifically required by the script. The other bones chosen as casting models included – in addition to several sizes of vertebrae – the mandible (jaw), the clavicle (collarbone), the scapula (shoulder blade), the humerus (upper arm bone), the pelvis, the sacrum (tailbone), the femur (thigh bone), the tibia (the larger lower-leg bone), and the calcaneous (the heel bone).

We settled on plaster as the best casting material because it would break convincingly when the bones were smashed with a large wooden mallet. To minimize the amount of shrapnel produced, we decided to use Polycast®, a plaster containing fiberglass fibers. That choice was a good one, for when the bones were smashed no fragments flew into the house.

All of the bones would be hard castings, all would be cast from two-part molds, and many would have undercuts of some magnitude, but they fell into groups that required different casting techniques and consequently different types of molds.

TYPE 1 AND TYPE 2 MOLDS

About 85% of the bones we made — the relatively compact ones, including the skulls — were cast in molds made of Smooth-On's Mold Max® 10 Silicone, which is reasonably priced and readily available. With a Shore A hardness of 10, Mold Max® 10 is so flexible that it will release even deeply undercut castings without significant damage. On the other hand, molds made of Mold Max® 10 are so flexible that they must be surrounded with temporary mother molds like that shown in Figure 2 until a casting has cured enough to maintain its shape.

For less-compact bones like the femur and tibia we used Smooth-On's Evergreen® 30 Urethane Casting Rubber. Evergreen® 30 is stiffer (Shore A 30) and can support Polycast® as it cures without being encased in a mother mold. For casting, we merely Quik-Clamped our semi-rigid Evergreen® 30 molds between two pieces of $\frac{3}{4}$" plywood, stood them on end, and filled them.

FIGURE 2: (LEFT TO RIGHT) TOP HALF-MOLD, BOTTOM HALF-MOLD, MOTHER MOLD

MAKING THE MOLDS

Our first step was to design the various molds. We laid individual bones (the femur and tibia, for example) or groups of bones (like vertebrae, clavicles, and mandibles) next to each other on a table to discover how many bones we could handle in a single casting. In all, we defined a total of 5 molds that would allow room for and support manageable groups of bones.

Having established the overall size of each casting, we half-buried each bone in a bed of Primo® Non-Sulfur Clay. The choice of clay was important because sulfur inhibits the curing of silicone. We made sure that the clay supported the entire length of each bone along its centerline, and we tilted each one as necessary to avoid the formation of air pockets during casting. We then fashioned pour spouts (rough cylinders of clay) and pasted one on the top of each bone model. Finally, we inserted short lengths of dowel in the clay beds to provide registration keys.

Next, we trimmed the clay beds into regular rectangles that we encased in mother molds like that shown in Figure 2. Many mold makers, the renowned Thurston James among them, use duplex nails as connecting hardware in mother molds, but knowing that we would repeatedly assemble and disassemble our mother molds, we chose to use bolts and wing nuts. We made each of the mother molds a full inch taller than the "terrain" formed by the clay-embedded bones. Before proceeding, we smoothed the edges of the clay beds into the mother molds and applied liberal amounts of Mann Ease Release 800® to the wood, clay, and plastic models as a release agent. Finally, we filled the mother molds, pouring the Mold Max® 10 and the Evergreen® 30 Urethane Casting Rubber over the models and clay beds, taking care not to cover the pour spouts.

A finished top half-mold is shown at the left in Figure 2. After the top half-molds had completely cured (approximately 16 hours), we removed them from the mother molds, flipped them upside down, and pulled the clay away. We were careful not to disturb the seal between the models and the top half-molds, for if we had, seepage would have ruined the detail in the bottom half-molds.

To make the bottom half-molds, we re-installed the models and top half-molds upside down in the mother molds, applied the release agent, and filled the mother molds with the appropriate mold material. After these bottom half-molds had cured, we removed the mother molds, pulled the two half-molds apart, and removed the plastic models. Finally, we flipped the two-part molds right-side up and cleared the clay from the pour spouts. (The pour spouts are clearly visible in the finished top half-mold shown at the left in Figure 2.) Once we had reassembled the mother molds around the Mold Max® 10 molds, we were ready for casting.

TYPE 3 MOLDS: SKULLS

The skulls were cast whole. After plugging the eye sockets and spinal-column opening with clay and weighting the model to keep it from floating, we put the skull in a mother mold and covered it completely with Mold Max® 10 Silicone. After the silicone had cured, we removed the mother mold and used X-Acto® knives to cut the mold into two halves along the skull's centerline.

CONCLUSION

Using these methods and materials, Milwaukee Repertory Theatre's Properties Shop produced nearly 1,000 anatomically correct bones in just a few weeks. We found that castings poured at the end of the day would be cured by the time we came in the next morning, and those poured first thing in the morning would be cured by mid-afternoon.

RESOURCES

Anatomical Chart Company: www.anatomical.com, 8221 Kimball Avenue, Skokie, IL 60076-2956, (800) 621-7500
Georgia Pacific (maker of Polycast®): www.gp.com/gypsum/industrial/artscrafts/products.html
Smooth-On: smoothon@smooth-on.com, 2000 Saint John Street, Easton, AP 18042, (800) 762-0744

❧❧❧❧

Part I in this series describes the construction of the molds the Milwaukee Repertory Theatre's properties shop used in reproducing nearly 1,000 human bones, some of which were dug up and smashed during performances of a 2002 production of *A Skull in Connemara.* This article details the casting and painting of those bones, some of which are pictured in Figure 1.

PRELIMINARIES

This project required two special preparatory steps. First, under normal use, Mold Max® 10 silicone needs no release agent but, concerned about the effects of repeated casting, we coated the inside of our molds with Mann Ease Release 800® to preserve finer details. Second, Polycast® is usually mixed in clear water, but since the inside of broken bones would not be plaster white, we used water tinted with earth-tone colors of Rit® dye.

FIGURE 1: BONES FOR *A SKULL IN CONNEMARA*

CASTING THE SKULLS

For the skulls, we mixed Polycast® powder and dye-tinted hot water into a fairly thick, quick-set plaster. We poured the plaster into the skull half-molds and spread it around with a spatula, taking care to fill undercuts and crevices and to keep the thickness as even as possible. The small air pockets we missed along the way were happy accidents that added to the skulls' look of decay.

In about 2 hours, the plaster had set up and we carefully pulled the castings while the plaster was still soft enough to carve. We trimmed the edges of the half-skulls so that they would mate as cleanly as possible and cut the hole where a spinal column would have entered the joined half-skulls. As Figure 1 illustrates, we did not cut the plaster away from the eye sockets. That would have weakened the pieces too much, and lighting and expert painting made it unnecessary. After trimming, we laid the still separate half-skulls in a well ventilated area to dry for at least 2 days. After the half-skulls had dried, we joined them together, using a two-part epoxy concrete cement that we masked under a paste of tinted Polycast®. We then let the skulls dry another full day before sanding the seam smooth in preparation for painting.

CASTING THE OTHER BONES

For the other bones, we filled a flexible mixing bowl half-full with tinted, room-temperature water and gradually added Polycast® until the water stopped absorbing the powder and a small island approximately $\frac{1}{2}$" tall was formed. Gentle hand mixing broke up the lumps of Polycast® while minimizing the introduction of air bubbles. Thoroughly mixed, this mixture looked more like a pancake batter than a batch of plaster: it had to be fluid enough to fill the mold properly or the finished castings would have been incomplete. During pouring we tapped and pressed on the silicone to force out any major air bubbles. We pulled these castings after only 2 hours or so. Even with practice and a delicate touch, some amount of damage was unavoidable, for they were fairly fragile; but we decided that small nicks were not a problem since they would add to the freshly-dug-up look of the bones. When a casting was completely broken, we stored the pieces together, let them dry, and glued them together as we had done with the half-skulls. We let the bones dry in a roadbox for 2 to 3 days before painting. We were able to produce three sets of bones each day by pulling the previous night's set first thing in the morning and immediately pouring another set. By noon we could pull and pour a third set and at about 4:30 that afternoon, repeat the process yet again.

PAINTING

The paint treatment developed by Margaret Hasek-Guy, Soft Props Artisan at the Milwaukee Rep, gave a very realistic pigmentation to the bones while allowing for individuality. The castings shared the same basic tone but no two pieces were identical, and this process was determined to be the best paint process for our exercise in mass production.

The process took a fair amount of time and table space, so we waited until we had made a large number of bones and skulls before spreading out the plastic. To keep later paint coats from being absorbed by the plaster, the first step was to dip each bone in a sealer made of 3 boxes of wheat wallpaper paste mixed with 24 pints of lukewarm water in a 5 gallon bucket. The bones were laid out to dry overnight.

The next day we mixed another bucket of wheat paste, adding 2 cups of Artists' Choice® Burnt Umber Saturated paint and small amounts of Cal-Tint®, a universal paint colorant. The resulting mixture looked like black coffee and had the consistency of pea soup. We dipped the sealed bones twice: first in a plain wheat paste mix to re-wet the exterior, and then into the tinted paste. Thick layers of paste were not desirable since they tended to flake up when dry and expose large areas of plaster, so we wiped each bone off with a terrycloth towel before laying it out to dry on the plastic for a second full night.

Hiding the seams in the skulls needed an extra step. The dye from skull to skull tended to vary a bit, so we mixed two "patch" colors of Artists' Choice® Burnt Umber and White in inverse ratios (1:2 and 2:1). Blending these two colors across the seams and feathering the edges of the patches with a brush masked all unwanted color variations and made the finished surface more uniform.

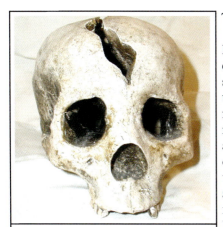

FIGURE 2: THE GASHED SKULL

THE PLASTIC REPLICAS

Plaster bones would not have survived being dug out of the ground during performance, so we made plastic copies of the skulls and some of the bones out of Smooth-On's Smooth Cast® 300. Wanting to avoid having to deal with any seams in the plastic skulls, we made a second skull mold, splitting this one only far enough to remove the model. We added a bottom to the 4-sided mother mold and poured just enough Smooth Cast® 300 into the mold to cover one small area at a time. When that area had set up, we turned the mother mold onto another side and poured in another small amount of plastic, in effect making a whole skull out of a series of fused plastic plates. The large gash needed in one skull (see Figure 2) was easily cut by a Dremel® with a cutting bit, and the plastic bones were painted with regular artist acrylics to match the plaster bones.

OVERVIEW

In a production of *The Unmentionables* at the Yale Repertory Theatre, one character coerced information from another using a stun gun. The director wanted to see a realistic portrayal of this action on stage. This prop stun gun solution emits a convincing simulated spark and realistic sound from a short distance away.

MATERIALS

	Material	Notes
1	P20 Flashlight Lamp	Spark Simulation
4	AAAA 1.5V Batteries	Power Supply 6V Total
1	8-Ohm Hi-Efficiency Speaker	Approximately 2" in Diameter
1	TDA 7052 Amplifier Circuit	Available pre-built at www.electronics123.com
1	iPod Shuffle	Holds and Plays Sound File
1	$\frac{1}{8}$" Minijack	Connects Amp to iPod
1	Stun Master 200-S	Provides Shell and Switch.

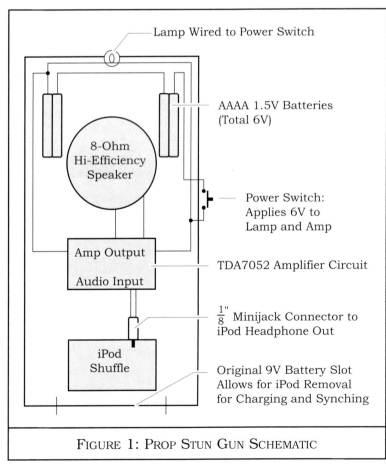

FIGURE 1: PROP STUN GUN SCHEMATIC

FIGURE 2: STUN MASTER 200S

CONSTRUCTION

1. Open the Stun Master 200S shell, and remove the transformer, wiring, and plastic dividers. Be sure to keep the momentary switch, and cap for the battery compartment.
2. Wire sound system (speaker, amplifier, minijack, and iPod) as shown in Figure 1.
3. Connect sound system, lamp, and momentary switch (see Figure 1).
4. Drill a $\frac{3}{8}$" hole in the top of the stun gun shell where the spark would occur, and install the lamp with its tip protruding through the shell.
5. Use double-sided tape to install the sound system, lamp, power supply, and switch into the stun gun shell.
6. Reassemble the stun gun shell sealing the seams with black gaffer's tape for easy access in case there is a need for repair.
7. Tape a small piece of gel over the protruding lamp tip. Rosco 40 provides a realistic color.

FINAL PRODUCT

Load a looping audio file of a stun gun effect into the iPod. The iPod can be removed and reinserted at will through the battery slot at the bottom of the stun gun shell for charging and file alteration. With the iPod in play mode at all times, the momentary switch will supply power to the Amp and Lamp simultaneously creating the sound and the "spark". When the switch is released both effects stop. The prop stun gun now functions as the real product would, except for generating a 20,000 volt output.

❧❦❧❦

During the Impetuous Theater Group's production of *Twelfth Night of the Living Dead*, it became clear that the death of Valentine would require a gory gunshot. The film industry's answer, the squib, is an incendiary device and getting the necessary permits to use one in live performance can be time-consuming. The production team set forth to develop the CO$_2$-powered gunshot wound described here.

As shown in Figure 1, this system relies on a CO$_2$ Load Discharger to function as both an air supply and pneumatic actuator, as well as Rubber Surgical Tubing to create a Reservoir for the blood and an Exit Port for the wound. To execute the effect, simply pull the trigger on the CO$_2$ Load Discharger and eject the liquid stored in the Rubber Surgical Tubing.

COMPONENTS

    1 CO$_2$ Load Discharger (available at www.cabelas.com)
    1 8-oz. CO$_2$ Cartridge
    1 Length of Rubber Surgical Tubing (length dependant on exit wound placement)
    1 Zip Tie
    Stage Blood

FIGURE 1: FITTING DIAGRAM

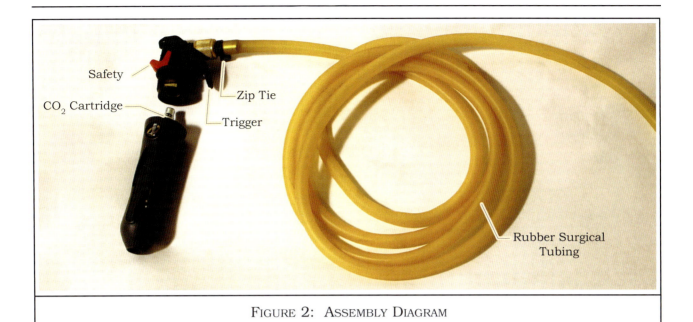

FIGURE 2: ASSEMBLY DIAGRAM

ASSEMBLY

Stretch the Rubber Surgical Tubing over the CO$_2$ Load Discharger air nozzle. Use the Zip Tie to secure the Rubber Surgical Tubing to the CO$_2$ Load Discharger air nozzle. Use a Sharp Blade to cut the Rubber Surgical Tubing to length. Please note the excess Rubber Surgical Tubing that forms a bend across the stomach area. When stage blood enters the system, it will pool at the base of that bend, which acts as a Reservoir. The extra bends on both sides of this Reservoir are meant to reduce the chances of blood shifting back into the CO$_2$ Load Discharger or prematurely out the exit port. Be sure to orient the exit port outward.

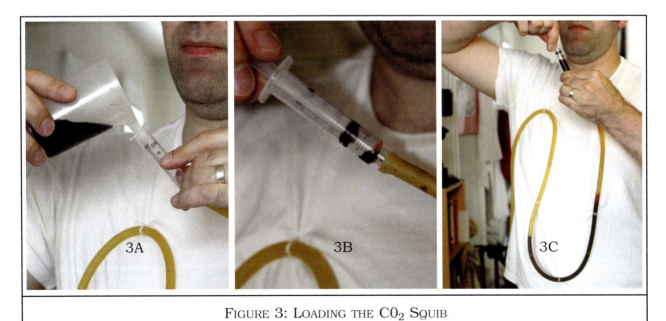

FIGURE 3: LOADING THE C0$_2$ SQUIB

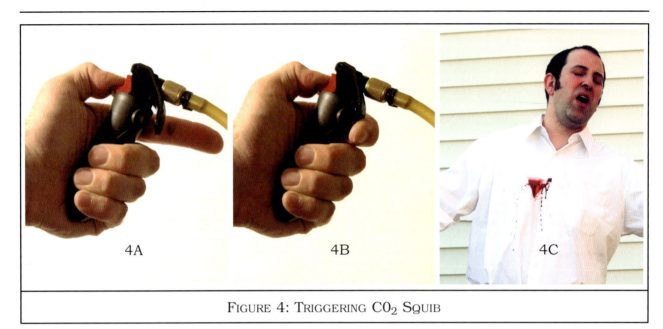

FIGURE 4: TRIGGERING CO$_2$ SQUIB

LOADING AND TRIGGERING THE CO$_2$ SQUIB

Straighten out the Rubber Surgical Tubing so there is direct access to the reservoir. Remove plunger from Syringe and insert Syringe into exit port (see Figure 3A). Pour Stage Blood into Syringe slowly, then replace plunger and inject blood into Rubber Surgical Tubing (see Figure 3B). Blood will pool at base of reservoir (see Figure 3C). Repeat until sufficiently loaded. Depress safety (see Figure 4A). Being mindful of exit port direction, squeeze trigger (see Figure 4B). React appropriately (see Figure 4C).

USE AND SAFETY NOTES

Assembly of the CO$_2$ powered squib is only part of executing a convincing effect. Incorporating the squib into the costume will take planning and interdepartmental communication. For this article, the Rubber Surgical Tubing was stitched to a T-shirt at several points (see Figure 1). The more subtle the better. Be sure to devote rehearsal time to executing the effect.

Reel Blood® was used at full consistency as blood for the squib, but diluting with water still looks great. Homemade blood will likely work with experimentation.

The CO$_2$ Squib ejects pressurized air at high velocities. Never trigger the CO$_2$ Gunshot Wound next to face or eyes. The 8 oz. CO$_2$ Cartridge will only engage if the base of the CO$_2$ Load Discharger is screwed in tightly. Depressing the safety as close to cuing of the effect will minimize the chance of premature discharge and mitigate CO$_2$ loss.

Special Thanks to Joe Mathers for his work in developing the CO$_2$ Gunshot Wound. Photos by Rachel Smallwood.

❧❧❧❧

In theatre productions, one of the most used special effects is blood. The following 3 recipes reliably produce good versions of thick or thin, edible or non-edible blood. They wash out pretty consistently, especially the ones that contain some detergent, but should always be tested on fabrics before being used in show conditions. They are easy to mix in small and large batches and are relatively cost effective.

CHOCOLATE BLOOD

This blood can be thickened by adding more dry ingredients and less water from the get go. It washes out of virtually everything, even most white fabrics (but still test on show fabrics when able). It is edible, works great in blood packs, and flows out of blood knives well. Mixing it in large batches is cost-effective since a full batch costs only about $15.00 and a quarter batch is enough to get through a 30-show run that uses one tablespoon (tbsp) sized blood pack per show.

Ingredient	Full Batch (50 oz)	Half Batch	Quarter Batch
Corn Syrup (light color)	32 oz (2 bottles)	16 oz (1 bottle)	8 oz
Chocolate Syrup*	500 mL	250 mL	125 mL
Water (half hot, half cold)	2 cups	1 cup	$\frac{1}{2}$ cup
Corn Starch	2 tbsp (heaping)	1 tbsp (heaping)	$\frac{1}{2}$ tbsp (heaping)
Coffee Mate creamer	3 tbsp	$1\frac{1}{2}$ tbsp	$\frac{3}{4}$ tbsp
Red and Blue food coloring	To desired color	To desired color	To desired color

*A variant of this recipe uses strawberry syrup for some of the red coloring. In this case, use one-third strawberry syrup, two-thirds chocolate syrup for your desired batch size.

Mix corn syrup and chocolate syrup in a large pot on high heat. Dissolve corn starch in cold water (one-half of the total water) and add to the pot. Dissolve Coffee Mate in hot water (the other half of the total water) and add to pot. Bring to a boil, stirring occasionally. Mix in food coloring to get the desired color. You will use far less blue (maybe only 1 drop) than red. Store final mixture in a refrigerator for up to 1 month.

PEANUT BUTTER BLOOD

This blood is edible and good for thicker applications, like a bloody lip or a blood pack that is broken in the mouth and thinned by the actor's saliva, but contrary to others' claims it can stain some fabrics. If the blood does not need to be edible, you can add a small amount of laundry detergent to help avoid staining. Use a bluish, slightly translucent detergent to enhance the color of the blood and avoid using a milky detergent. In any case, test the blood on any swatches of fabric it may contact. Two full batches (16 oz) can be made for less than $5.00. Mix together corn syrup and peanut butter until smooth. Add cornstarch in small amounts until mixed in thoroughly. Add food color to obtain the desired color. If a cast member is allergic to peanuts but not to hazelnuts, hazelnut butter or Nutella® (hazelnut butter and chocolate) can be used instead.

GLYCERIN BLOOD

This blood is pretty simple to mix as it is just the amount you need of glycerine and food coloring to the desired look. This can be made edible by using vegetable based glycerine. Glycerin and vegetable-based glycerin are available at some health food stores and also online for $6.00 to $8.00 per 16 oz, or $40.00 to $42.00 per gallon.

GENERAL BLOOD SUGGESTIONS

Always mix up a test sample and try it on swatches of show fabrics if available or something of similar color and composition before using blood in a show.

For edible bloods, always get a list of allergens from Stage Management for the actors who may eat the blood or will have any other contact with it.

When using blood that is non-edible (even factory brands like Reel Blood) adding a translucent detergent will help to pre-treat the blood so that it is less likely to stain. The color and clarity of the detergent is important. Slightly blue detergents are OK, for instance, while milky detergents are not. I recommend Oxi-Clean®.

When washing blood out of fabrics, use cold water to help prevent the stain from setting.

ALTERNATIVE RECIPES CAN BE FOUND IN...

Fullerton, Randy. *Stage Blood* in *Technical Design Solutions for Theatre, Vol 1*, edited by Bronislaw J. Sammler and Don Harvey, pp. 54-55. Woburn, Massachusetts: Butterworth-Heinemann, 2002.

Thoron, Ben. *More Stage Blood* in *Technical Design Solutions for Theatre, Vol 1*, edited by Bronislaw J. Sammler and Don Harvey, p. 60. Woburn, Massachusetts: Butterworth-Heinemann, 2002.

᪷᪷᪷᪷

This article describes three basic techniques for applying stage blood. The nature of the desired effect should determine the choice of technique. The techniques below include paintbrush for light applications, sponge for heavier applications, and blood packs for effects that are initiated onstage. Regardless of technique remember that applying stage blood is not an exact science and there will always be some level of trial and error. Be aware, too, that most blood recipes and products become sticky as they dry giving you limited working time.

PAINTBRUSH TECHNIQUE

The paintbrush technique is most useful for blood effects that require more control than volume. Likely candidates are small blood transfer patterns such as small wounds, dried blood, or healing wounds. The size of the brush should be based on the surface area being bloodied.

The process is as simple as dipping the brush into your blood container and applying gentle strokes to the desired area. As shown in Figure 1, the more pressure applied, the more the blood will pool creating darker spots (a) and small trails (b). This is especially true around joints in the body. For light to moderate volume blood transfers a wet scumble stroke pattern can be used (c). For smaller wounds, allow the blood to pool at the origin of the wound and then gently drag blood trails from it (d).

The paintbrush technique works best for thinner bloods and can be done with any quality of brush. As the viscosity of the blood decreases, the ability of the brush to realistically smear it does as well. The exception to this is if the desired effect is dried blood. For that look this technique can be paired with a thicker blood, perhaps peanut-butter-based, and a thin layer of glycerin can be applied as a top coat. If you are using blood with detergent in it do not use a stippling brush technique unless foaming of the blood will not detract from your desired look.

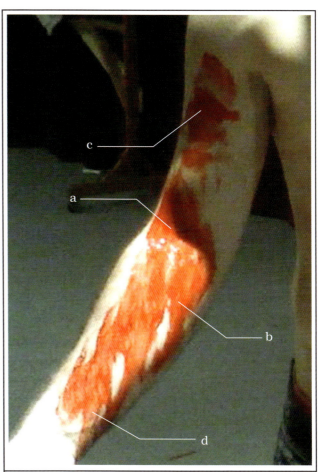

FIGURE 1: PAINTBRUSH APPLICATION

SPONGE TECHNIQUE

The sponge technique is most useful for effects that require high volumes of blood or to create a trail of blood left on stage. Likely candidates are offstage puncture wounds. Sea sponge is a common choice as a tool for its organic shape, but applications can also be done with a rectangular dish washing sponge, as was done in Figure 2 if attention is paid to smoothing out the corner shapes. For offstage applications, the sponge can be dipped directly into the blood container. If, instead, the blood is to drop into a trail onstage, it is easier to syringe the blood into the center of the sponge to avoid premature dripping.

The basic process for a high volume blood effect created offstage is to dip the sponge in blood and daub it onto the skin. This technique is substantially messier than the paintbrush. Gentle daubs should be used to avoid foaming the blood (a). The greater the pressure applied to the sponge, the more the blood will drip, leaving long trails across the body (b). For a true bloodbath effect it is probably easier to pour the blood on or dip appropriate body parts and costume pieces into the blood container.

For trails of blood onstage it is helpful to have a more accurate way to measure the amount of blood in the sponge. A turkey baster works well, as you can both control the amount

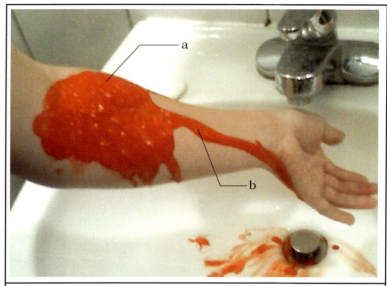

FIGURE 2: SPONGE APPLICATION SHOWN WITH DETERGENT-THINNED BLOOD TO SHOW FOAMING PROBLEM

of blood introduced and aim the blood into the center of the sponge. This allows the blood to soak into the heart of the sponge and be transferred to the stage as the bleeding person or prop is dragged. The blood can be forced from the sponge either by gravity or by squeezing at the appropriate moment.

The sponge technique does not work well for blood thinned with detergent because soap causes the blood to foam easily as it is daubed on. The exception to this is if the desired effect is a bubbling wound. Faster daubing with a detergent-thinned blood will create exactly that effect. For thorough sponge technique coverage, it would be wise to brush on a bottom layer prior to sponging. Achieving realistic results with the sponge technique takes practice.

BLOOD PACK TECHNIQUE

The blood pack technique is most useful for effects that require a wound to be created onstage. Likely candidates are sword wounds, onstage gun shot wounds, or punches to the face. The process for this can range from kitchen-made packs to hospital supplies and impulse sealers. The type of pack used should be based on the area the pack is hidden in. The larger and more easily concealed the hiding place the less fancy the application need be. As the blood amount increases it becomes more likely that the use of hospital equipment as your pack will yield the best result.

The basic low-tech blood pack is created by filling the corner of a plastic sandwich bag with the desired amount of blood. To close the bag, spin the bag so that the blood-filled section is isolated and pressurized, then start wrapping thread or floss about 2" above where the seal will reach the blood. Start with a looser wrap and tighten as you move closer to the blood. When you have wrapped it tight enough the blood pack will bulge from the pressure. If you wrap very tightly you will not need to knot the thread, but may do so for extra assurance. The more pressure within the blood pack the easier it will be to burst it at the right moment and the more dramatic the blood spill from it will be. A more high tech version of the same idea can be created with a tool called an impulse sealer pictured in Figure 3. This tool allows the same process but with a heat seal for blood packs rather than tying off. This method also allows you to create custom shaped blood packs with practice.

For larger blood packs using a plasma bag is common as it will stay relatively flat when hidden on the body. Hose clamps made specifically for catheters can be very useful both for filling and for making sure the effect is not triggered early.

Use a small squeeze bulb or needle-less syringe to fill the bags. These items can be found in the baby isle of most large department and grocery stores. Remember to take extra care when preparing a blood pack for the mouth. If you wouldn't want to put it in your mouth, chances are the actor shouldn't have to. Wash your hands thoroughly, wear gloves if possible, and work in a clean area on a piece of waxed paper. Store the packs in clean locations.

The blood pack application works with any blood that is not too thick. Peanut butter recipes will work if they are relatively liquid. As the blood viscosity decreases, the ability of the pack to give a dramatic burst increases. If you are using the blood pack in the mouth, be certain that there is no detergent in the blood recipe.

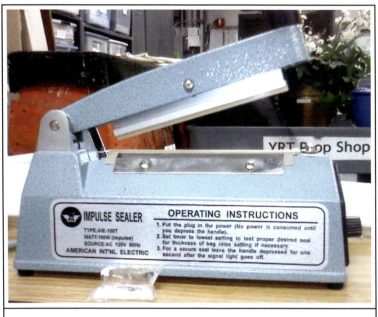

FIGURE 3: IMPULSE SEALER

RECIPES AND FURTHER READING:

Fullerton, Randy. "Stage Blood." *Technical Designs for Theatre, Vol. 1* ed. Bronislaw J. Sammler and Don Harvey. Woburn, MA: Elsevier Science, 2002.

Thoron, Ben. "More Stage Blood." *Technical Designs for Theatre, Vol. 2* ed. Bronislaw J. Sammler and Don Harvey. Woburn, MA: Elsevier Science, 2002.

For the 2006 production of *Urinetown* at the Florida State University School of Theatre, the design called for 3 urinal heads. We were on a tight budget and could not afford to purchase all of the urinal heads. In that the actors needed to be able to flush the urinals onstage in the production, we needed a way to quickly and cheaply reproduce a seemingly functional urinal head.

After consultation with the Master Craftsman program at FSU, our solution was to make reinforced plaster casts of the urinal heads using the Forton Modified Gypsum (FMG) casting system, making the molds using liquid poly skin wax. This is an inexpensive, readily available material that can be found in most sculpting supply stores at around $5.00 a pound or can be bought in bulk from companies such as Polytek. It is a molding material that can be recycled with low levels of material loss into new molds for future projects and, as detailed in the example of our urinal heads, is very easy to work with.

FIGURE 1: FINISHED FMG CASTING

We purchased 1 urinal head and sealed its joints and seams with artist's clay to prevent the wax from leaking inside (see Figure 2). This prepared urinal head was then dipped quickly in the heated liquid poly skin wax and cooled in ice water for about 30 seconds (see Figure 3). To ensure integrity of the mold once the original urinal head was removed, we repeated this dipping process 6 to 8 times until a thickness of approximately 1" had been attained. Wax may be brushed or poured on as well though care must be taken so that brush strokes do not cool into the wax. We found that dipping worked best for our needs. The process took approximately 15 minutes from the first dipping to when we were ready to remove the original urinal head from the mold, compared to a potential 48-hour wait time with an alternate material like a Poly Urethane liquid mold rubber.

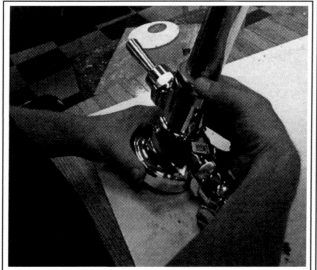

FIGURE 2: SEALING THE JOINTS

FIGURE 3: DIPPING THE ORIGINAL

The wax is a low-temperature wax that melts at 120° Fahrenheit and is safe for skin contact. To heat, all that is needed is a hot plate and a kettle or pot large enough to hold the liquid wax. We used a large insulated pot with a heating element on the outside and increased the efficiency of the system further, but this is not necessary for use of this wax. A large electric crock pot works well for quantities of up to 5 lbs or so. If the pot isn't large enough for a full immersion of the original, partial dips can be used to fully coat the piece.

After allowing the wax to cool fully (about 5 minutes), we carefully cut the mold in half using a utility knife and removed the original urinal head (see Figure 4). We could have used any type of razor blade tool as the mold was not so thick that we needed a specialized tool such as a mold-key knife. We cut the mold along the vertical axis to allow easier removal of the original urinal head by minimizing undercuts.

FIGURE 4

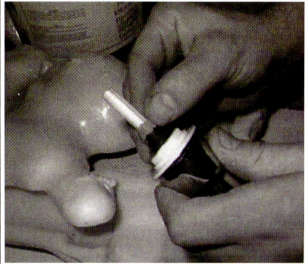

FIGURE 5

For our reproductions to flush, we needed working handles. We bought 1 replacement handle for each urinal at a local hardware store. Urinal handle stems extend into the heads and to form the corresponding cavities in the castings we encased the stem of each handle in a drinking straw and sealed the ends with clay to prevent the plaster from filling the straw (see Figure 5). The handles were placed into the molds along with the $1\frac{1}{2}$" couplers (see Figure 6).

While we could have used an alternate 2-part mold material, our process benefits from the speed and ease this wax offers. We cut the mold and pulled it apart in about 15 minutes, taking care as in all molds not to damage it in the process, and then re-sealed it around the handle in about 5 minutes, similarly to the first dipping process.

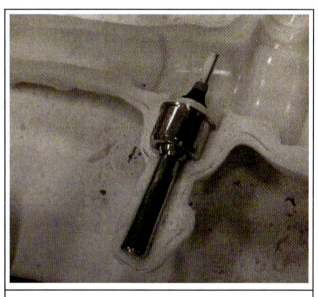

FIGURE 6

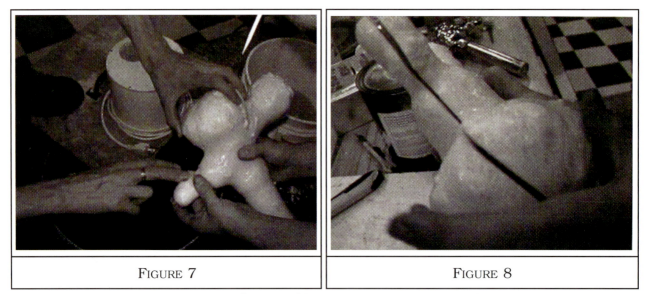

| FIGURE 7 | FIGURE 8 |

To repair the seams with this type of wax mold, one patches it back together by brushing on liquid wax (see Figure 7). Because the heating temperature was so low, we could dip our fingers into the wax and brush it onto the seams where needed. The mold was then dipped a final time to ensure that the seams were completely resealed.

We then mixed the reinforced FMG plaster and poured it into the mold. FMG plaster is a good choice of casting material to use with a thin wax mold, as the plaster expands very little as it sets up, unlike many 2 part foams or plastics. Using an expanding foam or plastic would have required a much thicker wax mold or plastic mother mold and would have taken longer. After the plaster set, the wax was removed to reveal our plaster urinal head (see Figure 8). A quick paint job, and it was ready to go.

This liquid poly-skin wax is non-toxic, non-staining, and working with it requires no special breathing protection. As when dealing with any hot liquid, standard goggles should be worn. One should take care with the heating element itself, as it may be hot enough to burn skin or start fires. While one can touch the heated wax with bare skin (in fact, one can do full immersion to make a hand mold), care should be taken to avoid sensitive skin areas.

In our specific production, we were already set up with the wax and plaster supplies, so our final total cost was significantly reduced from what it would have been had we needed to purchase all of the materials to start (detailed below). In any case, the wax is reusable and the cost can be spread out over several projects.

Original Urinal Head		$ 99.00
Replacement Handles	3 @ $7.97	$ 23.91
Poly Skin Wax	5 lbs	$ 32.00
FGM Starter Kit		$ 60.00
	Total	$214.91

ஐ ஐ ஐ

One of the scripts for the 5th International Play Festival at Ohio Northern University, required that a female character urinate onstage. When the action needed to happen, the actress, hand-cuffed and wearing a skirt, sat with her back facing the audience, The action needed to be actor-motivated so we built the device described below and shown in Figure 1.

PROCESS

We purchased a package of water balloons, 4' of fish-tank tubing, a fish-tank twist valve, and a sink-nozzle adapter, and we pulled the other parts from stock. Building a waterproof bladder was the most complicated step. Having discovered that a single water balloon would not produce the desired pressure, we slid one balloon inside a second one. We then slid both of them over one end of the tubing and closed the joint with a zip tie. We trimmed the zip tie, folded it as flat against the tubing as possible, and covered it with tape so that it could not puncture the balloons. As an extra hedge against leaking, we slid a condom over the balloons and zip-tied and taped it to the tubing below the balloons' zip-tie, and the bladder was complete.

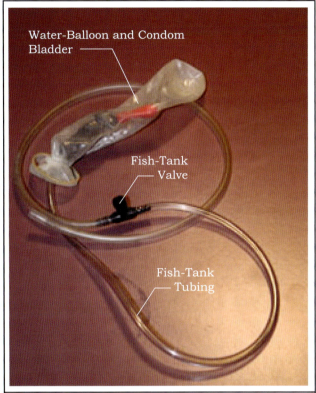

FIGURE 1: THE URINATION DEVICE

In any use of this or a similar device, blocking and staging will determine much of the design—including how much tubing will be needed and where the valve will be installed. The bladder must be placed where the performer can put pressure on it at will but also where it will be the least obvious and cumbersome. Since, in this case, the actress would be seated with her hands handcuffed behind her back, we enclosed the bladder in a microphone pouch located on her left inner thigh and under her buttock. The valve was located on her lower back where she could operate it discretely. We cut one piece of tubing to run from the bladder to the valve and a second to run from the valve down the performer's back and to her right inner thigh. While getting into costume, she taped the end to her leg so the water would fall as if she were urinating.

TIPS

Our experience suggests that it is best to fill the bladder with the unit completely assembled. The sink-nozzle adapter fits snugly inside the tubing, so the procedure involves opening the valve, filling the bladder, and bleeding any air out of the system before closing the valve. We built a back-up in case the device broke or leaked. The back-up was never used, but since this is such an inexpensive and simply-built device – and since predicting actors' and directors' needs is difficult – we recommend the practice.

ፚ ፚ ፚ

The piano to be used in the University of Central Arkansas fall 2004 production of *The Piano Lesson* had to satisfy two key requirements. First, it had to be correct in both period and type – a venerable paneled upright. Second, its panels needed to be decorated with raised African pictorial symbols tracing the cultural and family history of the Charles family.

A donated 1870s' piano we obtained was found to have trim panels along the front that could be easily removed and replaced with carved panels. Looking at the piano's beautiful wood finish and patina, we decided not to cut into the piano but rather to replace the panels with new sculptures that could be trimmed to match the rest of the instrument. We considered casting the items in some material, or perhaps vacuuforming and applying the results to the panels, but each of those ideas created problems of construction time, finish, and durability.

FIGURE 1: THE FINISHED PIANO

We decided to create bas-relief images by building up layers of Durham's Rock Hard Water Putty,® a material that would adhere to the wood fibers of the backing panels, could be sculpted and carved easily, and could take a wood finish. After experimenting briefly with the material, we developed a process that, depending on the water/powder mixture, has a varied open time and is somewhat like freehand sculpting with plaster. Here is the process we followed:

1. We cut lauan pieces to fit the removable front panels and the eight small panels (four for each side). We also purchased sticks of a small trim that matched the trim around the front panels and pre-cut them to fit each of the eight side panels. After some discussion about the extent of carving on the piano, it was decided to leave the front legs of the piano and the other surfaces as they were so as not to detract from the overall beauty of the instrument.

2. Designs for the panel were derived from African sculpture, early photographs of individual slaves and family groups and public sculptures of slave children. Sketches derived from the original images were scanned into Photoshop, reduced to line drawings, and adjusted to size.

3. Each panel was laid out and its line drawing transferred with carbon paper.

4. Wearing protective gloves, we deposited a thin mixture of putty (one part powder to two parts water and allowed to thicken slightly) to create a base level of the pattern, leaving the rest of the wood panel untouched to preserve the grain of the wood. We used baker's bags and various sized frosting tips to lay in this and other layers. Other tools used were clay sculpture tools and craft sticks.

5. We built up layers of putty and, as each began to set, we introduced finer details to the features. Various formulations allowed different effects. One and one-half parts water to one part powder created a creamy texture that could be extruded through a baker's bag and pulled and

pushed into shape but not carved. One part water to one part powder created a thicker mix that set up quickly and could be impressed with textures. Through this layering process eleven distinct sculptures were created. The images on the front of the piano were highly detailed and textured and panels on the side were very simple and of low relief.

6. After the panels dried for 24 hours, they were stained with an oil-based stain slightly lighter than the piano. After 10 minutes, a thin coat of black paint was sprayed on and rubbed off by hand to match the deep patina of the original finish. The same treatment was given the pre-cut trims. After another 24 hour drying time, a coat of polyurethane varnish was brushed on and let dry.

7. After everything was dry, the panels were mounted. The side panels were mounted with brads directly into the finished sides, and the trims were then affixed to fit the individual pieces. This would allow the pieces to be removed later with little harm to the original finish. The front panels were merely laid into the spaces in the front piece and backed with the original mounting hardware.

The result was a vintage piano with new sculptures that looked to be as old as the piano itself.

FIGURE 2: THE SCULPTED FRONT PANEL

ès ès ès

Shown in Figure 1 is the non-pyrotechnic flash we produced ourselves after discovering it would cost over $7,000.00 to hire a licensed pyrotechnician for the 4-week run of *The King Stag* at The Yale Repertory Theatre. The high cost of bringing someone in led us to explore using an air cannon to fire Cremora® non-dairy creamer into the air and allow it to drift down into a flame and ignite, as suggested in Steven A. Balk's *Technical Design Solutions* article "Remote Controlled Flash Effect".

Balk's article focuses on the remote control aspect of the device rather than the nature of the flash. During tests, we discovered that while his effect worked as described, it could not reliably produce the large, fast flash this production needed. In this case, widely variable air currents in the space caused the airborne Cremora® to drift away from the flame, causing misfires. With the modifications described in this article, the size and speed of the flash are governed solely by the air pressure and amount of Cremora® used: the higher the pressure, the taller the flash; and the greater the amount of Cremora®, the wider and brighter the flash. The flash shown in Figure 1 used 85 psi and less than $\frac{1}{8}$ cup of Cremora®.

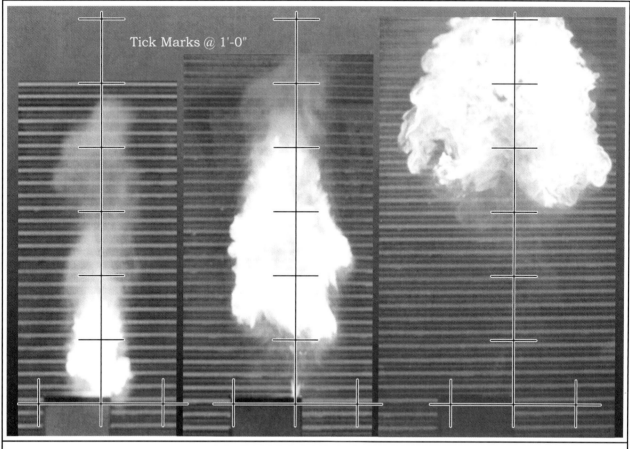

FIGURE 1: THE CREMORA® FIREBALL

CONSTRUCTION AND ASSEMBLY NOTES

As Figure 2 illustrates, the modified device has 3 main parts: a housing, an air cannon, and a Sterno®-can cradle. We built a steel housing measuring 6" x 12" x 12", but other materials and dimensions can be used as long as the housing keeps the flame away from any other objects, contains any Sterno® that might spill from the can, and shields the Sterno® flame from audience view and variable air currents. One side of the housing should be left open for ease of access.

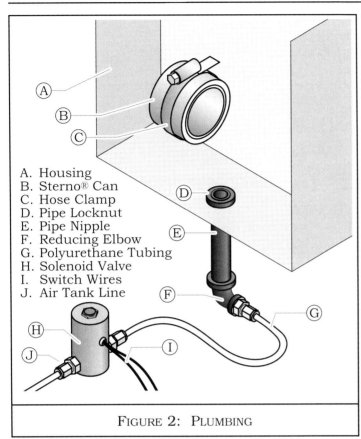

A. Housing
B. Sterno® Can
C. Hose Clamp
D. Pipe Locknut
E. Pipe Nipple
F. Reducing Elbow
G. Polyurethane Tubing
H. Solenoid Valve
I. Switch Wires
J. Air Tank Line

FIGURE 2: PLUMBING

THE AIR CANNON

See Figure 2 for details. First drill a $\frac{3}{4}$" hole into the base of the housing and use two locknuts to secure the pipe nipple to the base. Attach the reducing elbow with a quick-connect fitting to the other end of the nipple. Attach quick-connects to each port of the solenoid, connecting one end to the air supply and the other to the nipple assembly. Connect the solenoid to the switch and the switch to a power supply and the air cannon is complete.

THE STERNO®-CAN CRADLE

The cradle, a hose clamp attached to the side of the housing, holds the Sterno® can sideways and offset from the pipe nipple so that the flame is directly over the air cannon. We brazed the center of the clamp to the housing, $\frac{3}{4}$" back from the nipple and $2\frac{1}{2}$" above the base of the housing, but that location may need to be adjusted for other installations. The objective is to center the flame over the nipple.

In addition to centering the opening of the Sterno® can over the nipple, the cradle must allow the can to be slid closer to or farther away from the nipple. Complete adjustability is important because the position of the flame determines whether the air cannon will shoot Cremora® directly through the flame giving the desired result, or past it – putting the flame out. The correct placement is best found by trial and error.

FIRING THE EFFECT

Fill the air tank and load the measured amount of Cremora® into the pipe, light the Sterno®, and close the housing if one side was made removable. Stand back and depress the firing switch. The amount of time the switch is depressed will affect the amount of air released to the air cannon and, consequently, the height and spread of the Cremora®-fueled flame.

SAFETY REMINDERS

The flame this effect generates burns fast but it also burns hot enough to singe hair and ignite paper. Before using this effect in performance, we had it tested and approved by New Haven and Yale University Fire Marshals. The use of open flame onstage is governed by several codes, and permission to use this or any similar effect ultimately depends on local authorities. Even with approval, users are reminded to take all proper precautions, including keeping a safe distance between the performers and the effect and having an attended fire extinguisher nearby and ready for use.

MATERIALS

Quan	Part	Part #	Unit Cost	Other Information
McMaster-Carr				
1	medium-duty solenoid valve (NC)	4809K112	$99.44	5 psi min-150 psi max
4	gray acetal $\frac{1}{4}$" pipe $\frac{1}{4}$" tube male pipe adapter instant tube fittings	51055K12	$1.37	230 psi max
—	ether-based polyurethane tubing	5648K25	$0.33/ft	148 psi max at 75° F
1	22 mm panel cutout metal momentary pushbutton switch (SPST-NO) (not shown in Figure 2)	8382K21	$23.13	
Home Depot				
1	$4\frac{1}{2}$" x $\frac{1}{2}$" schedule-40 black pipe nipple	N/A	$0.97	150 psi max
1	90° black pipe reducing elbow $\frac{1}{2}$" to $\frac{1}{4}$" (female to female)	N/A	$1.58	150 psi max
2	$\frac{1}{2}$" black pipe locknuts	N/A	$1.23	
1	5"-dia worm-drive hose clamp	N/A	$3.50	
Others				
1	Sterno® Can (7oz)	N/A		
1	Cremora® Non-Dairy Creamer (32oz)	N/A	$2.15	

NOTES

Making the Sterno® cradle a separate stand would increase the adjustability of the can and, most likely, the effect's reliability in the long run. This effect's adaptability for repeated use might be improved by having an ignition source that could be turned on and off, rather than a constantly burning Sterno® pilot light.

RESOURCES

The Sterno® MSDS is available at http://www.sterno.com/sterno/sterno_retail/msds.aspx
Balk, Steven A. "Remote Controlled Flash Effect" *Technical Design Solutions for Theatre Vol. 1* ed. Bronislaw J. Sammler and Don Harvey. Boston: Focal Press, 2002.

❧❧❧

The fall 2006 Yale Repertory Theatre production of *The People Next Door* called for a fireball effect that had to be remotely ignited 25 minutes into the second act. Owing to the strict nature of local fire laws and the great expense of hiring a pyrotechnician, we decided to use Steven Balk's and Adam Dahl's *Technical Design Solutions* articles on Cremora®-fueled effects as a starting point for our effect.

INITIAL TESTING

We started by building a prototype to determine whether the effect would be suitable for the show. In testing we used Coffee-mate® Light as it is readily available. It worked, but the fireball was smaller than we anticipated and was also very picky about the conditions under which it ignited. After leaving a large bottle of creamer unsealed for a week or so, the effect stopped igniting altogether. To establish the reason behind this we tested new bottles of Cremora®, Coffee-mate®, Coffee-mate® Light, and a generic store brand. We found that Cremora® ignited more reliably and more spectacularly than any other brand, possibly because it has the right particle size and oil content.

SILO CONSTRUCTION

The enclosure that we arrived at used a copper conduit standoff with a hole drilled in it nestled inside of a short piece of $1\frac{1}{2}$" schedule-40 black pipe to hold the creamer over the air opening (see Figure 1). This assembly was welded inside of a piece of 4"-square tube intended to keep the flame going up rather than out. A piece of plate was welded to one side at the top of the tube to make a shelf for the can of Sterno® to sit on horizontally. Our testing showed that this orientation of the can allowed the flame to stay lit for more than twenty minutes. Angle brackets with tapped $\frac{5}{16}$" holes were welded on the shelf around the Sterno® can to provide adjustability of the can position with set screws, as well as to hold the can in place. This setup was placed inside a 16" tall aluminum tube that kept the Sterno® pilot flame enclosed and prevented the audience from seeing it.

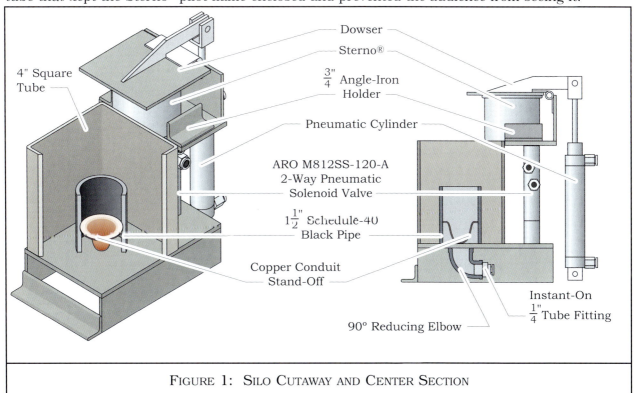

FIGURE 1: SILO CUTAWAY AND CENTER SECTION

STOP BUTTON

Because the flame had to stay lit for so long before the effect was triggered, a piece of aluminum was mounted to a hinge above the can of Sterno® to douse the flame if it grew too large or an actor got too close to it. A pneumatic cylinder was anchored to the deck outside the silo and attached to the dowser via an extension arm. The cylinder was plumbed to another ARO valve so that the dowser was open when power was applied to the solenoid. Power was cut to the valve when either of the stop buttons was pressed, which in turn reversed the direction of airflow and closed the dowser. Figure 2 shows a schematic of the system.

FIRING THE EFFECT

Before pressing a lighted momentary button to fire the effect, the operator first armed the system by turning a toggle switch. After the fireball had burned up, the operator pressed the stop button to extinguish the Sterno®. Confirmation that the effect fired was achieved by watching on a video monitor and listening for the satisfying whooshing sound the creamer made when it ignited.

Because there were a number of other pneumatically actuated effects in the show the operator was stationed at a centralized control panel underneath the platform where the effect was located. For safety, an additional stop button was located upstairs just inside the doorway leading to the platform. A crewperson was stationed here with a fire extinguisher while the Sterno® was burning in order to monitor the effect. A keyswitch that completely bypassed the arming circuit and fired the effect was also located at the upstairs station so that we could test the effect from stage level, *i.e.*, with the effect in full view.

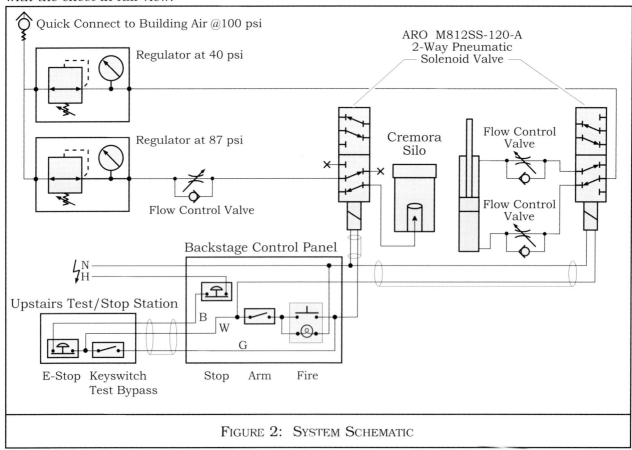

FIGURE 2: SYSTEM SCHEMATIC

REFINING THE SETTINGS

After the system was installed onstage, we tested the effect to set initial values for tech. We started by setting the air at 90 psi and loading the tube with 12.5 ml ($\frac{1}{2}$ Tbsp + $\frac{1}{3}$ Tbsp) of Cremora®. This produced a large fireball that, although spectacular, was judged by the Fire Marshal to be too large to be used onstage safely. We focused our efforts on finding the perfect balance between air pressure and the amount of creamer that would produce the smallest consistently repeatable fireball possible. After numerous tests, we concluded that anything less than 87 psi and 7.5 ml ($\frac{1}{2}$ Tbsp) of Cremora® would fail to produce a reliable flame. Results will certainly vary based on individual system design, humidity, and air currents.

SAFETY

Any sort of flame onstage is dangerous, so it is important to get approval from the local fire authorities before undertaking an effect like this. Precautions such as locating this effect well away from anything combustible and stationing a crewmember with a fire extinguisher nearby must be taken to prevent a fire.

One of the dangers that is unique to using a particle cloud for a fireball effect is that the flash fire does not burn all of the particles. Because the unburned particles settle on nearby surfaces and could potentially start their own flash fire, it is important to clean the apparatus and all surrounding surfaces after every show.

NOTES

It is important to note that there are many variables in the way this effect works. We tested the operation throughout the prototyping and build processes to ensure that any changes made did not affect the way the effect worked.

RESOURCES

Balk, Steven A. "Remote Controlled Flash Effect." *Technical Design Solutions for Theatre. Vol. I.* ed. Bronislaw J. Sammler and Don Harvey. Boston: Focal Press 2002.

Dahl, Adam J. "A Cremora-Fueled Pyrotechnic Alternative." *Technical Design Solutions for Theatre. Vol. III.* ed. Bronislaw J. Sammler and Don Harvey. Burlington, MA: Focal Press 2012.

☙❧❦❧☙

A Mechanism for a Battery-Operated Torch

Katherine Gloria Tharp

A Pennsylvania Shakespeare Festival production of *Henry IV* required a hand-held torch, but local regulations prohibited the use of live flame. Fortunately, DeSales University ATD Rob Napoli already had a plan for a battery-operated torch. Since the look of the torch had not been decided upon, we asked him to build the mechanisms for two torches, with the understanding that we would be putting a finished structural shell around the mechanism.

TORCH ASSEMBLY

There are four elements in the design of our mechanism, as shown in Figure 1: a Blue-LED-illuminated Computer Fan, a Kraft Foil Baffle Box, two White Torch Silks, and two Amber LED Bulbs.

The blue-LED-illuminated fan creates the airflow and provides an attractive blue glow at the base of the effect. The 2"-tall cross members in the baffle box keep the silks from twisting and stiffen the box. In addition to directing the airflow, the baffle box holds the elements of the mechanism together.

The bottom 1" of the 3"-tall baffle box sleeves down over the fan and is gaffer's-taped to it. The sides of the baffle box are bent inward at the top to hold the LED bulbs and direct their light at the silks. The bulbs are gaffer's-taped to the outside of the baffle box. The torch silks gradually fray and need to be replaced but they come with female (loop) Velcro® tabs. Mounting self-adhesive male Velcro® tabs on the outside of the baffle box simplifies attachment and replacement.

WIRING AND CONTROL

To meet the voltage and current needs of the components, we wired our components in parallel as shown in Figure 2. Measuring only 3" x $\frac{3}{4}$" x $\frac{3}{4}$", the terminal strip we used fit nicely into the handle of our torch and contained exactly the number of connections needed for the torch. We connected the components to one side of the paired terminals, and the batteries and a series of 6 jumpers to the other.

We used a latching push-button switch so that the operator could depress it once and not worry about keeping pressure on it – an advantage over the "deadman" switches generally needed in live-flame effects.

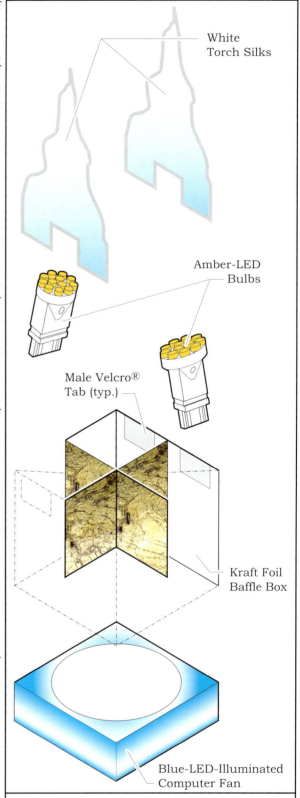

White Torch Silks

Amber-LED Bulbs

Male Velcro® Tab (typ.)

Kraft Foil Baffle Box

Blue-LED-Illuminated Computer Fan

FIGURE 1: TORCH MECHANISM COMPONENTS

FUNCTIONALITY

This mechanism can be used in any number of torch shells. We modified a Bamboo Tiki Torch from Jo-Ann Fabric and Crafts. We experimented with Fray-Check to eliminate the fraying of the torch silks, but that made the silks stiff and was neither successful nor worth the time it took. Though the silks need replacement after approximately 75 hours' use, they are relatively inexpensive. Onstage, the torch was convincing and attractive, particularly at lower overall levels of stage light. In very bright scenes, the white flame silks picked up a lot of the ambient light, and the effect was lessened. We did not experiment with different methods of dying the flame-shaped silks, but that might improve the look in brighter scenes.

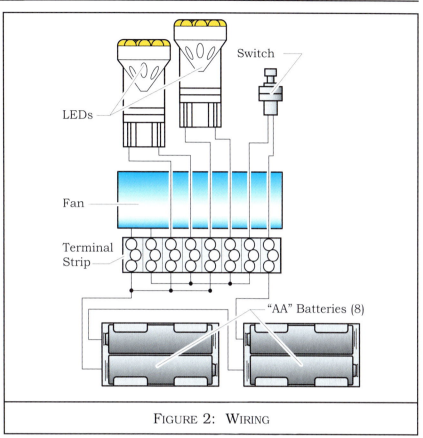

FIGURE 2: WIRING

MATERIALS AND COST

Item	Vendor	Cat #	Qty	Cost	Total
Antec 12V Fan: Blue-LED-Illuminated	antec.com	77042	1	$10.99	$10.99
Kraft Foil Refill Pack (use 2 blue sheets)	JoAnn Crafts		1	$2.99	$2.99
12V Amber-LED (wide angle)	superbrightleds.com	3157-A12	2	$3.99	$7.98
"Spare Set" White Torch Silks	superbrightleds.com		1	$4.99	$4.99
Adhesive-Backed Male Velcro	JoAnn Crafts		1	$1.99	$1.99
SPST Push On-Push Off Switch	Radio Shack	275-617	1	$2.29	$2.29
AA Battery Holders	Radio Shack	270-383	2	$1.59	$3.18
20ga wire (amount varies)	Radio Shack	278-1222	1	$5.49	$5.49
European-Style Terminal Strip, 8 positions	Radio Shack	274-678	1	$2.89	$2.89
AA Batteries (1.5V)	cheapbatteries.com		8	$.35	$2.80
				Total	$45.59

A Safe Glass Mirror Breaking Effect

John McCullough

This article describes a safe and reliable way to break a real glass hand mirror. The effect is easy to accomplish, leaves no debris, and produces a satisfying breaking sound. This mirror was created for a scene that required a small hand mirror be shown to audience, then smashed on the ground and broken. The needs of the play made staging the scene to hide a pre-broken mirror undesirable. There is no mechanism for the actor to operate; they simply drop it.

MAKING THE MIRROR

This effect uses a glass mirror that is $\frac{1}{8}$" thick. The mirrors can be purchased from an auto glass shop. The shop should be able to cut them to size and apply an adhesive sheet coating to the back. This prevents the mirror from breaking apart when it cracks.

The face of the mirror must also be covered with a clear, self-adhesive sheet to catch any small slivers that might crack off the front. Clear contact paper gives a dull, diffuse reflection. Laminating sheets (think office supplies) give a much clearer reflection. Experiment with the mirror face covering to achieve the desired look. Be sure to test your mirror face covering. Some materials may require two or more layers to adequately contain glass shards.

BREAKING THE MIRROR

The mirror, the masking plate, and the breaking plate are held in the hollow frame by a retaining ring, as shown in Figure 1. When the mirror is thrown or dropped face down, the masking plate and breaking plate will hit the mirror and each other. This breaks the mirror and sounds convincing.

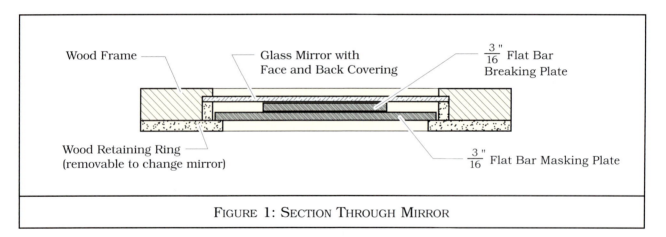

FIGURE 1: SECTION THROUGH MIRROR

FURTHER CONSIDERATIONS

It is important that the retaining ring and frame are durable enough to withstand the repeated impact of the break. The masking plate and breaking plate will slide around inside the frame while it is being handled. This can be overcome by the actor's holding them in place before the break (a simple squeeze will do). Another solution is to tape the breaking plate to the back of the mirror, reducing, but not eliminating, the handling noise.

❧❧❧

The 1970s' period pull tab Budweiser can is an essential prop in any production of Octavio Solis' *Lydia*, for at the end of the play the central figure commits suicide by swallowing a pull tab that her father has dropped on the floor. As the Yale Repertory Theatre Props Department learned while preparing for a production of the play, it's easy to find contemporary beverage cans – those with tabs that simply fold back on the lid – but finding sanitary, pull-tab cans is a different matter.

Through internet research, we found a number of sources of period beer cans. Typically, "collector copy" cans have been emptied through holes punched or drilled in their bottoms. We briefly considered buying as many as we needed, refilling them with seltzer, plugging the holes, and applying period labels. To ensure sanitation and safety, however, we decided instead to follow the procedure described here, which, with practice and experience, takes only about half an hour per can.

TOOLS AND MATERIALS

We estimated how many times the characters would "pop a top" and then bought enough vintage beer cans and 12-oz. cans of Goya juice to cover techs and performances. We chose the Goya juice cans because, in size and shape, they closely resemble 1970s' Budweiser cans. We bought seltzer to replace the juice so that we would get a convincing hissing sound when the tabs were pulled. We bought DAP Aquarium Sealant (silicone) to fasten the old lids to the new cans, and white Scotch Plastic Tape to fasten the color-laser-printed labels to the finished product.

To help us get the seltzer into the cans, we used a large plastic syringe. To keep the seltzer in the cans, we made corks out of rubber license plate bumpers that we bought from a local hardware store for about $0.68 each.

PROCEDURE

1.   The License Plate Bumpers. Trim each bumper as shown in Figure 1 for their use as corks.

2.   The New Cans. Drain the cans and cut off their tops with a Dremel® cutoff wheel, making the cut as close to the lid as possible (see Figure 2).

3.   The Period Lids. Drill a $\frac{7}{32}$" hole in the center of the pull-tab ring on each period can. Then, using a half-width ($\frac{1}{4}$"-wide) strip of spike tape as a guide, cut the lids off the period cans (see Figure 3).

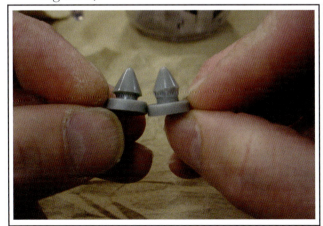

FIGURE 1: NEW (L) AND TRIMMED (R) LICENSE PLATE BUMPERS

FIGURE 2: CUTTING THE GOYA CAN

FIGURE 3: CUTTING THE PERIOD LID

FIGURE 4: LETTING THE SILICONE CURE

4. De-burr the cut edges and roughen the surrounding areas to provide tooth for the silicone. Wash the cans and lids thoroughly with soap and water.

5. Apply a bead of silicone to the inside edge of the lid and the outside edge of the can, and sleeve the lid over the can. After doing this to a number of cans, sandwich the cans between two pieces of plywood or MDF and weight them down with counterweights (see Figure 4). Let the silicone cure for 48 hours.

6. Trim off the excess silicone with a razor blade. After filling the cans completely with water to purge any silicone vapors, empty the cans and apply the labels with Scotch plastic tape as shown in Figure 5, locating the vertical seam wherever it can be most effectively hidden by the actor's hand.

7. Refill the cans with 10 to 11 ounces of seltzer (see Figure 6). To guard against premature leakage, do not fill the cans above the silicone joint.

8. Insert the corks, using a small screwdriver to seat them if necessary (see Figure 7). Finally, disguise the corks with tabs of metallic tape (see Figure 8).

FIGURE 5: APPLYING THE LABEL

FIGURE 6: FILLING THE CANS

FIGURE 7: INSERTING A CORK

FIGURE 8: THE FINISHED PRODUCT

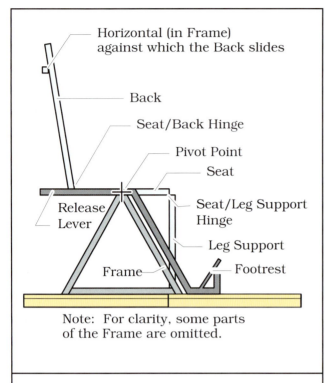

Horizontal (in Frame)
against which the Back slides

Back

Seat/Back Hinge

Pivot Point

Seat

Release
Lever

Seat/Leg Support
Hinge

Leg Support

Frame

Footrest

Note: For clarity, some parts
of the Frame are omitted.

FIGURE 1: SWEENEY BARBER CHAIR ESSENTIALS

Sondheim's musical *Sweeney Todd, The Demon Barber of Fleet Street*, has an interesting and challenging requirement: a barber chair that, having been brought onstage and installed during one song, converts into a chute that sends Sweeney's victims through a trap in the floor. For a production at the North Country Center for the Arts in New Hampshire, we needed to make the chair on a limited budget and a tight time schedule. We kept our design as simple and light as possible, using tube-steel frames covered only where necessary with plywood and upholstery. Its essentials are shown in Figure 1.

With a victim seated in the chair, Sweeney stepped on a release lever, raising the footrest out of the way as in Figure 2. Then as a stagehand in the traproom unlocked the trapdoor, Sweeney's victim shifted his weight forward, transforming the back/seat/leg support into a slide as shown in Figure 3. The victim kept his arms close to his body as he slid down the chute onto crash mats. After stabilizing the victim, the stagehand closed the trap, completing the action while Sweeney reset the chair.

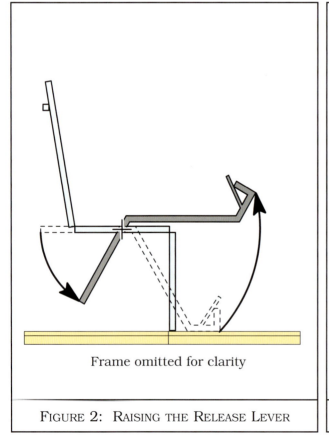

Frame omitted for clarity

FIGURE 2: RAISING THE RELEASE LEVER

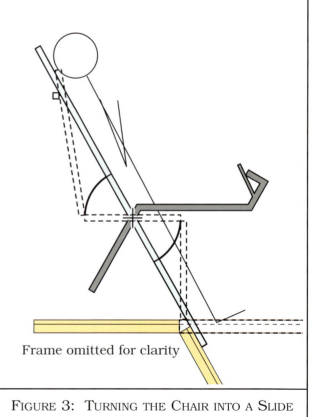

Frame omitted for clarity

FIGURE 3: TURNING THE CHAIR INTO A SLIDE

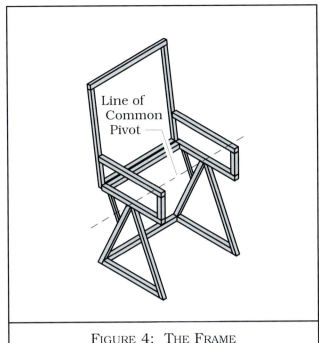

FIGURE 4: THE FRAME

The design we came up with took about a week to design and build and cost about $140.00, about $50.00 of which was for the upholstery.

Figures 4 through 6 illustrate the chair's three subassemblies: frame, back/seat/leg support; and release lever. All three subassemblies were framed in 18-gauge 1"-square tube steel and were joined along a common pivot represented here by the broken lines. The pivot itself was made of a length of $\frac{3}{8}$" round bar capped with pushnuts. Bronze bushings kept the subassemblies from binding on each other.

The frame and the release lever were rigid, welded structures. The back/seat/leg support, however, consisted of three welded rectangular frames joined by lengths of piano hinge. As the trap opened and the victim shifted forward tilting the seat, the leg support slid downward along the trapdoor, and the back slid upward against the frame's topmost member.

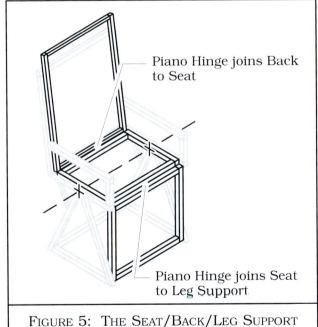

FIGURE 5: THE SEAT/BACK/LEG SUPPORT

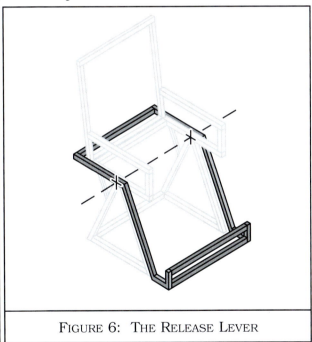

FIGURE 6: THE RELEASE LEVER

Our Sweeney chair's frame was 24" wide overall; the back, 24" tall; the seat, 16" deep; and the leg support, 16" tall. Other dimensions could certainly be used.

❧❧❧

This mechanism was developed while working on the Yale Repertory Theatre production of *Rough Crossing*, which called for a chair and table to slide offstage as though they were on a rolling ship. The chair and table only needed to slide offstage once, and the table, which was on casters, moved easily. The chair, on the other hand, promised to be more difficult since it was not castered, but building a tracking system to move it seemed a waste of resources. The simple, cost-effective, and time-efficient alternative was to use a trolling reel, as seen in Figure 1.

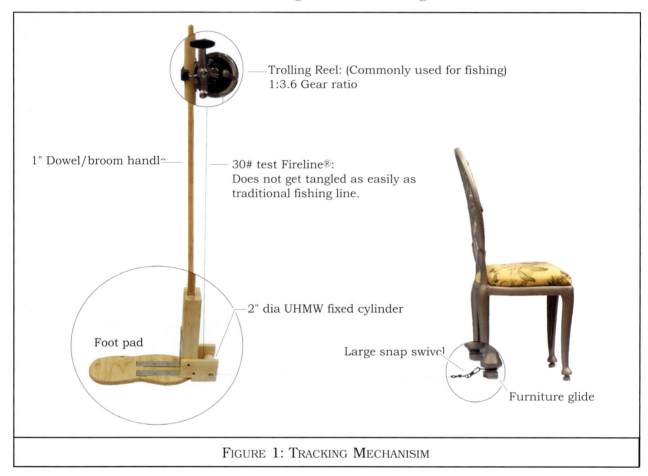

Trolling Reel: (Commonly used for fishing)
1:3.6 Gear ratio

1" Dowel/broom handle

30# test Fireline®:
Does not get tangled as easily as
traditional fishing line.

2" dia UHMW fixed cylinder

Foot pad

Large snap swivel

Furniture glide

FIGURE 1: TRACKING MECHANISIM

The reel's 1:3.6 gear ratio allowed the operator to move the 18-pound chair with a coefficient of friction (μ) of 0.25 (effectively 4.5 lbs.) at about 3.5 ft/sec. All fishing reels, *i.e.*, trolling reels, spinning reels, and casting reels, are built for speed: the spools always turn more times than the handles do. Casting and spinning reels have higher gear ratios than trolling reels, so we could have gained speed by using one of them instead of our trolling reel. They are also more affordable than the $100.00 trolling reel we bought. On the other hand, they are more likely to generate tangles if the operator is not extremely careful.

Fishing line is not rated for over-head lifting so any item rigged in this way must not be able to cause harm if the system were to fail. Still, fishing reels could safely be used to fly lightweight props *e.g.*, postcards, stuffed animals, or anything light and squishy.

❧ ❧ ❧

For a 2010 Yale Repertory Theatre production of *The Servant of Two Masters*, Director Chris Bayes, wanted a gradually increasing number of fireflies to appear slowly out of a blackout, gathering at last into a swarm of dancing lights. For this effect each of the eleven cast members carried two wand-like units containing a small lamp on each of two stems that joined in a shop-built handle. See Figure 1 for an overview.

CONSTRUCTION

For the stems, we used 3'-long, $\frac{1}{16}$"-diamenter brass rods, whose flexibility and responsiveness to motion amplified the actors' graceful movements. The rods are readily available at art supply stores.

We attached a standard Mini-Mag® krypton light bulb to each stem. From the house, the krypton lights seem about the same size as actual fireflies, and their two-pin construction needed no lamp base, allowing them to have the lowest possible profile. It also allowed the wires running down each stem to be soldered directly to the lamp pins. To dress the stems, we covered the wiring running along them with $\frac{1}{4}$" black shrink wrap, which also stiffened them a little.

We mounted the stems and lamps on handles made from 1"-diameter PVC tube. The assembly, which is shown in Figure 2, we found ideal in several ways. The tube fits nicely in the hand and its wall is thick enough that we had no trouble drilling a pair of $\frac{1}{16}$" holes parallel to its walls to slip the stems into. The approximately 1"-deep holes were snug enough that we had to force the stems in.

Additionally, the interior diameter is just large enough to hold a two-cell AAA battery holder, which was wired to two normally-open momentary pushbutton switches, each controlling one lamp. All of the electronic components are available at Radio Shack for less than $10.00 per unit.

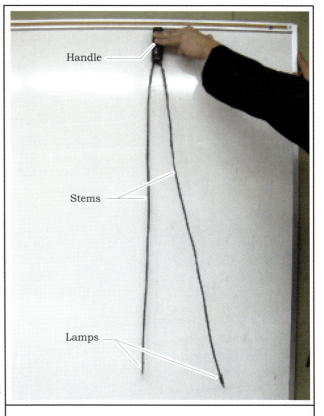

FIGURE 1: DANCING FIREFLY

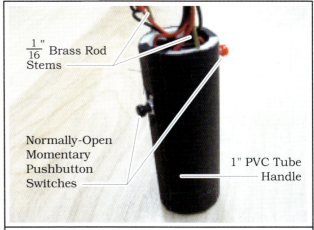

FIGURE 2: THE EFFECT'S HANDLE

REFINEMENTS

During the first technical rehearsal with the fireflies, we decided that the lamps were far too bright. We consequently removed one of the batteries from each handle and bridged the connections with a small jumper wire as shown in Figure 3, an approach we thought simpler than adding resistors.

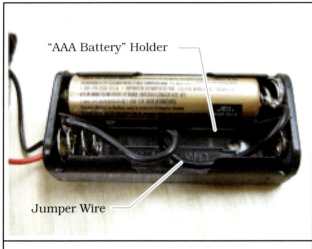

"AAA Battery" Holder

Jumper Wire

FIGURE 3: BATTERY HOLDER DETAILS

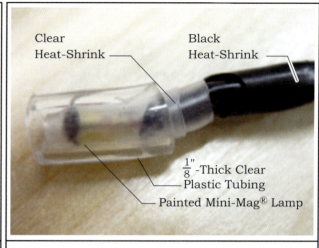

Clear Heat-Shrink

Black Heat-Shrink

$\frac{1}{8}$"-Thick Clear Plastic Tubing

Painted Mini-Mag® Lamp

FIGURE 4: A WRAPPED, COLORED LAMP

We also dipped the lamps in stained-glass paint to push the color temperature away from white and toward the yellowish amber of a firefly. As technical rehearsals continued, we discovered that the tips of the lamps needed to be covered with opaque black paint so that the only light from the lamps would be emitted through the sides.

Finally, to protect the fragile lamps from breaking, we encased them and their connections to the stems in two layers of clear plastic heat-shrink. As additional protection, we sleeved lengths of $\frac{1}{8}$"-thick clear plastic tubing over the heat-shrink-encased lamps. The multiple layers of protection diffused the light into a gentle realistic glow. The finished product is shown in Figure 4.

❧❧❧❧❧

TECHNICAL BRIEF

Rigging Hardware

An Adjustable Flat Hanger — *Moshe H. Peterson*

A Versatile Flat-and-Track System — *Rich Desilets*

A Convenient Shop-Built Mini-Arbor — *Joe Hamlin*

A Sleeve for Increasing Arbor Capacity — *Drew Becker*

Positioning Catches for Traveler Track — *Justin Elie*

Plans for a Double Kabuki Drop — *Kate Wicker*

An Inexpensive and Quiet Shop-Built Track System — *Shaminda Amarakoon*

A Simple Drop Rig for Small Payloads — *Andrew V. Wallace*

Centerline Studios' Roger Gray designed a device that can make flats hang plumb beneath their battens – an essential in tightly packed flies. As shown in Figure 1, the hanger's U-shaped base made from 3" x 3" x $\frac{3}{16}$" structural steel tube, bolts to the top of a flat. The hanger's $\frac{1}{2}$" x 4"-13 connecting socket cap screw passes through two slightly oversized holes in the base and a tapped hole in the hanger's $\frac{1}{2}$" x 2" flat-bar adjusting tab. Secured by a locking nut, the cap screw turns freely in the oversized holes in the base, driving the adjusting tab back or forward, moving the flat's pick point closer toward or farther away from its center of mass.

ACKNOWLEDGMENTS

Roger Gray, Centerline Studios
John Starmer, Yale School of Drama

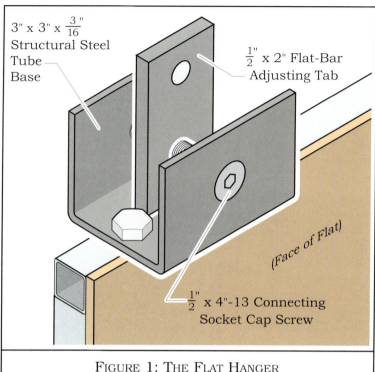

3" x 3" x $\frac{3}{16}$" Structural Steel Tube Base

$\frac{1}{2}$" x 2" Flat-Bar Adjusting Tab

(Face of Flat)

$\frac{1}{2}$" x 4"-13 Connecting Socket Cap Screw

FIGURE 1: THE FLAT HANGER

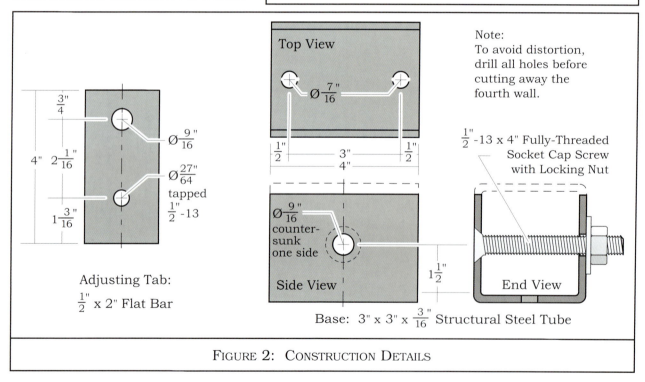

Top View

Note:
To avoid distortion, drill all holes before cutting away the fourth wall.

$\frac{3}{4}$"

$\varnothing \frac{9}{16}$"

$\varnothing \frac{27}{64}$" tapped $\frac{1}{2}$"-13

4" 2$\frac{1}{16}$"

1$\frac{3}{16}$"

Adjusting Tab:
$\frac{1}{2}$" x 2" Flat Bar

$\varnothing \frac{7}{16}$"

$\frac{1}{2}$" $\frac{3}{4}$" $\frac{1}{2}$"

$\varnothing \frac{9}{16}$" countersunk one side

Side View

$\frac{1}{2}$"-13 x 4" Fully-Threaded Socket Cap Screw with Locking Nut

1$\frac{1}{2}$"

End View

Base: 3" x 3" x $\frac{3}{16}$" Structural Steel Tube

FIGURE 2: CONSTRUCTION DETAILS

To help transform a movie theatre into a space for live performance, I designed a system of eight 4'-0" x 19'-0" flats that ride on 4 wheels each in a National "barn door" track, With one flat in the downstage rail of the track another flat can pass it on the upstage side as shown in Figure 1.

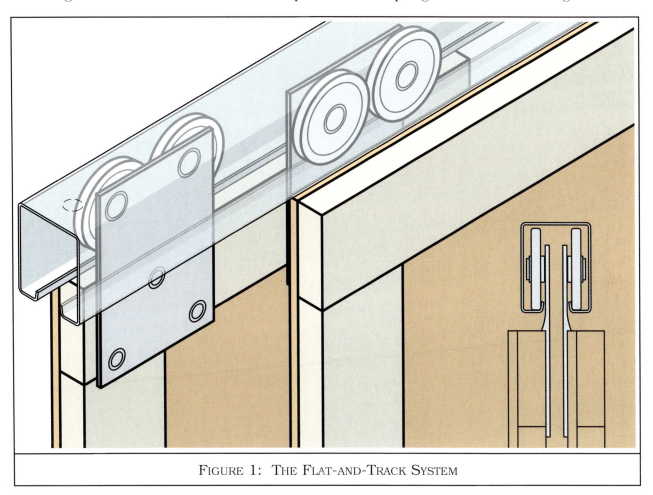

FIGURE 1: THE FLAT-AND-TRACK SYSTEM

We are using 4 rows of both 16' and 20' tracks hung parallel to the front of the stage and supported at 5'-0" intervals by threaded rod from the 2x10 beams above the ceiling. Some tracks extend all the way to the wall for storing pairs of flats when the theatre is used for music, etc. It was hoped that the flats could be moved from up and down stage rails by 2 people but in practice a third person on a ladder is needed to help align the wheels in the rail.

❧❧❧❧

A Convenient Shop-Built Mini-Arbor

Joe Hamlin

One of the challenges in the Yale School of Drama's flexible Iseman Theatre is the tight 9" clearance between the galleries and the side walls: it is just too narrow an opening for sand bags. In developing a temporary counterweight system for a new production called *Mirror, Mirror*, I designed and built a wire-guided mini-arbor, which has become a handy addition to the stock rigging gear.

This mini-arbor has two advantages: cost and design flexibility. The total cost of construction is about $30.00 and most of the parts are common stock items found in a scene shop. In contrast, the smallest commercially available wire-guided arbor is 4' tall and costs about $200.00. In addition to the price difference, commercial arbors lack some of the flexibility offered by this design.

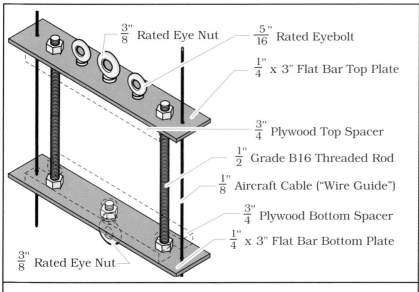

$\frac{3}{8}$" Rated Eye Nut

$\frac{5}{16}$" Rated Eyebolt

$\frac{1}{4}$" x 3" Flat Bar Top Plate

$\frac{3}{4}$" Plywood Top Spacer

$\frac{1}{2}$" Grade B16 Threaded Rod

$\frac{1}{8}$" Aircraft Cable ("Wire Guide")

$\frac{3}{4}$" Plywood Bottom Spacer

$\frac{1}{4}$" x 3" Flat Bar Bottom Plate

$\frac{3}{8}$" Rated Eye Nut

FIGURE 1: THE MINI-ARBOR (BOTTOM-PLATE HARDWARE OMITTED)

CONSTRUCTION

The mini-arbor's main parts are a top and bottom plate made of $\frac{1}{4}$" x 3" flat bar cut to a length of 1'-3" and 2 pieces of $\frac{1}{2}$" grade-B16 threaded rod. The other components include:

two $\frac{5}{16}$" rated eyebolts and Grade-5 nuts
two $\frac{3}{8}$" x 1" grade-5 bolts and Grade-5 nuts
eight $\frac{1}{2}$" grade-5 Nylock® nuts
two $\frac{3}{4}$" plywood spacers

Note: The plywood plates protect the bolt threads and keep the counterweights level.

ADAPTATION POSSIBILITIES

This arbor can be adapted in several ways. First, the top and bottom plates can be snugged down to keep a stack of counterweights quiet and securely in place. The arbor's capacity and height are easily adjusted by varying the length of the threaded rod. The eyebolts and nuts at the top and bottom of the arbor also provide various connection possibilities. For example, scenery with 2 pick points can be attached to the eyebolts on the top plate and a rope handline can be attached to the centered eye nut in the bottom plate and tied off to a pin rail. Alternatively, to run the handline like a single-purchase fly system the scenery would be attached to the eyebolts in the top plate and a handline would be attached to the eye nut in the bottom plate, run through a floor block, rope lock, and head block and tied off to the eye nut in the top plate.

INSTALLATION

There are a number of ways to rig the $\frac{1}{8}$" aircraft cable guide system. In this case, an I-beam provided rigging points for the head block and the aircraft cable guides (see Figure 3). I attached the aircraft cable to the I-beam with beam clamps and to the floor with D-rings that were lagged into the floor. Turnbuckles allowed me to add the appropriate amount of tension to the guide cables. The arbor traveled about 20' with minimal sway.

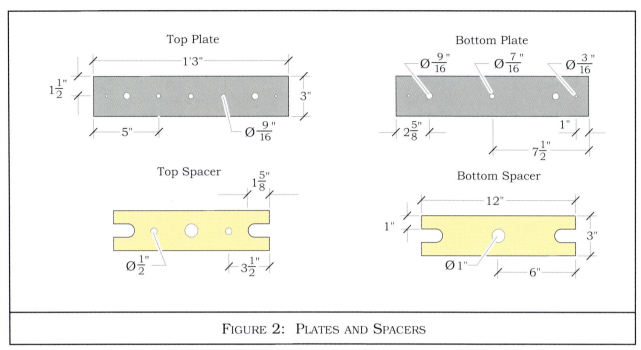

FIGURE 2: PLATES AND SPACERS

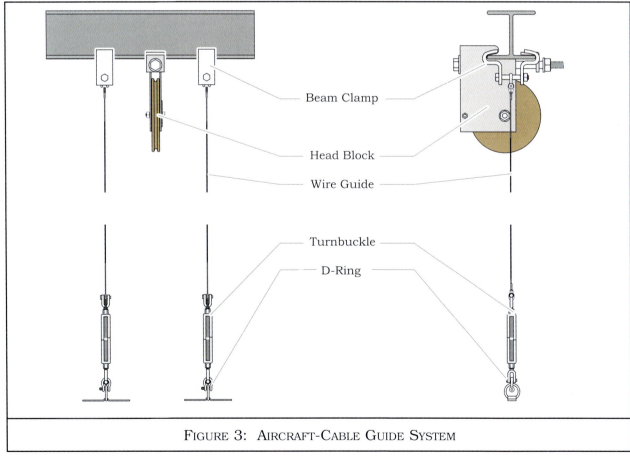

FIGURE 3: AIRCRAFT-CABLE GUIDE SYSTEM

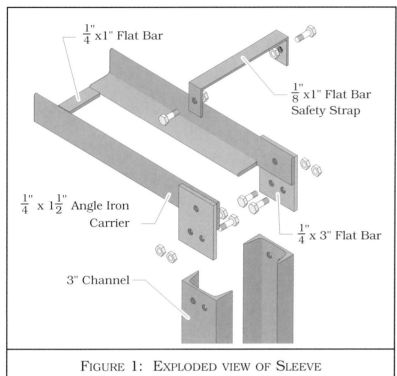

$\frac{1}{4}$"x1" Flat Bar

$\frac{1}{8}$"x1" Flat Bar
Safety Strap

$\frac{1}{4}$" x 1$\frac{1}{2}$" Angle Iron
Carrier

$\frac{1}{4}$" x 3" Flat Bar

3" Channel

FIGURE 1: EXPLODED VIEW OF SLEEVE

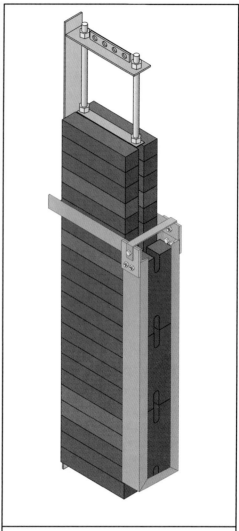

FIGURE 2: SLEEVE INSTALLED

Arbor size is usually the limiting factor for the capacity of counterweight linesets. Solutions currently exist, but many decrease travel by adding mass to the top or bottom, and others use multiple linesets. At the Utah Shakespearean Festival, our solution was to add weight to the rope lock side of the arbor in an arbor sleeve that held stock bricks vertically against the face of the arbor. The sleeve, detailed in Figure 1 and shown installed in Figure 2, required no modifications of the arbor and gained us a nominal 180 lbs. of capacity. The use of counterweights of a different size would affect sleeve size and the corresponding gain in arbor capacity.

INSTALLATION AND SAFETY NOTES

Load the system arbor until about 2' of open space remains. Place the carrier above the current top brick, then load the remaining bricks until the arbor is full. Bolt the channel to the carrier, and slide bricks into the channel. Bolt on the safety strap, and test the weight. Flying any piece of scenery is inherently dangerous. Follow all up-to-date standards for loading counterweight systems and plan the hang carefully to avoid out-of-weight conditions. The weakest link in our system was the batten. We overcame that weakness by distributing the load properly. Find the ratings of all components in your system and check that you are not overloading them.

The Glimmerglass Opera's 2009 festival season needed several pairs of framed masking legs to be moved into various positions on or offstage and locked into place. The legs were suspended from ADC Series 280 traveler track and, during changeovers, the tracks were flown out to allow scenery to move in and out of the space. To simplify resetting the legs and to keep them from shifting from side to side while being flown in and out, the Opera's lead rigger, Matt Cowles, built a number of positioning catches like the one illustrated in Figure 1.

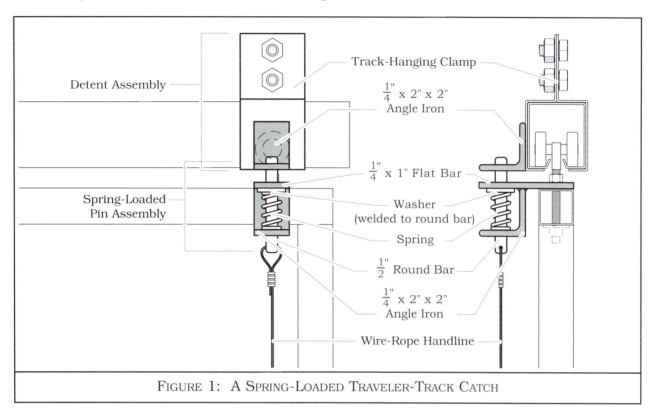

Detent Assembly

Track-Hanging Clamp

$\frac{1}{4}$" x 2" x 2"
Angle Iron

$\frac{1}{4}$" x 1" Flat Bar

Spring-Loaded
Pin Assembly

Washer
(welded to round bar)

Spring

$\frac{1}{2}$" Round Bar

$\frac{1}{4}$" x 2" x 2"
Angle Iron

Wire-Rope Handline

FIGURE 1: A SPRING-LOADED TRAVELER-TRACK CATCH

Each positioning catch consisted of two parts: an angle-iron detent assembly and a spring-loaded pin assembly. The former consisted of short lengths of $\frac{1}{4}$" x 2" x 2" angle iron welded to standard track-hanging clamps. A $\frac{5}{8}$" hole was drilled through the horizontal leg of the angle and counter-sunk on the bottom side.

The pin assemblies were made of $\frac{1}{2}$" round bar, $\frac{1}{4}$" x 1" flat bar, and $\frac{1}{4}$" x 2" x 2" angle iron. The first step in making these assemblies was to drill an $\frac{1}{8}$" hole through one end of a 4"-long piece of the round bar. The second was to weld a washer to the bar about 1" in from the opposite end of the bar. To form mounts for the pins, $\frac{5}{8}$" holes were drilled through short lengths of the flat bar and the angle iron as shown above. The springs were then sleeved over the pins and the pins were inserted through the holes in the angle iron. As a final assembly step, the springs were compressed and held by clamps on the pins, the angle iron and flat bar were welded together and the clamps were released. The finished spring-loaded pin assemblies were bolted to the masking flats as shown above, captured between the flat's carrier nuts. A $\frac{1}{16}$" wire-rope handline from the pin to the deck allowed a stagehand to pull the pin, slide the panel into its desired location, and lock it in place.

🔔 🔔 🔔

In *Servant of Two Masters*, a 2010 Yale Repertory Theatre production, the technical direction team faced a request for a drop that would fall quickly into sight and later drop just as quickly to the floor without harming an actor standing almost directly beneath it. To accomplish this move, they modified a Kabuki quick-release developed by Hudson Scenic Studio.

THE KABUKI DROP QUICK-RELEASE SYSTEM

This quick-release is activated by pulling on a $\frac{3}{16}$" wire rope operating line. For operator convenience, the lower end of the operating line terminates in a short length of sash cord and, to facilitate reset, the upper end in a bungee cord that allows the operating line to move while remaining attached. (The upper and lower ends of the operating line are not detailed in the accompanying illustrations.) A series of cotter pins connected to the operating line and inserted through beam clamps as shown in Figure 1 completes the device. The beam clamps are bolted in a line along a $\frac{5}{4}$x6 pine release batten at the same intervals that separate the drop's grommets. Zip-ties fastened through the drop's grommets are picked up by the cotter pins.

In preset, the batten is flown in, the drop is attached to the release system by running each cotter pin through its beam clamp and corresponding zip-tie, and the loaded batten is flown out. When the operating line is pulled, the freed cotter pins release the drop. When the operator lets go, the bungee cord resets the operating line.

DOUBLING THE SYSTEM FOR *SERVANT*

The top of the *Servant* drop was picked up by a Kabuki quick release. In addition, the team gathered the drop up in a canvas sling provided with its own quick release to arrange for the drop to fall into sight on cue. On its downstage edge, the sling was stapled to the 40'-long release batten. On its upstage edge, the sling was grommetted and picked up by a second Kabuki quick release as shown in Figure 2. Pulling the upstage operating line released the drop from the sling; pulling the downstage line let the drop fall.

NOTES ON THE DROP

For this production, the technical direction team chose scrim as the drop material as it wrinkles less than most other drop fabrics and doesn't

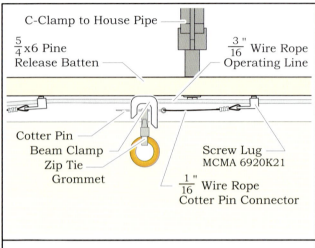

C-Clamp to House Pipe
$\frac{5}{4}$x6 Pine Release Batten
$\frac{3}{16}$" Wire Rope Operating Line
Cotter Pin
Beam Clamp
Zip Tie
Grommet
Screw Lug MCMA 6920K21
$\frac{1}{16}$" Wire Rope Cotter Pin Connector

FIGURE 1: QUICK-RELEASE DETAILS

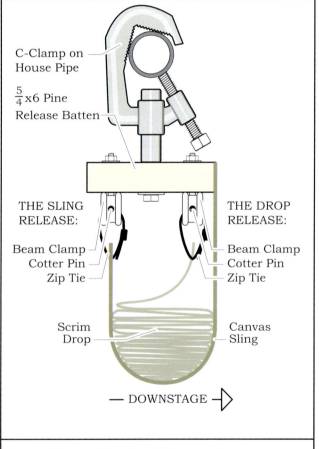

C-Clamp on House Pipe
$\frac{5}{4}$x6 Pine Release Batten

THE SLING RELEASE:
Beam Clamp
Cotter Pin
Zip Tie

THE DROP RELEASE:
Beam Clamp
Cotter Pin
Zip Tie

Scrim Drop
Canvas Sling

— DOWNSTAGE ⟶

FIGURE 2: END VIEW OF SYSTEM

cause the paint to crack when bunched up. The scrim needed some weight at the bottom but using a bottom pipe was out of the question for two reasons. First, an actor stood directly beneath the scrim both when it appeared and when it fell to the ground. Second, the use of a bottom pipe would have made it awkward to strike the scrim after the scene. Rather than a bottom pipe, the technical direction team decided on lead tape, which gave the bottom of the drop enough weight to fall into sight with a minimum of hang-ups or twists while keeping it from being so heavy as to cause serious injury should something go wrong and the drop land on or graze the actor.

ক্তক্তক্তক্ত

In the 2010 production of *Orlando* at the Yale School of Drama, sliding panels necessitated closely stacked tracking systems. Due to cost and space restrictions, the technical team developed a custom track that is a quiet, inexpensive and a reliable alternative to commercial track systems. The use of readily available materials makes this a viable alternative for many shops.

CONSTRUCTION MATERIALS

Figure 1 on the right shows a cross section of the system. The track was a length of 16-gauge 1" x 2" tube steel. Half-inch threaded rods spaced 6' apart and drilled close to the upstage edge of the tube steel supported the track. Washers and, wherever possible, Nylock® nuts on the threaded rod hanger kept the track from rotating.

A $2\frac{1}{2}$"-long section of 3" x 5" x $\frac{1}{4}$" structural steel tube with the top 1" cut off and ground down served as the main body of each carrier. Each carrier was fitted with a 65mm Senate Sinner® rollerblade wheel with standard bearings, installed opposite the tube's internal weld bead to maintain clearance for the wheel. A $\frac{1}{4}$" x $1\frac{1}{2}$" hex-head bolt capped with a Nylock® nut served as the wheel's axle and a narrow (N) style $\frac{1}{4}$" flat washer provided the clearance the wheel needed to roll freely. Two $\frac{1}{4}$" x $\frac{7}{8}$" UHMW pads were mounted below the wheel to maintain carrier/track alignment. A third UHMW block, this one measuring $\frac{1}{2}$" x $1\frac{1}{4}$" and milled to be a cable guide, was installed at the bottom. The carriers were locked to their $\frac{1}{4}$" wire-rope drive cable with Crosbies. (Wire rope and Crosbies are not shown.) Connection to the scenery panels was accomplished using fully threaded $\frac{1}{2}$"-13 grade-5 hex-head bolts.

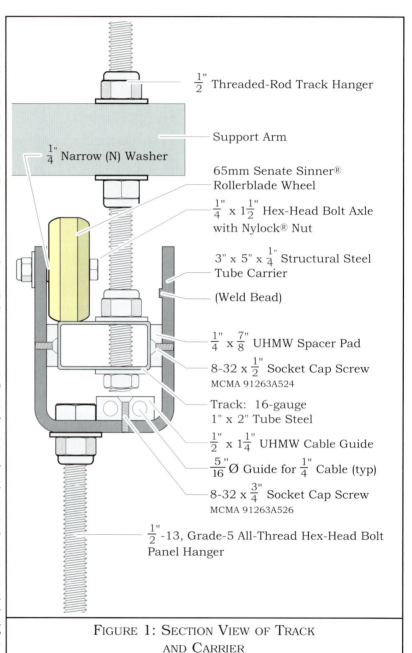

$\frac{1}{2}$" Threaded-Rod Track Hanger

Support Arm

$\frac{1}{4}$" Narrow (N) Washer

65mm Senate Sinner® Rollerblade Wheel

$\frac{1}{4}$" x $1\frac{1}{2}$" Hex-Head Bolt Axle with Nylock® Nut

3" x 5" x $\frac{1}{4}$" Structural Steel Tube Carrier

(Weld Bead)

$\frac{1}{4}$" x $\frac{7}{8}$" UHMW Spacer Pad

8-32 x $\frac{1}{2}$" Socket Cap Screw
MCMA 91263A524

Track: 16-gauge 1" x 2" Tube Steel

$\frac{1}{2}$" x $1\frac{1}{4}$" UHMW Cable Guide

$\frac{5}{16}$" Ø Guide for $\frac{1}{4}$" Cable (typ)

8-32 x $\frac{3}{4}$" Socket Cap Screw
MCMA 91263A526

$\frac{1}{2}$"-13, Grade-5 All-Thread Hex-Head Bolt Panel Hanger

FIGURE 1: SECTION VIEW OF TRACK AND CARRIER

ADVANTAGES

The three greatest advantages to this system involve cost, quietness, and close spacing. This system was built for about half the cost of comparable ADC and EEE track systems, and (subjectively)

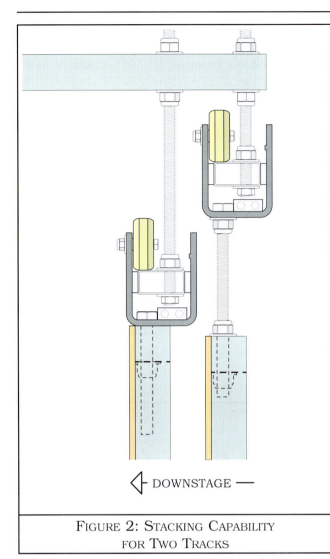

FIGURE 2: STACKING CAPABILITY
FOR TWO TRACKS

we judged it to be very quiet compared to the commercial tracks. The greatest advantage, however, was that panels hung on adjacent tracks needed as little as $1\frac{1}{2}$" clearance for reliable operation. Figure 2 demonstrates how that closeness was achieved.

TWO NOTES

First, keeping panels absolutely plumb while using a single wheel on each carrier requires that the panels be centered directly beneath the carrier wheels rather than the track. This requirement must be taken into account in developing the scenery hang. Maintaining plumbness may require that the connections at the top of the panels be slots rather than holes so that the panels can be shifted upstage or downstage as necessary. Second, the 1" x 2" tube steel will require more track hangers per 20' section than a typical ADC track. The weight of our panels allowed us to put one every 6', but smaller intervals would be required for heavier panels.

FUTURE IMPROVEMENTS

We were very pleased with the ease of fabrication, performance and cost of this system. With proper care, this is a system that could be added to a theatre's stock equipment along with commercially available systems. To be truly versatile, however, the system would have to be capable of handling heavier loads. One step in that direction might be to weld a 2" x 2" x $\frac{3}{16}$" angle iron along the top of the track – along the upstage side, if the carriers are mounted with their wheels downstage. Obviously, holes would have to be pre-drilled in the angle to correspond to the holes in the tube for the track hangers. Alternative approaches are possible of course.

A Simple Drop Rig for Small Payloads

Andrew V. Wallace

A 2009 Yale School of Drama Production of *Phaedra* called for a mechanism that would drop dust and small particles of debris from a hole in a suspended ceiling. This mimicked the effect of a tremor or shock to a building, as if it were falling apart. The effect was added during load in, after the ceiling had already been installed and was to be a single-use-per-show effect, which needed to be filled only once before each performance. Chris Russo, a first-year Technical Design and Production student created this effect with a low-tech but effective drop rig using a pull-top soup can modified as shown in Figure 1.

The bottom of the thoroughly washed can was cut off with a can opener, leaving a rim around the inside. One half of the can's bottom was trimmed back as shown so that when the bottom was placed back in the can, it cleared one side of the can by $\frac{1}{8}$". Later, when assembly was complete, the untrimmed edge would rest on the inner lip of the can to keep the can bottom from pivoting past its closed position. When the effect was actuated, the trimmed bottom would pivot open, much like the choke on a carburetor, and drop the debris.

A $\frac{5}{16}$" hole was drilled through the can $\frac{1}{2}$" up from the bottom. This hole received a $\frac{1}{4}$" hex-head bolt secured with a Nylock® (not shown) to allow the bolt to turn without loosening. This bolt functioned as the axle of the choke. The bolt was fitted with a coil spring that held the choke normally closed. One end of the spring was hooked into a small hole drilled in the side of the can and the other pressed down on the untrimmed half of the choke. Two U-bolts attached the choke to the axle.

As an operating line, a long piece of tie line was knotted to the choke. From the can, the operating line ran through a U-bolt attached near the top of the can and then up to a batten above the ceiling

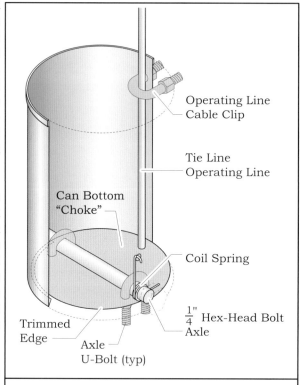

FIGURE 1: ISOMETRIC VIEW OF THE CAN (HALF OF BODY REMOVED)

that carried two sheaves. One sheave was positioned directly above the effect and the other carried the operating line offstage to an operator position. During preset, the operator lowered the can in to a comfortable working height, filled it, and pulled it out until it was snugged against the cheek plates of the sheave. The operating line was then tied off until the cue for the effect, when the operator overhauled the operating line, lifting one side of the choke and deploying the payload.

❧❧❧

TECHNICAL BRIEF

Rigging Techniques

Flying an Actor with a Ghost-Load Rig — Mark Prey

Hardware for a Ghost-Load Rig — Michael Madravazakis

An Inexpensive Controllable Drip System — Stuart Little

Fabric Swag Scene Changes Made Easy — Aaron Bollinger

Tilting a Wall — Greg Winkler

Pick-Length Calculator: A Quick Reference — Andrew James Gitchel

Rocking a Batten for *Pirates of Penzance* — Brian Frank

A Tricking Batten System for Stretched Panels — Aaron Verdery

Falling Leaves Effect for the Stage — Kellen C. McNally

A Temporary Lineset for Lightweight Objects — Amanda J. Haley

Automating a Snow Bag — Ryan Retartha

Soaker-Hose Rain Effect — Thomas R. Delgado

A Fan-Powered Confetti Drop — Alex Bergeron

A Device for Dropping Sand from Above — Mike Backhaus

Four Continuous-Beam Formulas for Stage Battens — Dan Perez

Flying performers in and then freeing them to move around onstage can impose a variable load on a lineset. Attempting to do so without a counterbalancing load would put performers and fly operators alike in danger, and the use of the traditional carpet hoist is only slightly less dangerous since it leaves a loaded arbor tied off several feet in the air. To avoid this condition in the Yale Repertory Theatre's 2000 production of *Heaven*, we used the alternate rig described here – the ghost-load rig.

CARPET-HOIST OPERATION

In the carpet-hoist rig shown in Figure 1, the flight arbor *F* – the arbor of the lineset carrying the actor – is loaded to pipe weight. All the actor-balancing counterweight rides in the adjacent carpet-hoist arbor *C*, which is tied off in the air (see Figure 1A). To clip an actor into the system, the flight arbor is raised until its connecting arms *A* pick up the bottom of the carpet-hoist arbor (see Figure 1B). Once they have untied the carpet-hoist arbor, fly operators use the flight-arbor's handline to control both arbors (see Figure 1C). So that the actor can be unclipped when the flight is over, fly operators must sometimes bull the arbors out. But whether such overhauling is needed or not, the heavily loaded carpet-hoist arbor must be securely tied off before the operators can take the rig back out of sightlines: the counter-weight is still in the air.

GHOST-LOAD RIG OPERATION

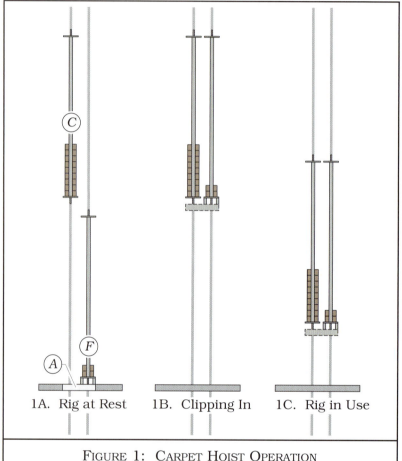

1A. Rig at Rest   1B. Clipping In   1C. Rig in Use

FIGURE 1: CARPET HOIST OPERATION

Though a ghost-load rig like that shown in Figure 2 also uses two adjacent arbors, it operates on an entirely different principle. (Note that, for clarity, the ghost-load arbor's handline and loft lines are not shown in the illustration. The flight arbor's loft lines are shown in red, and the wire rope joining the two arbors is shown in blue.) In place of connecting arms, the ghost-load lift line *L*, a wire rope reeved over a custom head-block *H* joins the flight arbor *F* and the ghost-load arbor *G*. The custom ghost-load headblock is mounted between the linesets and perpendicular to house headblocks. One end of the ghost-load lift line is attached to the flight arbor *F* at all times, but its other end is attached to a T-track guided trolley *T* weighing just enough to pull the ghost-load lift line down. The ghost-load arbor is clipped into the system only when the actor is not flying.

Both arbors are loaded to approximately the actor's weight. When the rig is not in use, as in Figure 2A, the counterweight in the ghost-load arbor balances that in the flight arbor. Raising the flight arbor so that the actor can clip in lowers the ghost-load arbor to the rail, where it is unclipped from the trolley (see Figure 2B). During flight, the weight of the actor balances the flight-arbor's counter-

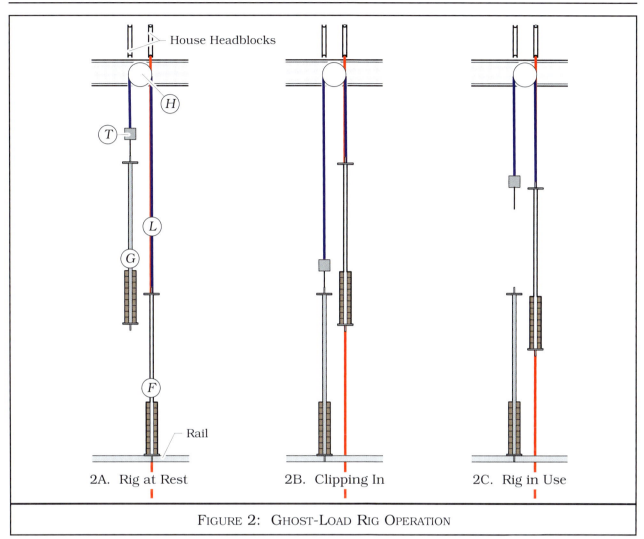

FIGURE 2: GHOST-LOAD RIG OPERATION

weight, and the ghost-load arbor sits safely on the rail (see Figure 2C). Once the flight is over, the ghost-load arbor is clipped back into the system and the actor is unclipped. Thus, when the flight arbor takes the rig back out of sightlines, its weight is again balanced by that of the ghost-load arbor. So long as the run crew clips the ghost-load arbor in before unclipping the actor – and clips the actor in before unclipping the ghost-load arbor – the rig is never out of weight, and no counter-weight is left hanging unbalanced in the air.

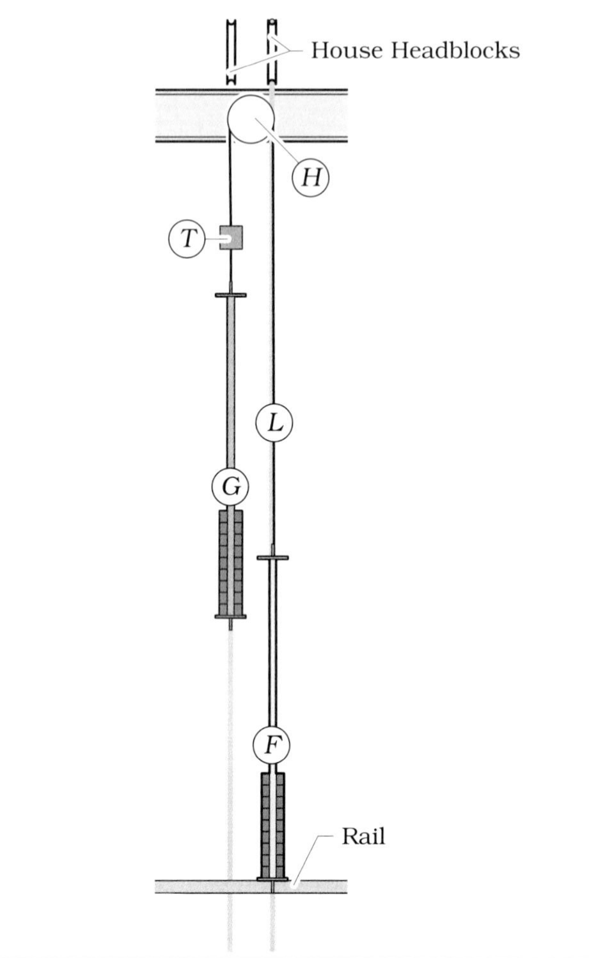

FIGURE 1: TYPICAL GHOST-LOAD RIG
COMPONENTS

For a two-minute-long scene of the Yale School of Drama's 2001 *Master and Margarita*, three actors had to be revealed "hanging on invisible crosses." Three actors could quickly bring the amount of weight on a lineset to 600 lbs, and not wanting to handle an equivalent amount of counterweight during the preceding scene change, we decided to use a rig based on that described in the preceding article, Mark Prey's *Flying an Actor with a Ghost-Load Rig.*

Prey's article, which describes the principles of ghost-load rigging, defines several key terms and includes the illustration reproduced here as Figure 1, in which

$F =$ the flight arbor, the arbor balancing the actor load.

$G =$ the ghost-load arbor, the arbor carrying the ghost load.

$L =$ the ghost-load lift line, the line joining arbors F and G.

$H =$ a ghost-load head block for line L. and

$T =$ a T-track guided trolley.

This article focuses on the construction of the ghost-load headblock and on an alternative to the trolley as used in the Yale School of Drama's University Theatre. The dimensions given here, as well as the choice of materials and construction and installation notes, can be modified for use in other theatres.

GHOST-LOAD HEADBLOCK CONSTRUCTION

We planned to mount our ghost-load headblock between the house headblock I-beams, clamping it securely to their bottom flanges and leaving only $\frac{1}{2}$" of clearance between their webs. Because house rigging would have to pass through it, we built it as three subassemblies: the frame and end cap, the blocks, and the clamp (see Figures 2 and 3). We made the frame from four pieces of 16-gauge 1" x 3" tube steel, butt-welding three 2'-2"-long pieces to a 10"-long piece at $3\frac{1}{2}$" intervals. Through the frame, we drilled a series of $\frac{7}{16}$"-diameter holes as shown in Figure 2 to receive the block, end cap, and clamp bolts. Two 4"-long tabs of $\frac{1}{8}$" x 3" flat bar welded to the ends of another 10" length of 16-gauge 1" x 3" tube steel made the end cap. We drilled $\frac{7}{16}$" bolt holes through the tabs for connection to the frame and welded a $\frac{1}{4}$" x 2" flat-bar fillet spacer along the tube steel to keep the cap from riding up the fillet weld of the house headblock's I-beam.

We made two blocks, the second one to carry a redundant ghost-load lift line for safety. Each block consisted of a 6" Ralmark sheave (MS24566-6B) sandwiched between sheave plates of $\frac{1}{4}$" x 8" flat bar welded to 10" lengths of $\frac{1}{8}$" x $\frac{1}{8}$" x 1" angle iron and 16-gauge 1" x 3" tube steel. Through the ends of the tube steel, we drilled four $\frac{7}{16}$"-diameter holes for mounting the blocks to the frame.

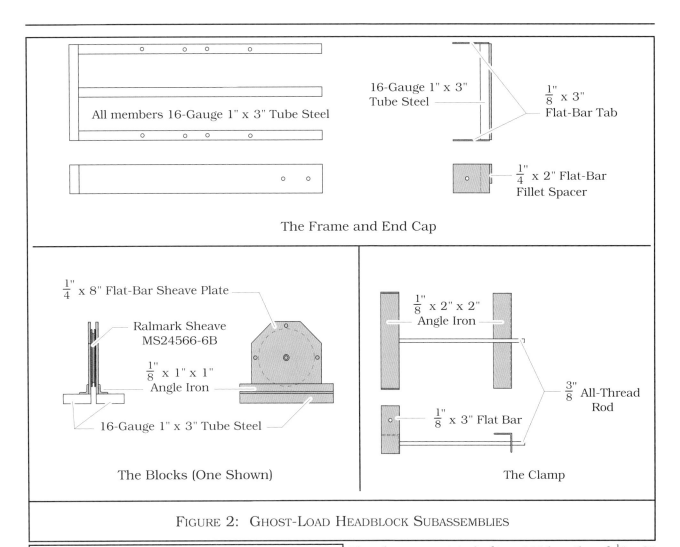

All members 16-Gauge 1" x 3" Tube Steel

16-Gauge 1" x 3" Tube Steel

$\frac{1}{8}$" x 3" Flat-Bar Tab

$\frac{1}{4}$" x 2" Flat-Bar Fillet Spacer

The Frame and End Cap

$\frac{1}{4}$" x 8" Flat-Bar Sheave Plate

Ralmark Sheave MS24566-6B

$\frac{1}{8}$" x 1" x 1" Angle Iron

16-Gauge 1" x 3" Tube Steel

The Blocks (One Shown)

$\frac{1}{8}$" x 2" x 2" Angle Iron

$\frac{1}{8}$" x 3" Flat Bar

$\frac{3}{8}$" All-Thread Rod

The Clamp

FIGURE 2: GHOST-LOAD HEADBLOCK SUBASSEMBLIES

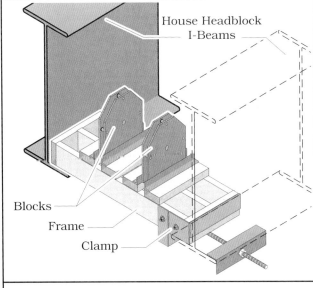

House Headblock I-Beams

Blocks

Frame

Clamp

FIGURE 3: GHOST-LOAD HEADBLOCK INSTALLED

The clamp consisted of two 10" lengths of $\frac{1}{8}$" x 2" x 2" angle iron, each drilled through one leg to receive a 14" length of $\frac{3}{8}$" all-thread rod. To the ends of one of the angles, we welded 5"-long pieces of $\frac{1}{8}$" x 2" flat bar, already drilled for bolt connection to the frame.

HEADBLOCK INSTALLATION AND RIGGING

To make our work easier, we began by freeing the ghost-load arbor from its house lift lines, chaining its batten to the grid and dressing its lift lines out of our way. After that point, the process became quite challenging and time-consuming because there was no convenient place to stand.

We carried the four subassemblies, the hardware, and the tools to the grid. Then, after feeding the frame through the house rigging and laying it in place on the house headblocks' bottom flanges, we bolted the end cap to the frame, the blocks to the top of the frame, and the clamp to the bottom of the frame. Finally, we tightened the clamp around the flange of the onstage head-block I-beam. Throughout the process, we worked in safety harnesses tied off to the I-beams with plenty of safeties.

After reeving ghost-load lift lines of $\frac{1}{4}$" aircraft cable through the ghost-load headblock and attaching them to the actor arbor with wire-rope clips, we raised the flight arbor out to low trim: the height at which the actors or the ghost-load arbor could be clipped into the system. We then pulled the free ends of the ghost-load lift lines down to the ghost-load arbor and formed nicopressed-eye terminations in each of them. This sequence saved us from having to calculate precisely the ghost-load lift lines' length in advance. Locking steel carabiners would serve as quick connects between the ghost-load lift lines and the arbor.

OUR ALTERNATIVE TO THE TROLLEY

At system low trim, the ghost-load lift lines were long enough to join the arbors. But at system high trim, with the actors' pickups raised beyond sightlines, the free ends of the ghost-load lift lines were several feet above the ghost-load arbor. Instead of installing a trolley, we cut and nicopressed eyes into another piece of aircraft cable just long enough to span that distance. Shackled between the ends of the ghost-load lift lines and the arbor, this last aircraft cable served two purposes. First, it eliminated the need for a trolley since its weight was great enough to pull the ghost-load lift lines down for attachment Second, it insured that no operator mistake would let the actors fly beyond system high trim, since beyond that point their weight would be supplemented by that of the ghost-load arbor.

CLIPPING IN

We deliberately left the flight arbor a little stage heavy. When the actors had clipped into the system, they lifted their legs slightly, letting the ghost-load lift lines go slack enough that an operator could unclip the ghost-load arbor. When the actors were flown back in after the scene, they kept their legs raised until we had clipped the ghost-load arbor back into the system and given them a signal to stand up slowly, letting the ghost-load arbor replace their weight.

SAFETY

To make sure that our system would be safe, we followed the single-failure-proof design principles and based our choice of materials and joining methods on careful structural analysis. We gave the frame a center member just to catch the lift lines if the sheaves were to break: the two outside members of the frame would easily have carried the load. We also used high-grade steel bolts as the sheaves' center bolts. Finally, we installed two aircraft-cable pickups for each actor and two ghost-load lift lines, each rated for 10 times the weight it could carry. Since human safety was at issue, we let redundancy be our guide.

ʑ🐧ʑ🐧ʑ🐧

In the fall of 2003, the University of South Dakota, Vermillion, produced Alan Aykbourn's *Taking Steps*. One of the technical requirements for this production was a controllable water drip system that could be turned on and off at specific moments in the show; once flow was set by the flow control valve (manually), one simply controlled the drip by switching it on or off. The drip was integral to the comedy of the production providing proof that the house involved in the plot had problems. The challenge was to create a small self-contained drip system (see Figure 1) that could be hung above the set.

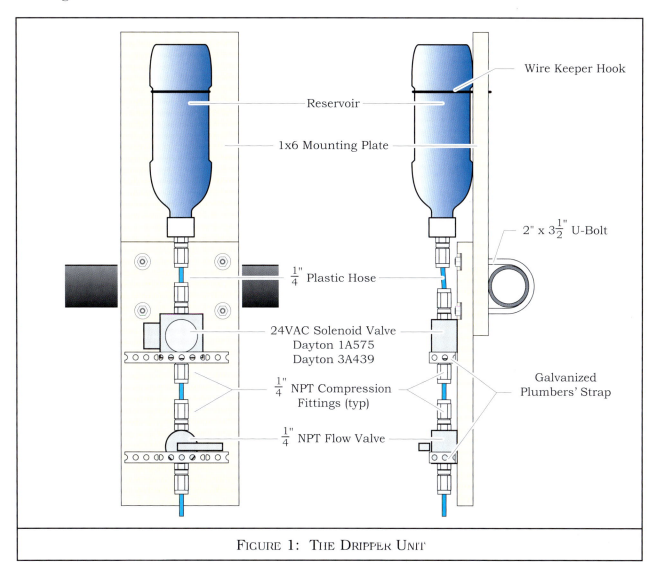

FIGURE 1: THE DRIPPER UNIT

I wanted electronic control of on and off and a flow control so that I could set the drip frequency. I purchased a solenoid valve from Grainger, Dayton part number 1A575, at a cost of $21.95 and a solenoid valve coil, Dayton part number 3A439, at a cost of $18.95. At the local Ace Hardware, I purchased a $\frac{1}{4}$" NPT brass flow valve and 5, $\frac{1}{4}$" NPT compression fittings. I had on hand the $\frac{1}{4}$" plastic hose which can be purchased at any hardware store for under $0.50 per foot. The major obstacle was finding a small reservoir bottle that would be able to supply enough water for approximately 60 minutes of drip time. This turned out to be easier than I predicted. I purchased a 20 oz. bottle of water from the soft drink machine across the hall, emptied the water, drilled a hole in the cap, cut off the bottom (which now became the top of the reservoir) and epoxied the cap onto the bottle. By epoxying the cap on, I formed a rigid, leak-proof end. I then inserted the male threaded end of the compression fitting into the cap and epoxied it on the bottle. From this point, it was simply a matter of cutting the hose to the needed length, attaching the fittings to the valves with Teflon tape to prevent leaking, and attaching the hose to the fittings. The whole system was then mounted to a 1x6 backer, holes were drilled in the 1x6 and U-bolts were inserted, and the system was mounted onto a batten and flown to height. The reservoir was filled with water, the solenoid valve was powered, flow was set, and the power was switched off. The power supply was a modular $15.00 24VAC converter unit from Radio Shack wired to a switch.

This Drip system worked flawlessly, once all the fittings were tightened down snugly and any leaks were overcome. It was an inexpensive solution (under $70.00) to an intriguing problem.

COSTS

Material	Cost
Water Reservoir (vending machine)	$1.00
Solenoid Valve - Dayton 1A575 (Grainger)	$21.95
Solenoid Coil - Dayton 3A439 (Grainger)	$18.95
$\frac{1}{4}$" NPT Flow Valve (local hardware)	$1.99
$\frac{1}{4}$" Plastic Hose (local hardware	$0.50
$\frac{1}{4}$" Compression Fittings (5) (local hardware)	$4.95
24VAC Power Supply (Radio Shack)	$15.00
Total	$64.24

A company of dancers darting quickly across the stage among swags of pastel sheers draped from the floor to the flies can look terrific. But issues arise when the dance ends and the fabric needs to disappear as quickly and gracefully as the dancers. To accomplish just such an effect, the Maine State Musical Theatre (MSMT) adapted a solution developed by ASI Production Services: a simple counterweight drop that pulls the swags safely and quickly into the fly loft.

SYSTEM OVERVIEW

In the MSMT system as in ASI's original, the move was driven by a sandbag tied to one end of a pick line as shown in Figure 1. The pick line, muled to a point above the swag's offstage storage location, reached down through a skeletal "swag well" of $1\frac{1}{2}$" schedule-40 black pipe and was tied into a grommet at the top of a swag. In MSMTs rig, the connections at the top end of the swag were hidden behind borders.

Before the move was triggered, the sandbag was held in place by a second line, a handline, that was tied off at the theater's midrail. The handline facilitated resets and, if the director had so desired, could have been used to slow the move.

MSMT used a third line - a length of galvanized aircraft cable (not shown in Figure 1) to limit the sandbag's travel and keep it from landing noisily. As shown in Figure 1, the midrail at MSMT is wide enough to accommodate a barrier that was built to keep stagehands and others away from the sandbag's path.

TWO SWAG WELL DESIGNS

MSMT made their swag well of 2'-0" squares of pipe rota-locked to pipe uprights and to the house mid-rail as shown in Figure 1. The mid-rail-level square established a smooth turn for the pick line and fabric and kept the fabric more or less contained when it was out. MSMT coated the pipe and all hardware with gaffer's tape to protect the fabric.

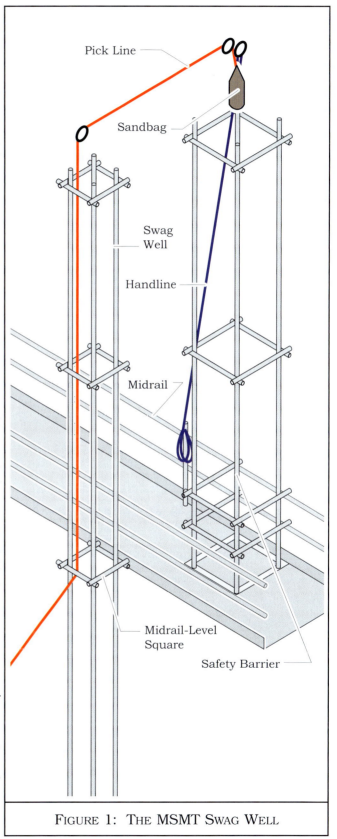

FIGURE 1: THE MSMT SWAG WELL

ASI Production Services had developed the original well design for an industrial. As shown in Figure 2, ASI's wells consisted of lengths of large-diameter PVC pipe mounted in horizontally rigged lighting trusses. There were no borders or other masking in this installation, but the PVC pipe completely hid the "offstage" swag and went unnoticed by most conventioneers, who assumed it was part of the building's HVAC system. The pipes and trusses also simplified shipping, load-in, and load-out.

FIGURE 2: ASI PRODUCTION SERVICES' SWAG WELL

A FINAL NOTE ABOUT ASI'S ORIGINAL RIG

Effects built for industrials are generally thought of as expensive, sophisticated, and hi-tech, but ASI drove their swag moves just as MSMT would some years later: by dropping a sandbag. They even allowed their sandbags to fall completely to the floor, though they clearly taped out the drop zones for safety. The thuds with which the sandbags landed were inaudible under the loud scene change music in the convention hall.

❧❧❧❧

A Yale School of Drama production of *The Skin of Our Teeth* in the fall of 2003 called for a section of the stage left wall to tilt over an actress as shown in Figure 1 and then return upright. Angled 12° off centerline and riding on a wagon raked at 2°, the tilting section was built as a single 8'-5"-tall and 10'-5"-wide Hollywood flat framed in 1x4 pine and covered in lauan. The use of loose-pin hinges allowed the 75-pound unit to be struck from the wagon for a later act. This article describes the cable rig that controlled the effect and the pneumatic systems that actuated it.

FIGURE 1: THE WALL IN ACTION

THE CABLE RIG

The onstage end of the rig consisted of a bridle and pickup, both made of $\frac{1}{8}$" black galvanized aircraft cable. The legs of the bridle, designed to keep the wall from wobbling as it tilted, terminated in thimbles at both ends. Small caribiners through the thimbles at the onstage end allowed stagehands to clip and unclip the bridle to the D-rings and keeper plates mounted on the back of the wall. At the offstage end, the bridle was joined to a pick line of $\frac{1}{8}$" black galvanized aircraft cable that was reeved through a small sheave mounted about 10' above the theater's locking rail. Above the rail, the pick line terminated in a thimble. Joined to this last thimble, a short length of $\frac{3}{8}$" black braided polyester line served as the operating line, which was tied off at the rail and operated by a stagehand.

THE LOCKING AND TILTING PNEUMATIC SYSTEMS

Figure 2 shows the system that held the tilting wall upright: a single-acting pneumatic cylinder mounted on the adjoining flat. The cylinder's rod protruded through holes drilled in both flats' frames and behaved like a pneumatically actuated barrel bolt. Figure 3 shows the system of three more single-acting cylinders that initiated the tilting action. These cylinder's rods pushed against the wagon through small holes drilled in the wall's frame. When triggered, the cylinders gave a slight push downward against the wagon deck to start the tilt motion, which was then taken over by the operator at the rail.

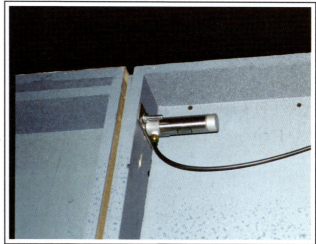

FIGURE 2: LOCKING CYLINDER

FIGURE 3: TILTING-CYLINDER SYSTEM

NOTES

Though the wagon played in the middle of a fairly open stage, a full-stage black upstage of the wagon made the bridle and pick line virtually invisible until the wall tilted. During the tilt, they were easily seen against the grey and white of the set and added to the theatricality of the moment.

❧❧❧❧

When planning the rigging of scenic elements, having all the pertinent information immediately available makes building precise lengths of rigging picks relatively easy. Many shops have taken an important first step by standardizing their rigging hardware. The next step is to collect and organize detailed dimension information about the hardware and to use that information methodically.

THE METHOD

One method of using such information is illustrated here. Starting from the upper end of a pick, each piece of hardware used in a pick is itemized and its effective length is listed, the effective length being the dimension that comes into play in the pick. For a trim chain, the effective length is one-half its total length, minus the amount used up in wraps; for a shackle, it is the distance included between the inside of the bell and the nearest edge of the pin; for an eye-to-eye turnbuckle, it is the inside eye-to-eye distance of the half-opened turnbuckle. Subtracting the sum of all these effective lengths from the distance between the top and the bottom of the rig reveals the length of the finished cable that will be needed.

Figure 1, a pick used to hang a Hollywood flat from a batten illustrates the approach. In this example, the distance from the top of the batten to the bottom of the flat is 42'-0". Working downward from the batten, the itemized list shows the total effective length of the components to be 2'-10$\frac{5}{8}$".

COMPONENT

Component	Effective Length (in.)
3' Trim Chain (1.5 wraps around 1$\frac{1}{2}$" schedule-40 black pipe	12.500
$\frac{1}{4}$" shackle	1.125
$\frac{1}{4}$" shackle	1.125
$\frac{3}{8}$" – 6" eye-to-eye turnbuckle	14.500
$\frac{1}{4}$" shackle	1.125
D-ring & plate	3.500
Bottom Rail (1x3)	0.750
Total Effective Length	35.675

Since the pick measures 42'-0" overall, the aircraft cable used should be terminated at a finished length of 39'-1$\frac{3}{8}$".

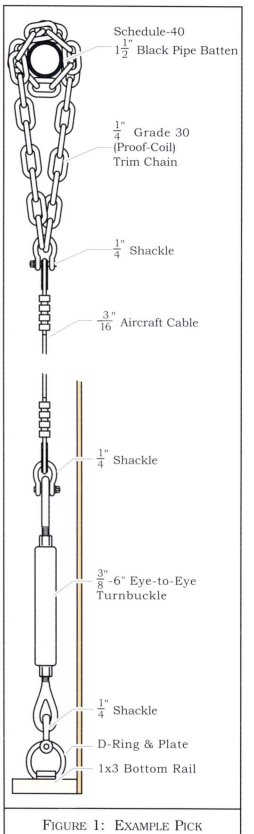

Schedule-40 1$\frac{1}{2}$" Black Pipe Batten

$\frac{1}{4}$" Grade 30 (Proof-Coil) Trim Chain

$\frac{1}{4}$" Shackle

$\frac{3}{16}$" Aircraft Cable

$\frac{1}{4}$" Shackle

$\frac{3}{8}$"-6" Eye-to-Eye Turnbuckle

$\frac{1}{4}$" Shackle

D-Ring & Plate

1x3 Bottom Rail

FIGURE 1: EXAMPLE PICK

HOW MUCH DETAIL IS TOO MUCH?

Even in this simple pick, the adjustable 6"-reach of the turnbuckle would not account for the combined $6\frac{7}{8}$" effective length of the shackles and D-Ring assembly, and using the methodical, detailed approach would save the effort, time, and frustration of having to make up a shorter cable during load-in. To encourage use of this approach, the tables below present a starter set of effective lengths

Type of Connection	Type of Wrap	$1\frac{1}{2}$" Schedule-40 Black Pipe	2" Schedule-40 Black Pipe	3"x4.1 C-Channel (Grid Steel)
$\frac{1}{4}$" Grade-30 Chain (Trim Chain)	1.5 wraps	(length − 11") ÷ 2	(length − $13\frac{3}{4}$") ÷ 2	(length − 15") ÷ 2
Polyester Sling	Choker	length − $6\frac{1}{2}$"	length − $9\frac{3}{4}$"	length − 9"
	Basket	length − $4\frac{3}{4}$"	length − $6\frac{1}{8}$"	length − 6"
$\frac{3}{8}$" Aircraft-Cable Sling	1.5 wraps	(length − 11") ÷ 2	(length − $11\frac{3}{4}$")÷2	(length − 15") ÷ 2

Screw Pin Shackle	Lengths - Pin to Bell
$\frac{1}{4}$" − $\frac{1}{2}$-ton WLL	$1\frac{1}{8}$"
$\frac{5}{16}$" − $\frac{3}{4}$-ton WLL	$1\frac{1}{4}$"
$\frac{3}{8}$" − 1-ton WLL	$1\frac{9}{16}$"
$\frac{1}{2}$" − 2-ton WLL	$1\frac{7}{8}$"
$\frac{5}{8}$" − $3\frac{1}{4}$ ton WLL	$2\frac{3}{8}$"
$\frac{3}{4}$" − $4\frac{3}{4}$-ton WLL	$2\frac{13}{16}$"

Drop-Forged, Hot-Galvanized Turnbuckles		Lengths	
		Closed	Open
Eye to Eye	$\frac{5}{16}$" x $4\frac{1}{2}$" − 800 lbs WLL	9"	$13\frac{1}{2}$"
	$\frac{3}{8}$" x 6" − 1200 lbs WLL	$11\frac{1}{2}$"	$17\frac{1}{2}$"
	$\frac{1}{2}$" x 9" − 2200 lbs WLL	16"	25"
Eye to Jaw	$\frac{5}{16}$" x $4\frac{1}{2}$" − 800 lbs WLL	$9\frac{1}{8}$"	$13\frac{5}{8}$"
	$\frac{3}{8}$" x 6" − 1200 lbs WLL	$11\frac{1}{2}$"	$17\frac{1}{2}$"
	$\frac{1}{2}$" x 9" − 2200 lbs WLL	$16\frac{1}{4}$"	$25\frac{1}{4}$"
Jaw to Jaw	$\frac{5}{16}$" x $4\frac{1}{2}$" − 800 lbs WLL	$9\frac{1}{4}$"	$13\frac{3}{4}$"
	$\frac{3}{8}$" x 6" - 1200 lbs WLL	$11\frac{1}{2}$"	$17\frac{1}{2}$"
	$\frac{1}{2}$" x 9" - 2200 lbs WLL	$16\frac{1}{2}$"	$25\frac{1}{2}$"

❧❧❧

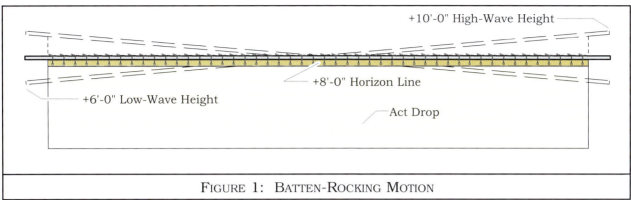

FIGURE 1: BATTEN-ROCKING MOTION

During the pre-show of the College-Conservatory of Music's 2005 *Pirates of Penzance*, the ends of a 50'-long shop-built batten were rigged to rock up and down as much a 4'-0" as shown in Figure 1. Dressed to look like the yardarm of a square-rigger, the batten carried the stage-wide act drop, most of which remained piled on the stage floor while the batten rocked. Just visible above the batten, a small ship on a stick was carried across the stage to enhance the audience's sense of looking at the horizon from the rail of a ship under full sail. Throughout the sequence the stage crew rocked the batten progressively more dramatically until, at last, they leveled it off and flew it to high trim to reveal the act drop.

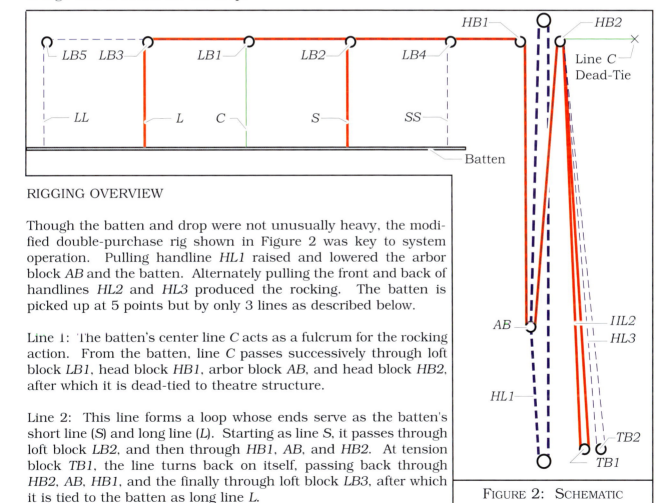

RIGGING OVERVIEW

Though the batten and drop were not unusually heavy, the modified double-purchase rig shown in Figure 2 was key to system operation. Pulling handline *HL1* raised and lowered the arbor block *AB* and the batten. Alternately pulling the front and back of handlines *HL2* and *HL3* produced the rocking. The batten is picked up at 5 points but by only 3 lines as described below.

Line 1: The batten's center line *C* acts as a fulcrum for the rocking action. From the batten, line *C* passes successively through loft block *LB1*, head block *HB1*, arbor block *AB*, and head block *HB2*, after which it is dead-tied to theatre structure.

Line 2: This line forms a loop whose ends serve as the batten's short line (*S*) and long line (*L*). Starting as line *S*, it passes through loft block *LB2*, and then through *HB1*, *AB*, and *HB2*. At tension block *TB1*, the line turns back on itself, passing back through *HB2*, *AB*, *HB1*, and the finally through loft block *LB3*, after which it is tied to the batten as long line *L*.

FIGURE 2: SCHEMATIC

Line 3: This line becomes the batten's short-short and long-long lines, and its rigging echoes that of Line 2. Starting as line *SS*, it passes through loft block *LB4*, and then in turn through *HB1*, *AB*, *HB2*, and *TB2*, where it reverses direction: back through *HB2*, *AB*, *HB1*, and then through loft block *LB5*, after which it is tied to the batten as line *LL*.

RIGGING AND OPERATION NOTES

The UCCCM theatre has a wire-rope counterweight system, and since this batten was hemp-rigged in keeping with the look of the show, assembling and operating this rig was far from simple. The head blocks were made up of single hemp blocks mounted as close together as possible to minimize fleet angles. The arbor block was a 5-sheave hemp block, and the arbor itself consisted of sandbags whose lateral movement was constrained by aircraft-cable guides specifically installed for the production.

As for the rig's operation, an unusually high amount of friction was generated by the use of so much hemp and by the unavoidable fleet angles. Consequently, operating the rig took 4 crew members, and coordinating their actions took a fair amount of rehearsal. There are, of course, other approaches to this problem – the use of a separate lift batten and automated reversible capstans springs to mind. Few, however, could match this approach for simplicity.

કોઈ

The scrim act drop that flew in and out 18 times each performance was a key element in a 2005 Off-Broadway production. The director and designer insisted that the scrim be tautly stretched as though on a rigid frame, but the grid was too low to permit the scrim to be framed. Instead, the scrim would have to be stretched between a pair of guide cables and an upper and lower batten, the latter of which would have to be tricked to fly the last foot or so out of sightlines. Many technicians are familiar with rigs of this type, but this article highlights the particularly successful design of the battens, which were made by temporarily modifying stock ADC track.

SYSTEM OVERVIEW

This system used $\frac{3}{16}$" wire rope as its lift lines and guide cables. The guide cables, dead-hung from the grid, connected to the stage floor, and tensioned by turnbuckles, ran through $\frac{1}{4}$" holes drilled through the ends of the upper and lower battens. The edges of the scrim slid along the guide cables on cable guide clips (not shown in the illustrations) purchased from Rosebrand. The upper and lower battens comprised modified sections of ADC 280 track 19'-0" long. Construction details of the upper batten are shown in Figure 1; the lower batten, in Figure 2.

The battens were hung from two adjacent linesets, whose sheaves had been kicked as close together as possible to minimize fleet angle. In both the upper and lower battens, the track was stiffened with an internal box beam of 1x lumber and hung with its carrier slot upstage. Though the box beam made the battens heavier, they provided two advantages. First, the exposed strip of wood inside the carrier slots served as a nailing strip for the top and bottom edges of the scrim. Second, they helped deaden the noise the track made as it slid up and down the guide cables.

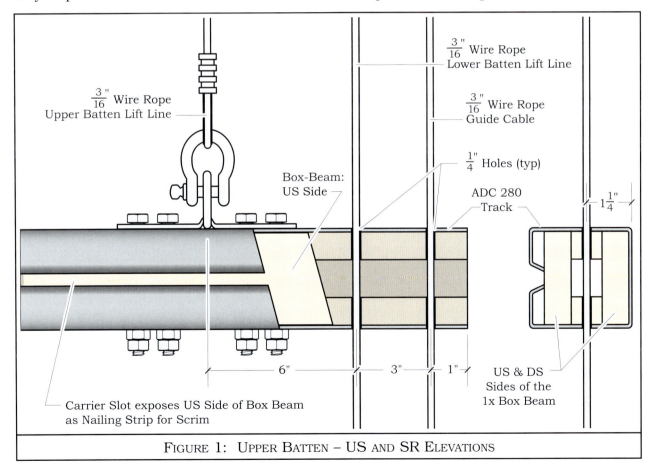

FIGURE 1: UPPER BATTEN – US AND SR ELEVATIONS

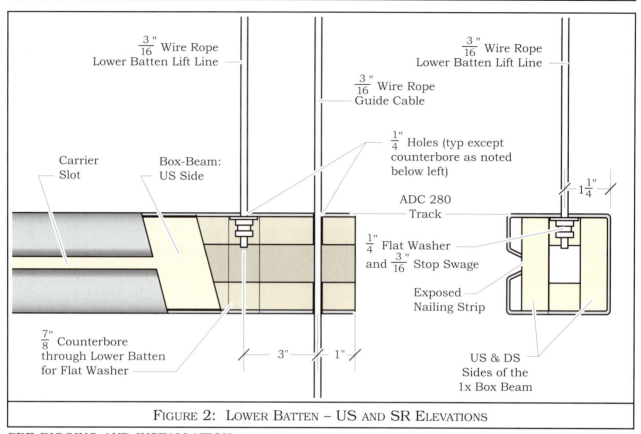

FIGURE 2: LOWER BATTEN – US AND SR ELEVATIONS

PRE-RIGGING AND INSTALLATION

Figures 1 and 2 detail the spacing between the lift lines and cable guides at the SR end of the system. This arrangement was reversed and repeated at the SL end, but the rig also included a centerline lift line that is not shown in either figure.

In pre-rigging, the box beams were made up and inserted into the ends of the track. The D-rings were through-bolted to the upper batten and the holes for the lift lines and guide cables were drilled through both battens. The lower batten was then flipped over and its lift line holes counter-bored as shown in Figure 2 to $\frac{7}{8}$" to facilitate the use of flat washers.

In installation, both battens were first laid out onstage, carrier slots up, with the lower batten placed upstage of the upper batten. The next step was to reeve the not-yet-terminated guide cables and lower batten lift lines through the holes in the upper batten and attach the upper batten to its lift lines. Once that had been done, the upper batten was dead-hauled to low trim, counterweighted, leveled, and tied off.

With the upper batten flown out, the lower batten was moved to saw horses placed beneath the upper batten. After the guide cables and lower batten's lift lines had been reeved through the batten, the guide cables were lagged to the stage floor and tensioned at the grid-hung turnbuckles. After the lower batten's lift lines had been cut to length, they were fitted with $\frac{1}{4}$" flat washers and stop-swaged. Once the batten had been counterweighted and tied off at its low trim, the rig was finished and ready for scrim installation.

ɛ⩗ɛ⩗ɛ⩗

For the University of Rochester's production of *The Hour We Knew Nothing of Each Other* the director wanted leaves to fall from the sky and cover an 8' x 8' area downstage. To perform this effect we modified a 5-gallon bucket with simple parts that anyone can purchase through a local hardware store.

First, remove the wire handle from the bucket and make a yoke so that the bucket can be hung on a pipe grid. Our yoke was made of 1" x $\frac{1}{8}$" flat bar as shown in Figure 1. We drilled two $\frac{7}{16}$" holes in the ends to receive $\frac{3}{8}$" flat-head bolts and a $\frac{9}{16}$" hole at the center so that the yoke can receive a standard lighting C-clamp (see Figure 1). Then we modified the bucket by drilling out the handle holes to receive the rated $\frac{3}{8}$" flat-head bolts.

Next, we installed the mechanism that pushed the leaves out of the bucket and into the air with a small variable-speed motor. The shaft of the motor ran through a hole in the bottom of the bucket and was attached to a threaded rod which spun inside the bucket. As the motor turned, the threaded rod pushed a plywood disk up by a nut that had been inserted in the center of the plywood disk. The disk had a notch cut into it for a keyway and a key was attached to the inside of the bucket. This allowed the disk to travel up and down the rod rather than just spinning. It was important that the bucket be as nearly truly cylindrical as possible. A tapered bucket would have required a tapered key and would have allowed leaves to fall below the disk and get caught.

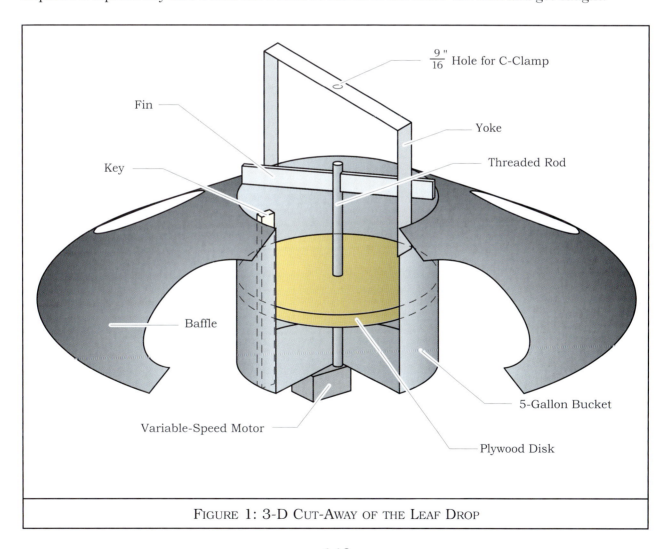

FIGURE 1: 3-D CUT-AWAY OF THE LEAF DROP

Once the motor assembly had been installed it was possible to push items out of the bucket and into the air, but there were two refinements to make. After mounting the motor to the bottom of the bucket we discovered that the bucket was acting as a large drum and creating a loud humming noise. We solved this problem by installing rubber grommets between the motor and the bucket. The second refinement involved dispersal. The leaves were coming out of the bucket in clumps and were not spreading to cover a large enough area.

To prevent clumping, we added a "fin" to the top of the threaded rod, which spun with the rod and pushed the leaves onto a baffle. The fin broke up most of the clumps. To achieve the desired dispersal, we attached a baffle to the outside of the bucket (see Figure 1). We made the baffle out of tin flashing and riveted it to the rim of the bucket. At random intervals along the surface of the baffle, we cut generously large holes to let the leaves either fall through the holes or slide farther down the baffle and drop over its outside edge. This gave us a much larger dispersal area: it doubled the size of our leaf drop from an 18" circle to a 36" circle.

FIGURE 2: ACTOR PLAYING IN LEAVES
PHOTO BY PAUL MILLER

❧❧❧❧

A rig we used during a production of *Finks* at Vassar College might be unfamiliar to some readers but it can be useful to all. Essentially, as shown in Figure 1 below, the object is dead hung, and its lift line is reeved through two sheaves, the spotting sheave mounted directly above the object and the handline sheave, which travels sideways, flying the object in and out.

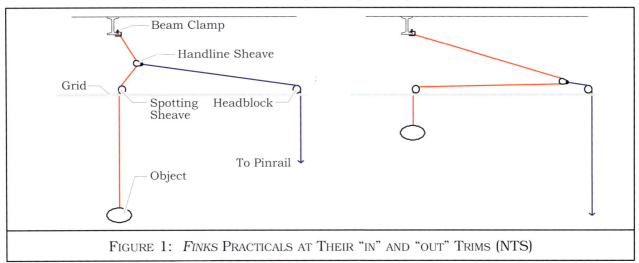

FIGURE 1: *FINKS* PRACTICALS AT THEIR "IN" AND "OUT" TRIMS (NTS)

FIGURE 2: CAMPBELL T7550401

RIG ASSEMBLY

1. In pre-rigging cut the aircraft cable roughly to length, leaving about a foot of "good luck".

2. Attach a rated single-sheave pulley to one end of a length of black polypro cut long enough to serve as a handline.

3. During the hang, mount the spotting sheave and handline headblock to the grid.

4. Run the cable through the spotting and handline sheaves and dead-tie it to suitable support in the ceiling.

5. Run the handline over the headblock and tie off at the pinrail.

THE RIG'S USE IN FINKS

Under the careful supervision of Andrew Wallace, Technical Director for New York Stage and Film, we used a version of this rig to fly a number of electrified practicals. Having determined that object weights, power requirements, and the amount of degradation that would result from a known number of technical rehearsals and performances, we knew that we could safely run both the lift lines and power lines together through the sheaves. We ganged both types of lines together with strips of electrical tape spaced about a foot apart. For our handline sheaves we used Campbell T7550401 $1\frac{1}{2}$" single-sheave pulleys like that shown in Figure 2.

❧❧❧❧❧

The director of a 2007 production of *The Mousetrap* at the University of Notre Dame wanted snow to fall across the entire stage throughout the play. The production team knew they could accomplish the effect with their stock full-stage snow cradle, but they wanted to automate the cradle's movement so that a flyman would not have to make it snow for nearly 2.5 hours every night for several weeks. To accomplish this goal, the team decided to move the lineset with pneumatic cylinders.

THE RIG

For the effect, the snow cradle was hung conventionally on two linesets. Three 8" double-acting pneumatic cylinders were ganged together as illustrated in Figure 1 to operate one of the linesets. The tops and bottoms of the cylinders were bolted onto triangular steel plates. The bottom plate was attached to the house system's midrail with aircraft cable and Crosby clips, an arrangement that kept the cylinders in line and even with each other but let them move somewhat freely.

At the top end of the cylinder assembly, a length of hemp rope was tied through a hole in the top plate and Crosby clipped to the handline of the actuating lineset, the one that would move to operate the cradle. As Figure 1 shows, we made that connection on a bight in the hemp to avoid having to shorten it and we hung the extra over an adjacent lock on the rail. To guard against overtravel, we ran a length of aircraft cable from one of the headblock I-Beams to the top of the actuating lineset's arbor.

Once the rig was installed, flown out, and secured, the actuating lineset was loaded to be slightly arbor-heavy. The cylinders were plumbed to retract when actuated. As they pulled the arbor up its batten flew in 8". When the air

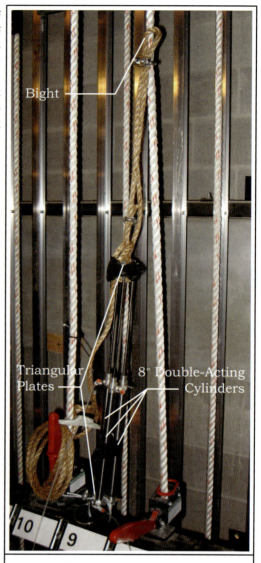

FIGURE 1: THE RIG

was switched off the weight of the arbor pulled the batten back up 8" as it brought the cylinder rods back to their extended position. The surgical-tube air lines that fed the cylinders were daisy chained together so that air flowed into and out of all three cylinders simultaneously, causing them to share the work equally. The air source was the theater's built in pneumatic system, operating at about 80 psi.

ROOM FOR IMPROVEMENTS

While the effect worked well enough, it could have been improved. Using a prusik knot to secure the hemp rope to the handline would cause less damage to the handline. Better yet, hanging the cylinders from the headblock I-Beam and attaching them to the top of the arbor with aircraft cable would have avoided damaging the handline.

Here is a simple and effective rain effect that can be built with inexpensive materials found at any hardware store. Using the materials listed here, a technician can build a 20'-long rain pipe in just a few hours — which is useful to remember since artistic teams often find it difficult to describe the amount of rain they'd like to see, and "more" is a familiar request.

Quan.	Item	Unit Cost	Line Cost
6 ea.	$\frac{1}{4}$" x $1\frac{1}{2}$" Threaded Forged Eye Bolts	$3.74	$22.44
20'	1"-Square Tube Steel	$0.47	$9.40
1 roll	$\frac{1}{2}$" Teflon® Tape	$0.97	$0.97
1 ea.	$\frac{5}{8}$" Garden Hose	$21.98	$21.98
	$\frac{1}{4}$" Nylon Nuts and Washers	$0.50	$0.50
1 pkg.	Zip Ties	$2.98	$2.98
1 ea.	2" PVC Pipe 10' length	$5.79	$5.79
2 ea.	$\frac{5}{8}$" Soaker Hose 10' length	$6.99	$13.98
	TOTAL COST		$78.04

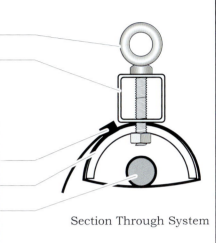

Section Through System

FIGURE 1: MATERIALS AND SECTION

PROCEDURE

1. Drill six $\frac{5}{16}$" holes in the 1"-square tube steel at the following intervals from one end: 0'-6"; 5'-0"; 9'-6"; 10'-6"; 15'-0"; 19'-6".

2. Using a table saw, rip the 2" PVC into half sections. (Note that ripping the PVC pipe did not trigger our table saw's Saw Stop®.)

3. Lay the PVC half sections end-to-end and cut side down on a workbench. Lay the tube steel on top of them and align the ends of the tube steel with those of the PVC half sections. Using the holes in the tube steel as a guide, drill six $\frac{5}{16}$" holes through the PVC. Loosely join the PVC half sections to the tube steel with the $\frac{1}{4}$" x $1\frac{1}{2}$" eyebolts.

5. Lay the assembly on its side. Slide zip ties between the PVC half sections and the tube steel at intervals of about 1'-0". Put the soaker hose in place and fasten the zip ties. Finally, tighten the eyebolts.

6. Apply Teflon® tape to the end threads of the soaker hose and fasten the end cap. Repeat the process to the connection of the soaker hose to the garden hose to eliminate potential leaks.

7. Do a trial set-up of the system, outdoors if possible. Demonstrate it for the director, set designer, lighting designer, and stage manager. Once they have approved the look, dismantle the set-up and install the system in the theatre.

❧❧❧❧❧

The final song in the 2009 production of *The Marvelous Wonderettes* at Northlight Theatre in Skokie, Illinois, required a drifting confetti effect. A traditional fabric sling confetti drop would have been too noticeable in the space, so the production manager, Christopher Fitzgerald, came up with a simple, reliable solution.

THE DROP

The confetti drop, shown in Figure 1, is a $\frac{3}{4}$" plywood box made to hold many performances worth of confetti while supporting a 20" box fan face down on top of it. The box fan, connected to a non-dim and controlled through the light board, pushes the confetti out through the opening on the front of the box, sending confetti a short distance forward in a gentle snowfall that measures anywhere from 4' to 8' left to right and about 3' upstage to downstage depending on trim height, the air currents of the particular space, and the type of confetti. Using two of these units, the confetti drop, in this case loaded with paper confetti, covered about two-thirds of the stage for *The Marvelous Wonderettes*.

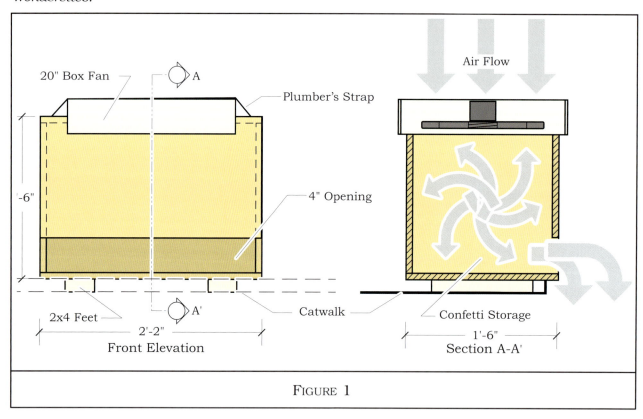

FIGURE 1

Northlight's confetti boxes were built to sit on 2x4 feet and rested on top of a catwalk above the grid pipes, but modifications can be made to rig to any landing, gallery, or catwalk. Alternatively, two standard side arms can be bolted to either side to allow easy attachment to a batten or dead hung pipe.

ADVANTAGES

Loading the unit is accomplished by removing the box fan and placing more confetti in it. The fan's three speed settings can be used to increase or decrease air flow, adjusting how much confetti comes out. Since the confetti is forced out the front rather than straight down, the risk of confetti falling at inopportune times is kept to a minimum. Finally, controlling the unit through the light board saves using an extra crew member.

DISADVANTAGES

There are three disadvantages to be aware of. The first is the potential for noise. While a running fan 20' in the air during a musical is hardly noticeable, noise during a quiet show may be a concern. Also, because of its size, this device may not be suitable for a tightly packed fly system. Finally, some packing of the confetti may occur due to the downward direction of the air current. A light "fluffing" of the confetti beforehand prevented any problems in our case.

❧❧❧❧

For the Yale Repertory Theatre's 2010 production of *Battle of Black and Dogs* by Bernard Marie Coltez, the artistic team wanted red sand to fall from 3 separate 12"-diameter by 4' high metal tubes to be dead-hung from the grid in full view of the audience. Sonotube® was used as an inner cylinder in which to mount the apparatus, and 24-gauge sheet metal, rolled and painted black, provided a good exterior finish. Granulated cork, available from Maryland Cork in a wide variety of coarseness, was chosen as the "sand" to be dropped because it could be dyed to the desired color and produced virtually no dust while falling.

THE DEVICE

Inspired by Kellen McNally's "Falling Leaves Effect for the Stage" (see pages 143–144), the device uses a plywood disc, as shown in Figure 1, to drive sand up and over the top of the cylinder. The disc is actuated by a variable-speed AC motor coupled to a $\frac{3}{4}$"-13 threaded rod that runs up the length of the Sonotube®. This device incorporates two discs routed from $\frac{3}{4}$" plywood to match the I.D. of the Sonotube®. The *mounting disc* has the motor bolted to its underside to protect it from the cork. The *push disc* pushes sand over the top of the tube as the motor turns the threaded rod. The push disc is topped with a 2" piece of $\frac{1}{8}$" flat bar with a $\frac{3}{4}$"-13 nut welded to it as detailed in Figure 2. The nut allows the push disc to thread up and down the rod. A $\frac{3}{4}$" x $\frac{3}{4}$" pine key, attached up the length of the inside of the Sonotube® as shown, meshes with a keyway in the push disc, so that when the rod rotates, the push disc moves up or down.

In our case, to prevent the push disc from threading too far up or down, the key was cut 4" short from the top and bottom limits, and the run crew used a stopwatch when running the motor up. Once it neared the limit of its travel (about 3 minutes at 70% speed), they ran the motor down for the same amount of time and refilled the tube between shows, eliminating the added complexity of limit switches.

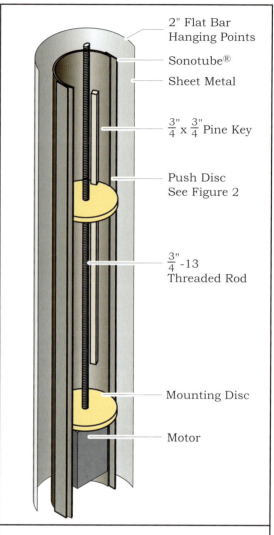

FIGURE 1: MOTOR DEVICE

Labels:
- 2" Flat Bar Hanging Points
- Sonotube®
- Sheet Metal
- $\frac{3}{4}$" x $\frac{3}{4}$" Pine Key
- Push Disc See Figure 2
- $\frac{3}{4}$"-13 Threaded Rod
- Mounting Disc
- Motor

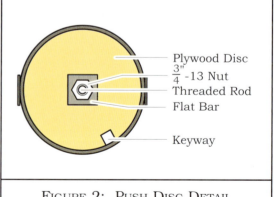

FIGURE 2: PUSH DISC DETAIL

Labels:
- Plywood Disc
- $\frac{3}{4}$"-13 Nut
- Threaded Rod
- Flat Bar
- Keyway

The reactions for linesets with evenly distributed loads and evenly spaced pick points have been solved in Jay Glerum's *Stage Rigging Handbook* and other publications. The published case formulas do not, however, apply to the reactions in asymmetrically loaded and/or supported linesets, and solving them by hand involves tedious calculations. This article provides a set of case-formula solutions for four asymmetric and/or unevenly supported battens.

Case 1: Border, Full Stage Drop

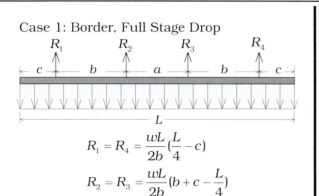

$$R_1 = R_4 = \frac{wL}{2b}\left(\frac{L}{4} - c\right)$$

$$R_2 = R_3 = \frac{wL}{2b}\left(b + c - \frac{L}{4}\right)$$

Case 2: Legs, Side Lights

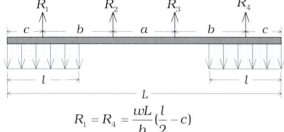

$$R_1 = R_4 = \frac{wL}{b}\left(\frac{l}{2} - c\right)$$

$$R_2 = R_3 = \frac{wL}{b}\left(b + c - \frac{L}{2}\right)$$

Case 3: Center Tab

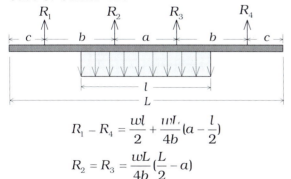

$$R_1 = R_4 = \frac{wl}{2} + \frac{wl}{4b}\left(a - \frac{l}{2}\right)$$

$$R_2 = R_3 = \frac{wL}{4b}\left(\frac{L}{2} - a\right)$$

Case 4: Border with 3 Reactions

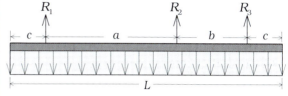

$$R_1 = \frac{wL}{(a+b)}\left(\frac{L}{2} - \frac{L^3 - 2La^2 + a^3}{8ab} - c\right)$$

$$R_2 = \frac{wL}{8}\left(\frac{L^3 - 2La^2 + a^3}{ab(a+b)}\right)$$

$$R_3 = \frac{wL}{(a+b)}\left(\frac{L}{2} - \frac{L^3 - 2La^2 + a^3}{8b^2} - c\right)$$

In all 4 cases...

R_1, R_2, R_3, R_4 are reactions, lbs
w is a distributed load, plf
l is the length of a distributed load, ft
L is the length of the batten, ft
a, b, and c are distances along the batten, ft

FIGURE 1: FOUR CONTINUOUS-BEAM CASE FORMULAS FOR STAGE BATTENS

TECHNICAL BRIEF

Safety

An LED and SPST Safety Feedback — *Jim Siebels*

Introducing a Live Animal to the Stage — *Kristan Falkowski*

Comparison of Safety-Wrap Techniques for Counterweight Linesets — *John Starmer*

Stoneham Theatre's 2002 production of *A Christmas Carol* incorporated a trap approximately 3' square in the stage floor, through which an actor needed to disappear quickly. The actor, who was inside a 10'-tall "Ghost of Christmas Yet to Come" puppet, would place himself upstage of the center of the trap, which would open in front of him under the control of a stagehand in the traproom. The actor would then transfer control of the puppet to the stagehand and climb down a ladder through the trap. With the actor out of the way, the stagehand then dropped the puppet, letting it free-fall into the trap – a spectacular effect enhanced by about 6" of trap-obscuring dry ice fog.

The actor's safety was our major concern. His placement precisely at the upstage center of the trap was essential to ensure that the trap's opening would be masked by the ghost's voluminous black costume, yet if the actor stepped a few inches too far downstage and onto the trap door, he risked falling in as it opened. The ghost's costume and the near-darkness on stage obscured the actor's vision. A heavy layer of dry ice fog hampered his ability to find glow-tape spikes, and made it impossible for the stage manager to verify that the actor was in place before calling the trap open.

Our solution involved a single, two-color LED holder recessed into the floor at the exact spike location. The LED was invisible to the audience, but clearly visible to the actor looking straight down at it. Adjacent to the LED holder we recessed a submini SPST momentary-on pushbutton switch into the deck. At a long "standby," the stagehand in the trap room flipped a toggle switch, illuminating the floor-recessed LED and a second LED below the stage, both red. The actor placed himself on spike and tapped the pushbutton switch with his foot, turning both LEDs to green. This verified for both the actor and the stagehand that he was on spike, and that the trap could be opened safely.

A small aluminum enclosure, a clip for a pair of "C" cells (could just as easily have been a transformer), a power switch, a pushbutton switch, a pair of dual-color LEDs, and some heat-shrink tubing totaled about $24.50 from Radio Shack; assembly took about an hour.

Ours was a busy show, with a great deal of stage traffic – both feet and casters – over the switch. The rig worked trouble-free for about 20 performances, after which the contacts in the switch became unreliable and needed to be replaced. A heavy-duty switch would likely have extended the period of reliability. In all, however, this solution worked beautifully and made all concerned more comfortable with the actor's safety, which made for a better and smoother performance.

ია ია ია

In the spring of 2003, the Yale Repertory Theatre premiered David Rabe's *The Black Monk.* Our designer's first request was to have a miniature horse in the opening scene. After locating a willing miniature horse (and even more importantly, a willing miniature-horse owner) and discovering that associated costs would fit into our budget, we proceeded to cast Melody, the miniature horse. Though we had used live animals previously, we used this opportunity to discover how to make tech rehearsals even more animal-friendly.

Please note that this article focuses on familiarizing an animal with the tech process: it does not address all issues involved in using an animal in a production. What you will find here are suggestions for establishing a safe situation for the animal. Our experience with Melody gave us a clear understanding that animals respond best to familiar situations, feelings of security, and basic conditioning (the repetition of actions with similar starting and ending points and consistent reward patters). Knowing that each situation will have its own specific needs and challenges, we suggest the following process as a starting point.

FIGURE 1: MELODY AND FRIENDS

1. Select and train a sole handler.
2. Animal-proof the space.
3. Establish a plan for the first day.
4. Establish a routine.
5. Plan emergency egress.

Selecting and Training a Sole Handler. One and only one person should be chosen as the animal's handler – someone who is thoroughly familiar with the tech process and who is interested in becoming comfortable with the animal itself. The handler will need non-rehearsal time with the animal and owner. The handler and the animal would also benefit from time in which they can get to know each other's regular behaviors. The handler should form a true liaison with the animal's owner, to learn what might scare the animal; what might make it sick or uncomfortable; and whether food rewards are allowed or not. If the handler will not be participating in tech notes or will not have the authority to make requests in matters that affect the animal, someone with that authority should be designated as the animal's advocate and should work with the handler to ensure all conditions set forth in the contract with the owner are met.

Animal-Proofing the Space. In the space – and with a member of the management team – the handler and owner should discuss the layout of and any inherent hazards in the theatre. Hazards may include the presence of toxic substances like paint or cleaning supplies within the animal's reach. Some less obvious hazards include dim stairway lighting and the presence of radiators or other protrusions at eye level and softgoods within mouth's reach. Once measures have been taken to mitigate those hazards, inviting the owner to inspect the space will provide all parties with added reassurance – and the owner may even identify hazards that you have missed.

Establishing a Plan for the First Day. Having a clear first-day plan is essential because the calmer and more organized the situation is, the more comfortable the animal will feel – and, ideally, greater comfort will lead to more controlled behavior. It is also essential to set aside time to acclimate the animal to the rehearsal setting, including a few minutes for the cast and crew to introduce themselves and time for the animal to roam backstage with the handler, investigating the space. Include in the first-day plan a limit to the number of hours the animal can work. Animals grow restless and hard to control over long periods of confinement or inactivity. Carefully limiting the animal's first-day call is vital in avoiding this potential problem, keeping in mind that, ultimately, the length of its call will be determined as much by the animal's temperament as by the number of scenes in which it is involved. The length of the first-day's call especially should be set with the animal's owner.

Establishing a Routine. Animals respond well to conditioning, To get the most consistent results, set up a routine that encompasses everything you will ask the animal to do and then follow those steps exactly every time the animal is in the theater. The routine should provide consistency in transportation methods, time schedules, walking paths, holding areas, and rewards for a job done well. By following a pattern, you will provide a sense of security and familiarity to the animal and are more likely to get the behavior you want. The initial plan will be refined during tech and, like other details, should be confirmed with the owner. Note that the first time a routine is run, even if the animal has performed previously, every new production will be new to the animal. It is a good idea to run the routine for the first time under work light and then gradually add lighting and other technical elements to accustom the animal to changes in conditions. Example routine:

7:30pm	Handler picks animal up at its home in company van.
7:45pm	Handler and animal stay in Dressing Room A.
8:20pm	Handler and animal walk DSL for a handoff to Actor A, who leads the animal across the set and holds the animal's lead during dialog with Actor B. Dialog over, Actor A walks US and hands the animal off to the handler.
8:30pm -	Handler returns animal to dressing room and provides a treat.
8:45pm -	Act I ends. Handler returns animal to its home in company van.

Planning Emergency Egress. In most cases, the animal will be able to use the same egress as your cast and crew, but if the animal would have trouble navigating stairs or otherwise have difficulty with emergency routes, plan a safe alternative.

NOTES

Whether the animal you work with is difficult or quite pleasant, one thing is for certain – the animal doesn't really understand theatre. Your handler and advocate have the essential job of catering to the sense of safety and familiarity an animal needs, and that, coupled with a practiced show routine, will lead to greater happiness among animals, technicians, and, ultimately, producers and the audience.

ঽ঺ঽ঺

When loading and unloading counterweight linesets the system becomes unbalanced – a very dangerous condition. For years, theater technicians have employed various types of safety wraps to secure a system during loading and unloading. In fact, Jay O. Glerum's well-known *Stage Rigging Handbook* is adamant in warning "WHEN LOADING OR UNLOADING, ALWAYS HAVE A SAFETY WRAP ON THE HAND LINE....NEVER RELY ON THE ROPE LOCK TO HOLD AN UNBALANCED LOAD!" (emphasis in original text). Mr. Glerum describes a few types of safety wraps, and this article attempts to quantify the effectiveness of a selection of safety wraps, some but not all of which are included in *Stage Rigging Handbook, 2nd Edition.*

THE SAFETY WRAPS

All of the safety wraps described here can become very fast to apply and control, even second nature, with practice and attention to detail.

FIGURE 1: THE STOPPER HITCH

FIGURE 2: THE PRUSIK KNOT

The stopper hitch, described on pages 148–150 and 194 of *Stage Rigging Handbook, 2nd Edition*, is tied around the front purchase line only (see Figure 1). Once the lineset has been loaded, the stopper hitch can be slipped down until the load is balanced. This technique involves overhauling the weight to get enough slack, making it more suitable for lighter loads that can be bulled out manually. Tying a stopper hitch is cumbersome and learning to tie and slip one reliably takes practice.

The *prusik knot* (see Figure 2), much like the stopper hitch, provides the ability to slip the purchase line through the knot until the load is balanced. Like the stopper hitch, the prusik is tied to the front purchase line only and can be slipped or untied only if the weight is over-hauled. The prusik is, however, an easier knot to tie, and using a rated shackle or snap hook between the safety wrap

FIGURE 3: THE SNUB HITCH

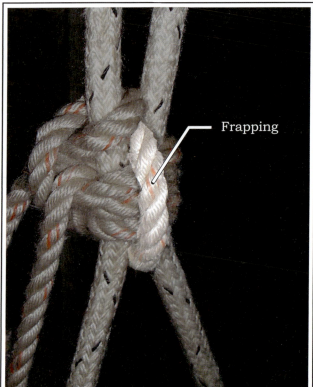

FIGURE 4: FRAPPING

and the rail as seen in Figure 2 makes the process even easier by eliminating the need to tie the line around the locking rail.

Unlike the previous two knots, the *snub hitch*, is tied around the front and back purchase lines as shown in Figure 3 and finished with a single frapping (omitted from Figure 3 for clarity but shown in Figure 4). The snub hitch is the easiest of the knots to tie and untie, and tying (or wrapping) the purchase lines together increases useful friction. Still, the snub hitch also increases the stress on the lineset's tension block and can cause the block shoes to bend or deform.

The *Line Lok®* (see Figure 5) is a device which also uses friction produced by holding the front and back lines together in compression. Like the snub hitch, the Line Lok® can overstress tension block shoes. The Line Lok® can be applied quickly and easily but can just as easily "fly off" during unbalanced removal. As shown in Figures 3 and 5, the back purchase line needs to be "dog-legged" to ensure proper friction, for both the snub hitch and Line Lok®.

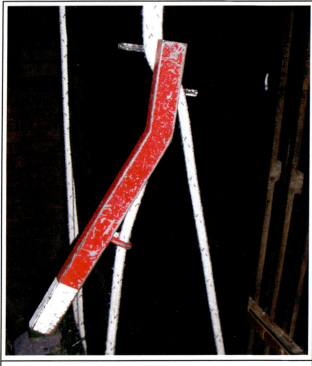

FIGURE 5: THE LINE LOK®

THE TEST

The arbors of four counterweight linesets were secured to have only one foot of travel from the loading bridge. With the system rope lock open, each of the linesets was loaded with counterweight until the arbor moved. This loaded weight became the control weight for each lineset. Then, four safety wrap methods – stopper hitch, prusik hitch, snub hitch, and Line Lok® – were each employed on the four linesets. Each set was loaded, again with the system lock open, until the arbor began to move under the unbalanced load. Having the system rope lock open was for control purposes only. In normal practice, no lineset should ever be loaded with the rope lock disengaged. Each method was employed three times on each of the four linesets (a total of twelve applications for each method) to account for possible human error and lineset differences. Note that, to establish a control for this limited experiment, all four of the purchase lines were Stage Set X polyester parallel-core sleeved rope, and all the tied safety wraps used $\frac{1}{2}$" Multiline II polyester/polyolefin 3-strand twisted rope. The Line Lok® was shop-built using the specifications on page 153 of *Stage Rigging Handbook, 2nd Edition*. Other rope combinations could return significantly different results.

SAFETY WRAP TEST RESULTS

	Lineset 1	Lineset 2	Lineset 3	Lineset 4	Average
Control Weight	40	30	40	50	40
Stopper Hitch	480	450	400	520	462.5
Prusik Hitch	400	460	480	500	460
Snub Hitch*	355	340	380	355	357.5
Line Lok®**	600	600	600	600	600

All Weights given in pounds.
*Finished with a single frapping.
**Held fully-loaded arbor.

RESULT NOTES

The stopper and prusik knots became very difficult to untie or slip down the line when loaded with more than 150 lbs. Before a frapping was added, the snub hitch held only 100 to 150 lbs. During Line Lok® tests the arbor dropped about 2' because of line stretch and tension block stress.

SOURCE

Glerum, Jay O. *Stage Rigging Handbook, 2nd Edition*. Carbondale: SIU Press, 1997.

TECHNICAL BRIEF

Scenery

Pneumatically Actuated Caster Planks — Drew Monahan

Making Oversized Cove Moulding on the Table Saw — Nick Bria

Using 18-Gauge $1\frac{1}{2}$"-Square Tube Steel to Build Taller and Longer — Annie Jacobs

Compound Miters Simplified — Peter Malbuisson

Kerfing Steel for Larger Arcs — Andrew Farrow

"Pacing" Groundrow Elements — Kevin Hines

Building Stairs from Scrap Plywood — David A. Griffith and Gerald Kawaoka

Isolating Door Vibration in Flats — Sam Michael

Changing Portraits with Ganged Sunroofs — Andrew F. Southard and Don Harvey

Eleven Quick Tips — Craig Martin

Flexi-Pitch Handrail — Dorian James Robison

Fauxberglass: An Inexpensive Alternative to Fiberglass — Kalen Larson

Setting Up an X-Ref Master File — Ted Griffith

Providing a Column Shaft with Entasis — Dan Perez

Using stock materials and a handful of inexpensive new parts, we built a set of pneumatically actuated caster planks that easily lifted a half-ton 200-square-foot raked platform off its legs, allowing us to move it and set it on spike quickly and with little effort. Figure 1 illustrates the parts of a typical caster plank: 2x6 top and bottom plates, two square steel-tube and flat-bar frames, and a bladder made from general-duty PVC water-discharge hose. In addition to providing caster-to-plank and plank-to-platform mounting locations, the lumber plates sandwich the PVC bladder, distributing the load equally over the casters. The frames constrain the movement of the lower plate, stabilizing the casters when the bladder is inflated and serving as additional legs when it is deflated.

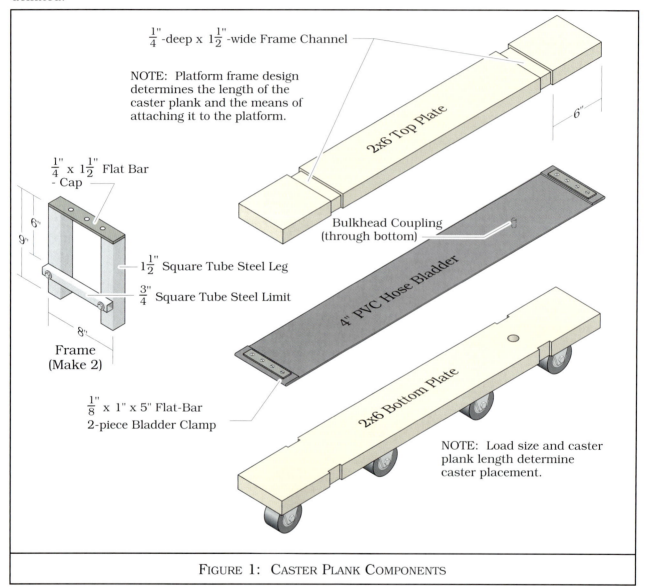

$\frac{1}{4}$"-deep x $1\frac{1}{2}$"-wide Frame Channel

NOTE: Platform frame design determines the length of the caster plank and the means of attaching it to the platform.

$\frac{1}{4}$" x $1\frac{1}{2}$" Flat Bar - Cap

6"

9"

$1\frac{1}{2}$" Square Tube Steel Leg

$\frac{3}{4}$" Square Tube Steel Limit

8"

Frame (Make 2)

$\frac{1}{8}$" x 1" x 5" Flat-Bar 2-piece Bladder Clamp

2x6 Top Plate

6"

Bulkhead Coupling (through bottom)

4" PVC Hose Bladder

2x6 Bottom Plate

NOTE: Load size and caster plank length determine caster placement.

FIGURE 1: CASTER PLANK COMPONENTS

ASSEMBLY

The Bladder: Cut a piece of PVC hose 3" longer than the caster plank will be. Near one end, punch a $\frac{3}{8}$" hole for a bulkhead coupling through one wall. Apply silicone sealant around the hole and tighten the coupling in place. Lay a generous bead of sealant inside the ends of the hose, fold the ends back, and close each end with a bladder clamp – two 5" pieces of $\frac{1}{8}$" x 1" flat bar.

Plates and Frames: After cutting two 2x6s to length for the plates, cut the frame channels $\frac{1}{4}$" deep and a little more than $1\frac{1}{2}$" wide across their edges and across one face of the top plate as shown in Figure 1. Cut the steel for the frames. Drill $\frac{5}{16}$" holes in the legs and limits and countersink $\frac{1}{4}$" holes in the caps. Weld the caps (countersinks up) to the legs. Slide the leg and cap assembly over the top plates and screw the caps and plates together.

Connections between these caster planks and a platform depend on the platform's design. Screwing or lagging the top plate directly to a platform at this point is one option. Alternatively, custom-designed connecting tabs may be fastened to the top plate before proceeding with assembly.

Turn the top plate and partially completed frame assembly on its back, and lay the bladder, bulk-head coupling up, on the top plate. Locate and drill a 1" access hole for the bulkhead coupling through the bottom plate. Attach the casters to the bottom plate, and slip the now-complete bottom plate into the frame, pushing the bulkhead coupling into the access hole. Finally, bolt the $\frac{3}{4}$"-square tube steel limits in place on the legs.

SYSTEM DESIGN CONSIDERATIONS

The PVC hose we used has an outside diameter of 4.13" and a maximum working pressure of 70 psi. The amount of lifting force it can supply when used as a bladder depends on the pressure supplied to it and the size of its footprint on either one of the plates.

Even at maximum working pressure, our 5'-0" end-clamped bladders would have had an effective contact length of at least 4'-0". As Figure 2 illustrates, applying enough pressure to press the lower plate against the $\frac{3}{4}$"-square-tube steel limit would press about $1\frac{9}{16}$" of the bladder's circumference against a plate. Under these conditions, the bladder-plate footprint would measure 48" × 1.5625", or 75 sq. in., making a single caster plank capable of lifting a whopping 5250 lbs. Total system pressure of less than 20 psi would lift a wagon weighing 1200 lbs. (1200 lbs. ÷ 75 sq. in. = 16 psi).

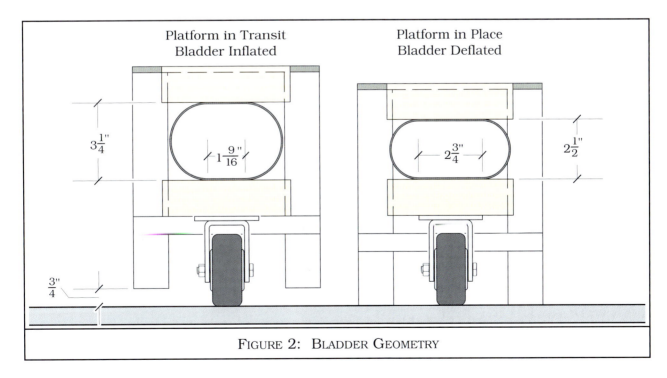

FIGURE 2: BLADDER GEOMETRY

Deflating these bladders just enough to lower the platform onto its legs increases the width of the bladder-plate contact area to $1\frac{3}{4}$", producing a footprint of 48" x 2.75", or 132 sq. in. Consequently, bringing a platform to spike requires near-complete exhaustion of the bladders. A 1200-pound caster-planked platform could only be set on spike, for instance, if total bladder pressure were reduced to 9 psi (1200 lbs. ÷ 132 sq. in. = 9.09 psi).

To a degree, the width of the bladder-plate contact area also affects caster stability. Zero-throw casters and straight casters attached along the bottom plate's centerline are the least likely to rotate the bottom plate and cause it to bind between the frame legs. Swivel casters can be used, however, as long as the air pressure pushes the bottom plate hard enough against the limit to prevent rotation.

MATERIALS

Like ours, many shops stock the basic materials for these caster planks, and all other materials are easily obtained locally and/or through the internet. Our costs per plank are illustrated below:

Component	Quan	Material	Cost
Top and Bottom Plates	2	2x6 - 5'-0"	(stock)
Frame Caps	2	$\frac{1}{4}$" x $1\frac{1}{2}$" flat bar, 8" long	(stock)
Frame Legs	4	18-gauge $1\frac{1}{2}$"-square tube steel, 9" long	(stock)
Frame Limits	2	18-gauge $\frac{3}{4}$"-square tube steel, 8" long	(stock)
Bladder Caps	4	$\frac{1}{4}$" x $1\frac{1}{2}$" flat bar, 4" long	(stock)
Bladder	1	4"-I.D. "Lay-Flat" PVC Hose, 5'-3" long McMaster-Carr: 5295K41	$9.54
Bladder Connection	1	Bulkhead Coupling (for $\frac{1}{4}$" O.D. Tube) McMaster-Carr: 51055K3	$2.67
Bladder Sealant	1	Tube – Silicone-Rubber Sealant	$2.23

RESOURCES

McMaster-Carr: http://www.mcmaster.com/
    for PVC hose, follow links to /catalog/108html/0160.html
    for bulkhead coupling, follow links to /catalog/108html/0126.html

¿▲¿▲¿▲

While I was in my undergraduate studies at Rutgers University, Technical Director Tim Pickens introduced me to the time-tested technique of making oversized cove moulding on a table saw. While the ready availability of products like custom-cut foam moulding and even Sonotube® has largely made this process obsolete, theatre technicians will find it useful – even if only in a pinch. This article describes how it's done.

INITIAL CONSIDERATIONS

First, there are limits to the size of coves this technique can or should be used to produce. It can't produce coves with radii larger than the maximum height setting of the table saw's blade, and using it to make coves that can be bought at the local lumber yard would be a waste of time and money. Second, using a table saw to process foam blocks – this technique's most appropriate material – poses two significant safety hazards: it releases harmful vapors and it requires the removal of blade guards. Third, the cross section of a table-sawn cove, which is dictated by trigonometry, may closely approximate design intentions but it probably won't match them exactly.

PLANNING AND SET-UP

From the designer's drawings you can determine the height and depth of the cove itself as well as the height and thickness of the foam blanks needed. Figure 1 represents an example cove section, here a 3" x 3" cove cut in a block of foam 4" tall and 4" wide.

Figure 2 illustrates the relationships between the radius of a blade r, exposed height of the blade h, and dimension x, half the length of the chord of the exposed blade segment. According to the formula, setting a standard 10" table saw blade set to a height of 3" yields an x value of about $4\frac{9}{16}$" – over an inch and a half wider than the depth of the desired cove.

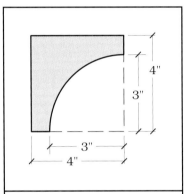

FIGURE 1: PROPOSED COVE

$$x = \sqrt{h(2r\text{-}h)}$$

$$x = \sqrt{3"[(2)(5")] - 3"}$$

$$x = 4.58" \text{ or } 4\frac{9}{16}"$$

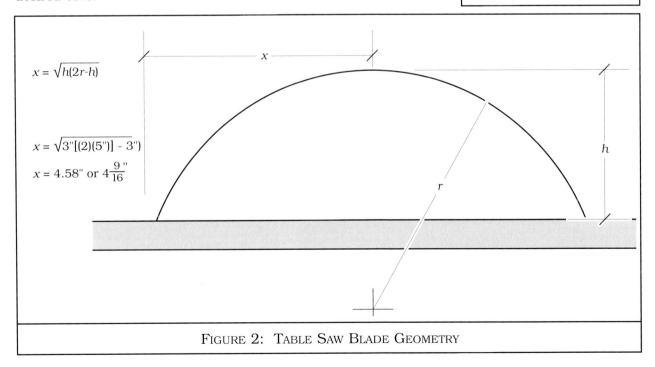

FIGURE 2: TABLE SAW BLADE GEOMETRY

Making Oversized Cove Moulding on the Table Saw

Nick Bria

Traditionally, table-sawn cove mouldings are produced by running blanks past a temporary rip fence set at an angle to the table saw's blade. Dividing the desired cove depth by x and finding the arcsine of the result tells us the angle at which the rip fence will need to be set. In this case, as illustrated in Figure 3:

$$\text{arcsine}(3.00" \div 4.58") = 40.9° \approx 41°$$

The set-back at which the fence should be clamped to the saw table can be determined in either of two ways. As Figure 4 illustrates, the perpendicular distance between the fence and the already-set saw blade is equal to the width of the blank minus the depth of the cove – in this case, 1". Measuring along the blade at the top of the table is the other approach, The distance between the fence and the point at which the blade enters the table equals the value of x (found in the first step) minus the depth of the cove – here $1\frac{9}{16}"$.

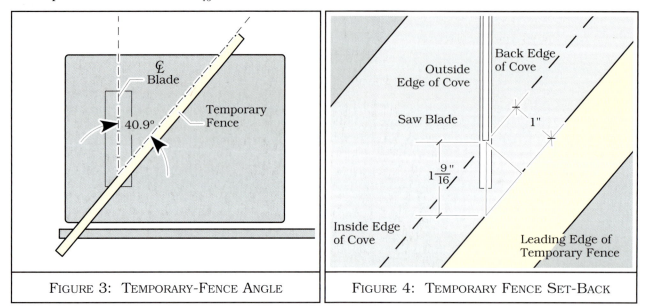

| FIGURE 3: TEMPORARY-FENCE ANGLE | FIGURE 4: TEMPORARY FENCE SET-BACK |

SET-UP AND PROCEDURE

Clamp the fence securely to the saw table – behind the blade, where rotation will push the blanks downward toward the table and back toward the fence, Drop the blade to $\frac{1}{8}"$ above the table and slowly run all the blanks. Raise the blade $\frac{1}{8}"$ ($\frac{1}{4}"$ above the table saw surface) and run all the blanks through again. Repeat this sequence until reaching the desired cove depth (3" in this case).

❧🙶🙶❧

When we frame units in 16-gauge 1"-square tube steel (0.065" thick), we lose out on several advantages we might gain by using 18-gauge 1½"-square tube steel (0.049" thick). The switch to a tube with a thinner wall but larger cross-section can decrease overall unit weight and the number of required supports while increasing weight allowances and the length of spans between supports.

BEAMS AND THE VALUE OF *I*

In a steel beam or horizontal steel frame, failure is said to occur when deflection in the form of a sag becomes noticeable. Of the several geometric properties engineers have defined for the cross section of a beam, one in particular – the moment of inertia or the *I* value – is directly proportional to a beam's resistance to deflection. The greater a beam's *I* value, the greater the load it can support, or for a given load the greater a beam's *I* value, the longer its span can be.

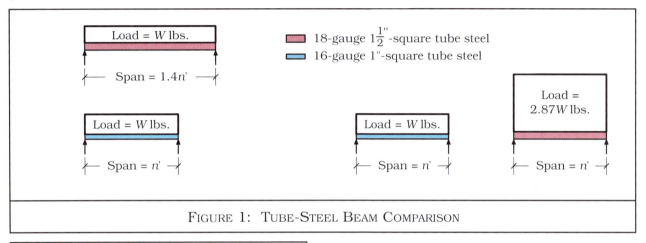

FIGURE 1: TUBE-STEEL BEAM COMPARISON

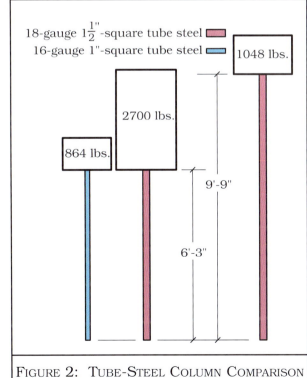

FIGURE 2: TUBE-STEEL COLUMN COMPARISON

The *I* value of 18-gauge 1½"-square tube steel is 0.0982 in⁴ but that of 16-gauge 1"-square tube steel is only 0.0342 in⁴. Thus, as shown in Figure 1, a platform supported only at each end and framed in 18-gauge 1½"-square tube steel can either be 1.4 times longer than or carry 2.87 times the load of a similarly supported platform framed in 16-gauge 1"-square tube steel.

COLUMNS AND THE VALUE OF *r*

Legs or columns fail by buckling, and the radius of gyration (*r*) relates directly to a column's resistance to buckling. Columns with larger *r* values can carry heavier loads or be taller than those with smaller *r* values. As Figure 2 shows, for example, a column made of 16-gauge 1"-square tube steel (*r* = 0.3797") can carry 864 lbs. at a maximum unbraced length of 6'-3", but a 6'-3" column made of 18-gauge 1½"-square tube steel can carry over 2700 lbs. At its maximum unbraced height of 9'-9", an 18-gauge 1½"-square tube steel column (*r* = 0.5908") could carry a load of 1048 lbs.

ON THE OTHER HAND....

Since theatrical loads rarely approach the capacity of carefully engineered units, many technical designers consider a unit's weight to be more important than its strength. True, carefully engineering a unit framed in 18-gauge $1\frac{1}{2}$"-square tube steel to reduce the number of supports it needs can optimize its weight. But 16-gauge 1"-square tube steel still weighs about 16% less per linear foot than 18-gauge $1\frac{1}{2}$"-square tube steel.

FINAL NOTES

This article is meant to suggest some possible advantages of using 18-gauge $1\frac{1}{2}$"-square tube steel in place of the more common 16-gauge 1"-square tube steel. The discussion presented here is general and far from complete. Careful technical design requires that, for safety's sake, all forces and loading conditions not mentioned here be taken into account, and the use of a book such as *Structural Design for the Stage* by Alys Holden and Bronislaw J. Sammler is advised.

RESOURCES

Holden, Alys E. and Bronislaw J. Sammler. *Structural Design for the Stage*. Boston: Focal Press, 1999.

ই▲ই▲ই▲

How many times has a set design come across your drafting table with the deck raked and walls plumb to the Earth and you've thought, "Oh no, more compound miters to deal with!" Searching for help in fine-carpentry textbooks or on the internet will yield several formulas that use the functions Cosine, Sine, and Tangent. Unfortunately these formulas are arranged for cutting cornices for your house – not for cutting rails and stiles for scenery. This article translates the formulas for cutting compound miters into scenic terms familiar to technical directors. The formulas that follow have been tested and proven using 3D AutoCAD.

THE TERMS

Four terms must first be defined. Two terms, *off-axis angle* and *rake angle*, relate to the scenery as a whole. The other two terms, *side angle* and *front angle* relate to the stiles and rails of the flats. Figure 1 illustrates the Off-Axis Angles of two Hollywood flats standing on a raked deck. Their faces and stiles are mitered and beveled as shown in Figure 2 to achieve the cleanest possible joints. No compound miters are involved in cutting rails: side angles are ripped into the rail's downstage edges on a table saw and front angles are cut into their ends on a compound-miter saw. The side

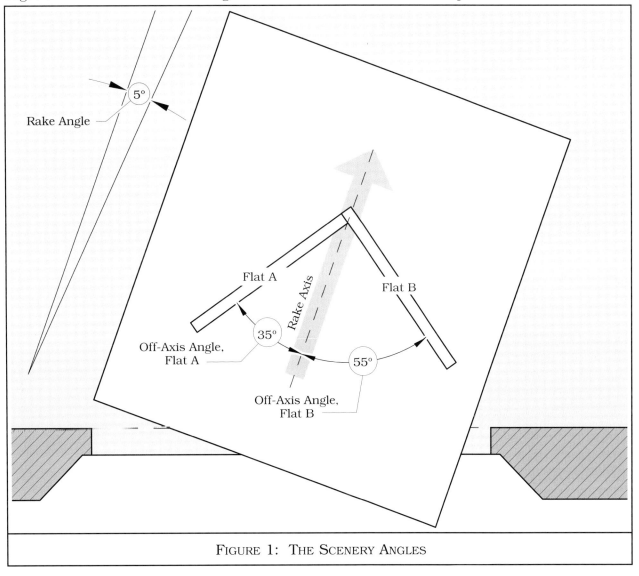

FIGURE 1: THE SCENERY ANGLES

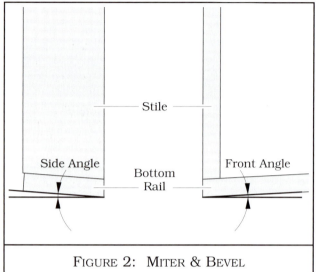

FIGURE 2: MITER & BEVEL

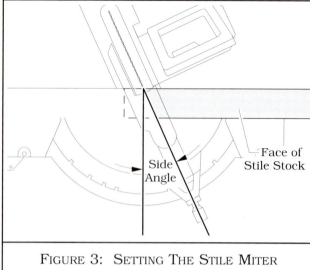

FIGURE 3: SETTING THE STILE MITER

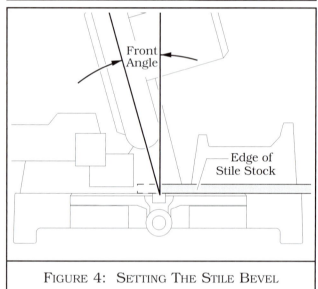

FIGURE 4: SETTING THE STILE BEVEL

and front angles are, by contrast, cut into stiles in a single compound-miter cut as illustrated in Figures 3 and 4. Swinging the head of a compound-miter saw as shown in Figure 3 produces the side angles; tilting the head as shown in Figure 4 produces the front angles.

THE FORMULAS

For brevity, the formulas use two abbreviations: *rake* for rake angle, and *offax* for off-axis angle. For any flat, the leading edge of the bottom rail is ripped at the side angle, and its end is trimmed at the front angle. The formulas for cutting the bottom of a stile are as follows:

Side Angle = arctan (tan(rake) * sin(offax))
Front Angle = arctan (tan(rake) * cos(offax))

EXAMPLE

The deck shown in Figure 1 has a rake angle of 5°. Flat *A* sits on the rake with an off-axis angle of 35°. The compound-miter saw settings used to cut the stile are found as follows:

The end of Flat *A*'s bottom rail is beveled at 4.10° and the edge is beveled at 2.87°. Since the two flats in this example play at 90° to each other, the side angle found for Flat *A* is the same as the front angle for Flat *B*, and the front angle for *A* is the side angle for *B*. Obviously, thought still needs to be put into the carpentry. The formulas don't tell you which direction to turn the compound-miter saw bed or tilt the blade. In addition, some CAD work must be done to determine the lengths of the stiles and rails, but the formulas can help scene shops reduce the amount of scrap wood that is generated.

NOTES

Rake angles are often described in rise-to-run ratios – *e.g.*, $\frac{1}{2}$" to the foot, or 0.5:12 – rather than in degrees, and a spreadsheet like the one shown in Figure 5 can speed all the calculations involved in framing Hollywood flats to fit a rake. Follow these steps to duplicate the one shown here:

1. Open a blank Excel worksheet and name two data ranges: *rake*=F1, and *offax*=$B:$B.

2. In cell F1, enter the formula =DEGREES(ATAN(B1/B2)).

3. Enter the labels shown in cells A3 through D3. Starting in row 4, work down the spreadsheet, entering the names of flats in column A and their off-axis angles in column B.

4. To calculate the side angles, enter the following formula in each row of column C: =IF(ISBLANK(offax),"",DEGREES(ATAN(TAN(RADIANS(rake))*SIN(RADIANS(offax)))))

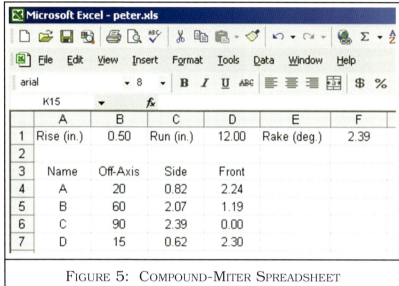

	A	B	C	D	E	F
1	Rise (in.)	0.50	Run (in.)	12.00	Rake (deg.)	2.39
2						
3	Name	Off-Axis	Side	Front		
4	A	20	0.82	2.24		
5	B	60	2.07	1.19		
6	C	90	2.39	0.00		
7	D	15	0.62	2.30		

FIGURE 5: COMPOUND-MITER SPREADSHEET

5. To calculate the front angles, enter the following formula in each row of column D: =IF(ISBLANK(offax),"",DEGREES(ATAN(TAN(RADIANS(rake))*COS(RADIANS(offax)))))

❦❦❦❦

The accurate and efficient construction of large curved steel frames can be complex and problematic for scene shops that lack access to rollers and benders. For such shops, kerfing is still the only practicable technique, and unfortunately the more widely-known approaches to kerfing don't seem to apply universally. The approach suggested in Daniel J. Culhane's *Technical Design Solutions* article "A Measured Approach to Kerfing", for instance, works very well but, as PCPA Theatrefest Shop Carpenter Steve Henson discovered, it is best suited to smaller-diameter arcs. In response, Henson developed two formulas that repeatedly yielded accurate results.

THE FORMULAS

Formula 1:   Number of Kerfs (k) Required: $k = \dfrac{2\pi t}{b} \times \left(\dfrac{a}{360°}\right)$

where   t = stock's top-face width, inches

b = kerfing blade thickness, inches

a = angle of arc, degrees

Formula 2   Distance (s) between Kerfs: $s = \dfrac{c}{k}$

where   c = outside circumference, inches

k = number of kerfs required, unitless

APPLICATION EXAMPLE

A 10'-0"-diameter turntable is to be framed in 16-gauge $1\frac{1}{2}$"-square tube steel.

Formula 1:   Number of Kerfs (k) Required: $k = \dfrac{2pt}{b} \times \left(\dfrac{a}{360°}\right)$

t =   1.5"

b =   0.125"

a =   360°

$k = \dfrac{2\pi t}{b} \times \left(\dfrac{a}{360°}\right) = \dfrac{2\pi\,1.5}{0.125} \times \left(\dfrac{360°}{360°}\right) = 75.40$

Formula 2   Distance (s) between Kerfs: $s = \dfrac{c}{k}$

c = $2\pi r = 376.99$

k =   75.40

$s = \dfrac{c}{k} = \dfrac{376.99}{75.40} = 5"$

The calculated value of *k* is used in determining the distance between kerfs, but that value is rounded up as necessary in construction. Further, assuming that all the blades a shop uses in kerfing are the same thickness, the number of kerfs required for circles of any size can be represented in a table rather than recalculated for every new project. The table in Figure 1 lists the number of $\frac{1}{8}$"-thick kerfs required to bend 1"-wide, $1\frac{1}{2}$"-wide, and 2"-wide tube steel into full circles.

Stock Width	k	Number of Kerfs
1"	50.27	51
$1\frac{1}{2}$"	75.40	76
2"	100.53	101

FIGURE 1: A K-VALUE TABLE

NOTES ON KERF DEPTH

As general practice, kerfs may be cut halfway through the top and bottom faces of arc stock, but kerf depth should suit particular needs. Kerfing always weakens stock, and deeply kerfed stock is useless as framing material unless the kerfs are welded shut after an arc has been bent. On the other hand, stock with overly shallow kerfs can deform significantly during bending, making the attachment of a skin difficult or impossible. Kerfing halfway through the stock optimizes the tradeoff between flexibility and material strength.

THE MATH BEHIND FORMULA 1

Figure 2 and the following table illustrate why the expression $2\pi t$ represents the difference between an arc's outside and inside circumferences (m).

$$
\begin{aligned}
m &= c_{outside} - c_{inside} \\
&= 2\pi r_{outside} - 2\pi(r_{outside} - t) \\
&= 2\pi(r_{outside} - (r_{outside} - t)) \\
&= 2\pi(r_{outside} - r_{outside} + t) \\
&= 2\pi(0 + t) \\
&= 2\pi t
\end{aligned}
$$

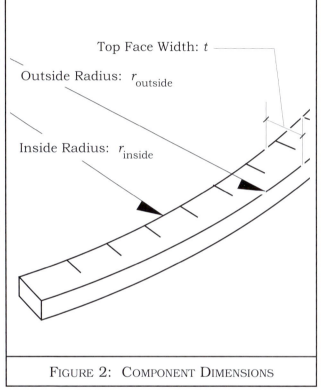

Top Face Width: t

Outside Radius: $r_{outside}$

Inside Radius: r_{inside}

FIGURE 2: COMPONENT DIMENSIONS

RESOURCES

Steve Henson
Culhane, Daniel J. "A Measured Approach to Kerfing", *Technical Design Solutions for Theatre, Vol. I* ed. Bronislaw J. Sammler and Don Harvey. Woburn, MA: Elsevier Science, 2002.

For a Spring 2000 Production of *The Country Wife* at Carnegie Mellon School of Drama, David Henderson designed a set of three groundrows, each consisting of individual human silhouettes that would "pace" back and forth, each one pivoting 180° on its base to face forward before crossing the stage. This would need to be a surface-mounted effect, as the show was played on the stage floor, but we decided that the presence of a cable running across the deck was acceptable, as long as it could be kept as close to the floor as possible.

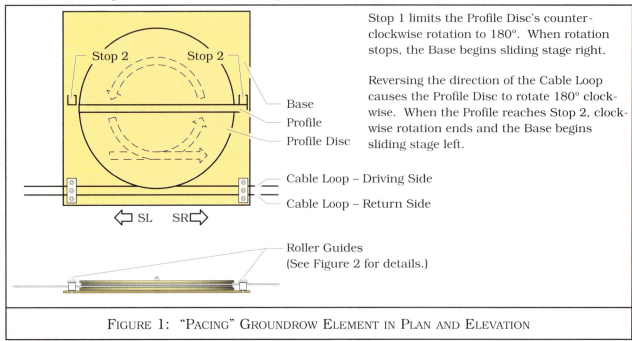

Stop 1 limits the Profile Disc's counter-clockwise rotation to 180°. When rotation stops, the Base begins sliding stage right.

Reversing the direction of the Cable Loop causes the Profile Disc to rotate 180° clockwise. When the Profile reaches Stop 2, clockwise rotation ends and the Base begins sliding stage left.

Stop 2 — Stop 2

Base
Profile
Profile Disc

Cable Loop – Driving Side

Cable Loop – Return Side

⇐ SL   SR ⇒

Roller Guides
(See Figure 2 for details.)

FIGURE 1: "PACING" GROUNDROW ELEMENT IN PLAN AND ELEVATION

RIGGING OVERVIEW

Figure 1 illustrates the essentials of the rig's components and operating principles. As the drawing shows, the driving side of a simple closed-loop cable drive muled close to the deck passes through a first set of roller guides, wraps 360° around a disc carrying one of the profiles, and then through a second set of roller guides. From there, it is reeved around a return mule on the far side of the stage to become the loop's return side.

The key to successful operation was the design of the silhouettes' bases, which responded to drive cable movement first by rotating the profiles into the desired "forward" orientation, then by dragging the base across the stage. When a rank of profiles reached the point of "counter-march," the cable drive (driven, in our application, by a simple hand crank) was reversed. The profiles responded first by rotating and then by moving back in the opposite direction.

The biggest challenge for implementation was controlling the sliding friction between the disc and base, and the base and floor. For the sequence to work properly, the friction between disc and base needed to be minimized to guarantee that drive tension would be transformed first into disc rotation, then into base movement. The bottom of the disc was clad with UHMW tape, which ran smoothly on the Masonite® base. Even so, the bases frequently slid before the discs rotated. We eventually added weight to each base to increase its friction with the floor, thus increasing the necessary friction differential between the two movements, giving us consistent operation.

The overall thickness of the bases was kept to a minimum. Unwanted rotation of the square base plates was prevented by routing the return line through a set of vertical roller guides which used the tensioned return cable as a linear guide.

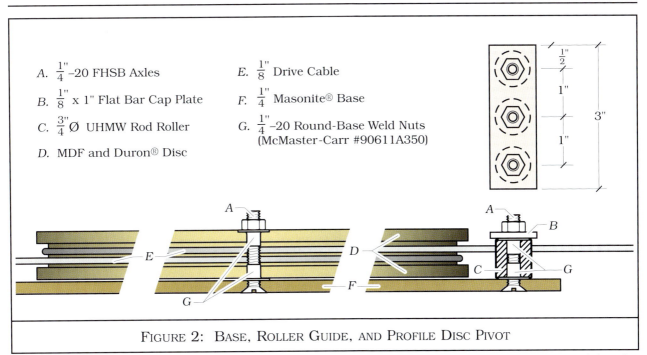

A. $\frac{1"}{4}$–20 FHSB Axles

B. $\frac{1"}{8}$ x 1" Flat Bar Cap Plate

C. $\frac{3"}{4}$ Ø UHMW Rod Roller

D. MDF and Duron® Disc

E. $\frac{1"}{8}$ Drive Cable

F. $\frac{1"}{4}$ Masonite® Base

G. $\frac{1"}{4}$–20 Round-Base Weld Nuts
(McMaster-Carr #90611A350)

FIGURE 2: BASE, ROLLER GUIDE, AND PROFILE DISC PIVOT

All hardware choices were made to simplify the fabrication of the twenty units required by the design. Disc pivot and roller axles were all $\frac{1}{4}$"-20 FHSB, countersunk flush to the underside of the base and nutted with inverted $\frac{1}{4}$" round-base weld nuts. Rollers and disc were bored to the O.D. of the weld nut cylinders. The discs were three-layer sandwiches with $\frac{1}{2}$" MDF "meat" and $\frac{1}{4}$" Duron "bread." The "meat" was $\frac{1}{2}$" smaller in O.D. to provide a reliable cable tread, Cable-wrap tension proved sufficient to avoid making cable terminations at each unit, which made relative adjustment of the units' spacing a simple matter of slacking the system, sliding each unit to its desired position, and re-tensioning.

The same rig might also be used to effect a groundrow element that spins continuously as it travels by removing the disc stop, connecting the return line to the base, and using it as the drive line.

❧❧❧❧

Building Stairs from Scrap Plywood

David A. Griffith and Gerald Kawaoka

To make the most of his scenery budget, the Associate Technical Director for our production of *Man of La Mancha* found a clever way to build two major staircases of scrap $\frac{3}{4}$" plywood, providing both a huge cost savings and a way to clean up the shop.

Our design includes a series of tread/riser supports cut from scraps of $\frac{3}{4}$" plywood. As shown in Figure 1, the supports are glued and screwed to the wider faces of the staircase's 2x4 stringers. Once the supports have been attached to the stringers, the shorter tread/riser reinforcements are glued and stapled to the insides of the supports as shown. This allowed the majority of the stress to act on the 2x4 stringers and not the screws.

The finished stairs worked safely and well in our production and I saw no problems with their construction. Depending on the size of your stairs this approach can save your budget quite a bit of money and put the scraps of $\frac{3}{4}$" plywood that can clutter a scene shop to good use.

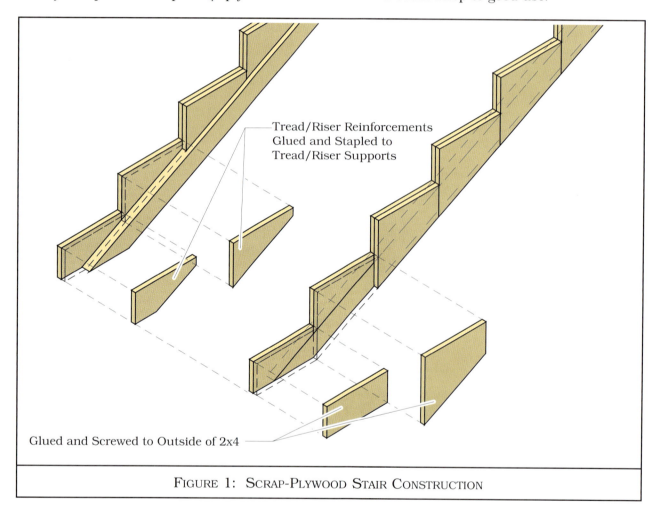

Tread/Riser Reinforcements Glued and Stapled to Tread/Riser Supports

Glued and Screwed to Outside of 2x4

FIGURE 1: SCRAP-PLYWOOD STAIR CONSTRUCTION

The opening and closing of doors on stage often causes undesirable vibration and movement in adjacent flats. It is most prevalent in soft covered flats such as muslin or scrim, although it is a concern in larger hard-covered flats as well. A remedy for this is to isolate the door unit from the flat.

DESCRIPTION

Separating the unit into two components, the door unit and the flat, produces an air gap, as illustrated in Figure 1. The opening in the flat is constructed to be marginally larger than the door unit. A $1\frac{1}{2}$"-square tube steel framed door unit and flat similar to that illustrated in Figure 1 only needs $\frac{1}{4}$" to $\frac{1}{2}$" for the face and return air gap for a standard size door that is properly braced under normal operation. In a recent production of *The Autumn Garden* at Williamstown Theatre Festival, we employed this separation for two sets of French doors mounted in scrim walls. Because the doors were 10' tall and 30" wide, we increased the face air gap to $\frac{3}{4}$" and the return air gap to 1" to allow for more variance in frame movement. Because of the doors' position onstage, the designer and director did not have any issues with the gap as long as the scrim on the flats did not shake.

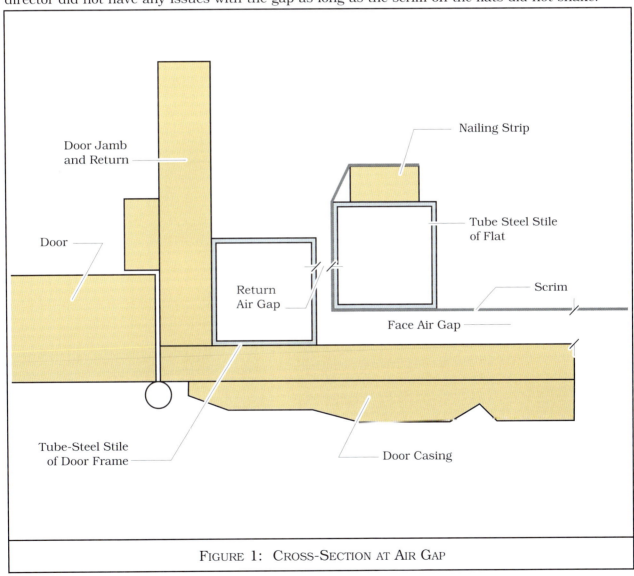

FIGURE 1: CROSS-SECTION AT AIR GAP

DESIGN CONSIDERATIONS

There are 4 key points to consider in sizing the return air gap and the face air gap: the nature of action the doors will receive, the materials used in the adjacent flats, the size and type of door, and the type of bracing used. Together, the nature of the action and the type of bracing used most heavily influence the size of the air gaps. Heavier action on the door increases the size of both air gaps while stronger bracing reduces them.

Determining the type of use the door will receive can be a difficult task since construction is likely to start before the director can determine blocking. Looking at the actions that are described in the script can provide a solid basis to determine the usage of the doors. Often, the designer and director will already have discussed special blocking needs and can provide information as well.

Bracing of both the flat and the door unit can prove challenging due to sight lines through the door and through the flats depending on their covering. The designer can be a great resource in solving this issue. They can incorporate easy solutions such as a return flat or a set of fake doors opened offstage to adequately brace the units without compromising the design. If options such as these are not viable, the designer can assist in placement of traditional bracing to help minimize its visibility.

COST

Additional costs are minimal. The only added materials are the extra door frame on the door unit and the additional bracing required. Extra time is needed in planning, but there is minimal change to the drafting or build time.

ぉ&ぉ&

In a Yale Repertory Theatre production of *A Woman of No Importance*, a 4' x 6' opening in a downstage portal was to be filled by alternating portraits. For various reasons, we didn't want to see a stagehand replacing one portrait with another during a scene change, and there was insufficient clearance to mount one, double-faced portrait on a center pin and flip it over. The change was accomplished by use of ganged sunroofs.

Theatre sunroofs are perhaps most commonly used to move trap plugs into place to cover the openings that are left when lifts are lowered into traprooms. During their travel on and offstage, they always stay parallel to the surfaces they fill and, when not in use, they are still close to those surfaces. These qualities made them the ideal mechanism to meet our needs.

SYSTEM OPERATION

As shown in Figure 1, we fastened the portraits to a pair of sunroofs bolted to a carriage that rode in a straight track mounted vertically upstage of the portal. The carriage was driven up and down by a closed-loop cable, which, to reduce graphic clutter, is not shown. As the cable lowered the carriage, the carriage simultaneously drove *Portrait A* into the portal opening and *Portrait B* down into its storage position. When the carriage was raised, it brought *Portrait B* into the opening while it took *Portrait A* into storage.

SYSTEM DESIGN ESSENTIALS

Though a carriage riding in a straight track drove the system up and down, the portraits were guided into the portal opening by pairs of cam followers riding in curved tracks on either side of the portal opening.

We used shop-built UHMW cam followers and we CNC-routed the curved tracks into lengths of MDF that we mounted on either side of the portal opening. All four of these tracks were cut to the same width just a little larger than the diameter of our cam followers. The curve in each track was a quarter-circle, but the radii of those circles were determined by the different clearances required for the two portraits. As indicated in Figures 1 and 2, *Portrait B* had no frame at all

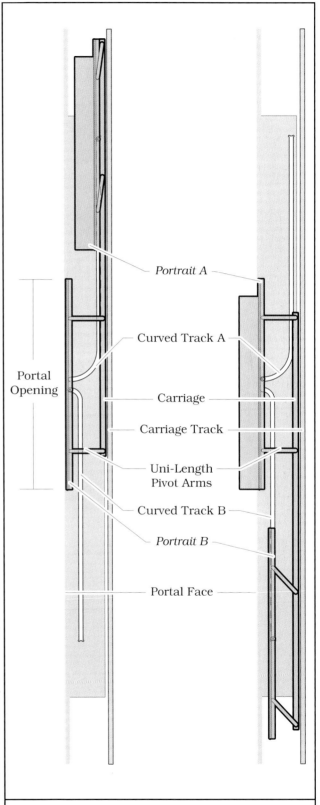

FIGURE 1: SYSTEM OPERATION SEEN FROM SL

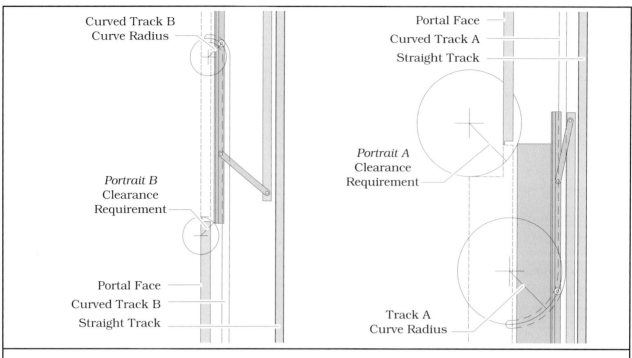

FIGURE 2: MATCHING TRACK CURVES TO PORTRAIT CLEARANCE REQUIREMENTS

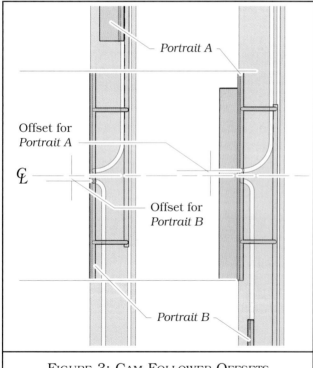

FIGURE 3: CAM FOLLOWER OFFSETS

while *Portrait A* had a thick frame. Consequently, before *Portrait A* could move out of the portal opening, it had to recede far enough behind the portal for its thick frame to clear. Figure 2 illustrates how the curve of each track met the clearance requirements.

As Figure 3 shows, the cam followers had to be offset above and below the portal opening centerline to allow the curved tracks to be separate from each other.

Two final features are not shown here but are essential nonetheless. First, we beveled the edges of the sunroof panels and counter-beveled the edges of the opening to produce nearly invisible seams. Second, we made the curved tracks just a little wider than the diameter of the cam followers to minimize friction.

ACKNOWLEDGEMENT

Thanks to Alan Hendrickson for suggesting this device and guiding its development.

Some ideas need little explanation but are so helpful that they ought to be recorded for posterity. Here are eleven of them:

1. Paint the long slot side (neutral) of female extension cord ends as a clue to which way to plug in two-prong plugs (see Figure 1).

2. Knowing your eye height makes estimating scenery heights quick. With a tape measure, measure from the top of the scenery to your eye level and add your eye height to estimate the overall height of the scenery.

3. For small, accurate moves, apply movement at right angles. For example, to move lumber slightly left or right on a pull-over saw, slide it in and out to "walk" it to the exact cut alignment needed.

4. For estimating scenery weights it's easy to remember that 4'x8' sheets of plywood weigh about 100 lbs per inch of thickness.

5. Small clamps can be used as wrenches for screwing in small hooks etc (see Figure 2).

6. Leave price tags on shop-owned equipment to help students learn the costs of tools.

7. Rough-set stage lights by lowering the light pipe five feet below trim and making the pattern on the floor that you want it to be at head level.

8. To mark half an angle for mitering, trace the full angle on paper and fold it in half.

9. To find the center of a small circular object, trace its outline on paper, then fold the circle in half. Use that fold to mark two diameters on the object. Their intersection marks the center.

FIGURE 1: A PAINTED NEUTRAL

FIGURE 2: A SMALL-CLAMP WRENCH

10. To mark 2, 4, 8, etc. equal intervals, mark the overall length on adding machine tape, tear the tape off and fold it end-to-end once, twice, three times, etc., then unfold it and mark at the folds.

11. WD-40® can remove many sticky substances, from wood sap to duct tape residue.

❧❧❧❧

In "Flexi-Pitch Escape Stairs" in *Technical Design Solutions for Theatre, Vol. 2*, Kevin Hines describes the adjustable staircase illustrated in Figure 1. Since it has only a single bolt at each tread-to-carriage connection, this staircase can be set at various angles as needed to accommodate escape platforms of different heights. This article describes the design and construction of Flexi-Pitch Handrails for use with the versatile staircase.

OVERVIEW

Flexi-Pitch Handrails, which are essentially a third pair of stringers running parallel with those of the staircase itself, have four components. The railings and flexi balusters, shown in blue in Figure 2, are connected to each other and to the top stringer and treads with single bolts that act as pin joints, allowing the railings to fold with the staircase. At the top of the staircase, the railing is attached to the stable baluster (shown in red-orange), again with a bolt acting as a pin joint. The stable baluster is an extension/addition to the stemmed ledger of the Flexi-Pitch Stairs. Its function is to provide rigidity and to keep the handrails in the correct relationship to the treads. Finally, the stabilizer tabs (shown in green) added to the bottom edge of the top stringer keep the Flexi-Pitch Handrails from wiggling excessively left to right in use.

All of the materials and hardware are in common use. Construction details for the railings and stabilizer tabs are shown in Figure 3; those for the flexi-balusters and the stable baluster, in Figure 4.

NOTES

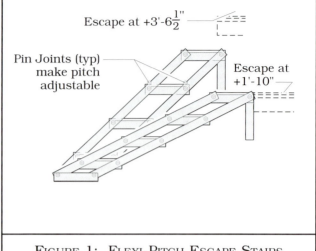

FIGURE 1: FLEXI-PITCH ESCAPE STAIRS

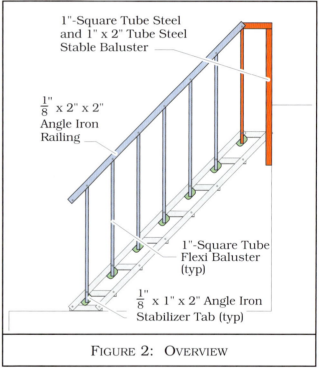

FIGURE 2: OVERVIEW

The added weight of the steel stairs and handrails can make larger units difficult to handle. A chain hoist or block and tackle is recommended for the installation of larger units. I would also recommend the addition of casters on the stairs so that when the stairs are lowered for storage the unit can simply roll away. Placement of the casters is critical: the casters must be placed so that they are unobtrusive at the Flexi-Pitch Stairs' most extreme pitches. With larger units, the 1" x 2" tube steel will deflect quite a bit, so the addition of a central support for the stringers is recommended. Either traditional 2x4 legs or 1" x 2" tube steel could be added to the stringer and made collapsible with another pin joint. Another thing to remember during installation is that larger units will sway side to side when being walked on, so the addition of lateral supports or cross bracing is necessary.

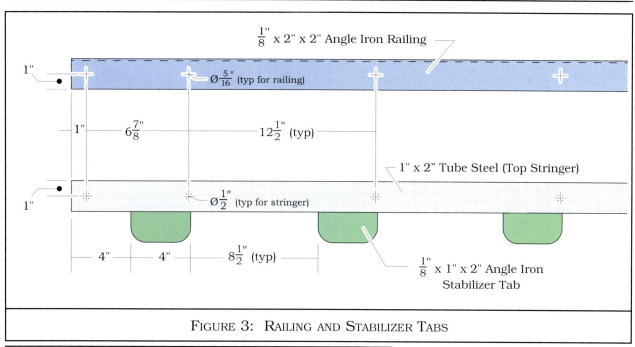

$\frac{1}{8}$" x 2" x 2" Angle Iron Railing

$\varnothing \frac{5}{16}$" (typ for railing)

1"

1" $6\frac{7}{8}$" $12\frac{1}{2}$" (typ)

1" x 2" Tube Steel (Top Stringer)

$\varnothing \frac{1}{2}$" (typ for stringer)

1"

4"   4" $8\frac{1}{2}$" (typ)

$\frac{1}{8}$" x 1" x 2" Angle Iron
Stabilizer Tab

FIGURE 3: RAILING AND STABILIZER TABS

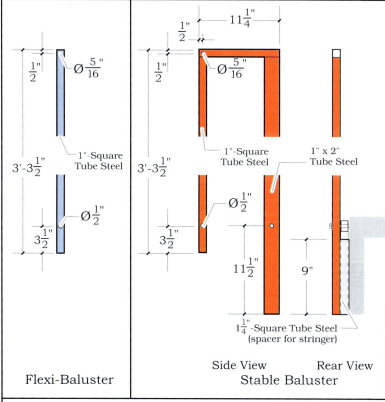

Flexi-Baluster

$\frac{1}{2}$" $\varnothing \frac{5}{16}$"

1"-Square
Tube Steel

3'-3$\frac{1}{2}$"

$\varnothing \frac{1}{2}$"

3$\frac{1}{2}$"

11$\frac{1}{4}$"

$\frac{1}{2}$" $\varnothing \frac{5}{16}$"

1"-Square
Tube Steel

1" x 2"
Tube Steel

3'-3$\frac{1}{2}$"

$\varnothing \frac{1}{2}$"

3$\frac{1}{2}$"

11$\frac{1}{2}$"   9"

1$\frac{1}{4}$"-Square Tube Steel
(spacer for stringer)

Side View   Rear View
Stable Baluster

FIGURE 4: BALUSTERS

The railings are connected to the balusters with $\frac{1}{4}$" hardware, but the balusters are connected to the top stringers with $\frac{3}{8}$" hardware. Using nylon lock nuts to lock down the stairs after installation minimizes noise.

AN ALTERNATE TREAD DESIGN

The original staircase uses stressed-skin treads but we've found success with a simpler tread design – frames of $\frac{1}{8}$" x 2" x 2" angle iron topped with $\frac{3}{4}$" plywood. The solid metal frames last longer, can handle the extra stress caused by the Flexi-Pitch Handrails, and more effectively resist the twisting that occurs if the staircase is lifted unevenly. After several productions, this tread design is holding up well, and with the Flexi-Pitch Handrails, the stairs can be installed and safely walked on in a matter of minutes.

A principal design feature of Michigan Tech's 2009 production of Ionesco's *The Lesson* and *The Bald Soprano* was a surround of thin translucent walls that "seemed to melt into the stage." In exploring cost-effective ways to achieve the desired objective, we discovered that fiberglass resin can be applied to a wide range of fabrics to produce self-supporting though non-weight-bearing structures. Figure 1, for instance, shows the walls we built out of ordinary scenic muslin.

FIGURE 1: *THE LESSON* REHEARSAL PHOTO

These walls were made by draping successive layers of muslin over a lumber-and-chicken-wire armature, coating each layer with a generous amount of resin, and letting it cure before adding the next layer. Deep contours in the fabric gave many areas of the surface the rigidity necessary to be self-supporting, but in some areas we deliberately included sections of chicken wire in the layer. As illustrated above, the finished four-layer walls could be made either opaque or translucent through the placement of lighting instruments.

CONSTRUCTION SEQUENCE AND NOTES

Since it was not to be part of the finished product, we built our armature out of scraps of 2x4 and irregularly sized and shaped pieces of chicken wire. Except where we wanted to include chicken wire in the finished product, we covered the completed armature with plastic sheeting to keep it from sticking to the muslin. We then draped the armature with pieces of muslin cut as necessary to follow the contours, safety-pinning the fabric to the armature wherever necessary.

We then mixed the 2-part fiberglass epoxy resin and brushed it onto the muslin with disposable glue brushes until the fabric was completely saturated. We allowed the resin to cure overnight before adding the next layer of muslin, and we applied 4 layers of fabric in most areas.

After the last layer had cured, we cut the armature away from the inside. The areas we had not covered with plastic sheeting stuck to the fabric as we had intended. We strengthened those areas by adding a layer of fabric and resin to the inside. Since the resin is designed to shed water, we primed the finished walls with a base coat of oil-based paint.

NOTES

- Muslin-based fauxberglass – and presumably others – is brittle and more prone to breaking than is fiberglass. It has limited structural strength and cannot be treated as weight-bearing.

- The frequency and depth of the surface contours has a significant impact on any fauxberglass structure: the more numerous and deeper the contours are, the stiffer the structure will be.

- In our experience, one gallon of resin covered approximately 32 sq. ft. of muslin. Big box store prices for the resin ranged from $25.00 to $75.00 per gallon, so it pays to shop around.

HEALTH AND SAFETY

Not all fiberglass resin epoxies are created equal. The vapors of 3M's Bondo resin, for instance, are flammable, while the MSDS for Elmer's fiberglass resin claims that the product presents only a "slight fire hazard" and is essentially "not flammable".

Despite the manufacturers' assurances that "adequate ventilation" will suffice, users should wear respirators – if only for comfort and peace of mind. Both products' MSDSs admit skin and eye irritation as possibilities and recommend that users wear splash-resistant safety goggles and PVA gloves.

Organizing a drawing assembly for a show can be challenging. To avoid element overlap and provide the most accurate groundplan possible, the Technical Director needs to follow a procedure that saves time while producing entirely reliable results. One such procedure is the use of custom and pre-loaded buttons along with the x-reference function provided in AutoCAD.

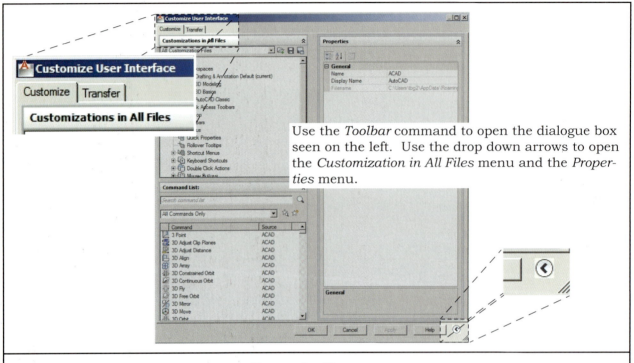

Use the *Toolbar* command to open the dialogue box seen on the left. Use the drop down arrows to open the *Customization in All Files* menu and the *Properties* menu.

FIGURE 1: TOOLBAR

Search for *Copy with Base Point*. Right click and duplicate the *Copy with Base Point* command. Click on the duplicated command icon and make the following modifcations:

Name: Copy with Base Point 0,0,0
Macro: ^C^C_copybase;0,0,0

Right click the *Toolbars* icon under the *Customization in All Files* drop-down menu and create a new toolbar. Drag the commands *Copy with Base Point 0,0,0* and *Paste to Original Coordinates* into your new toolbar. Hit *OK*. A new toolbar will appear on your screen with your two new commands.

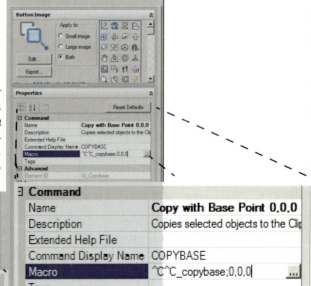

FIGURE 2: COPY WITH BASE 0,0,0

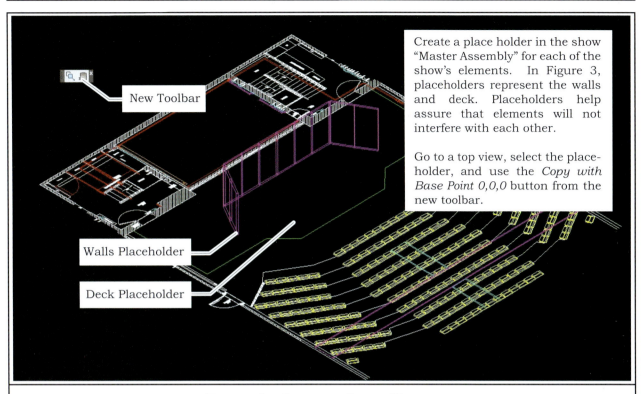

Create a place holder in the show "Master Assembly" for each of the show's elements. In Figure 3, placeholders represent the walls and deck. Placeholders help assure that elements will not interfere with each other.

Go to a top view, select the place-holder, and use the *Copy with Base Point 0,0,0* button from the new toolbar.

New Toolbar

Walls Placeholder

Deck Placeholder

FIGURE 3: CREATE A SPACE HOLDER

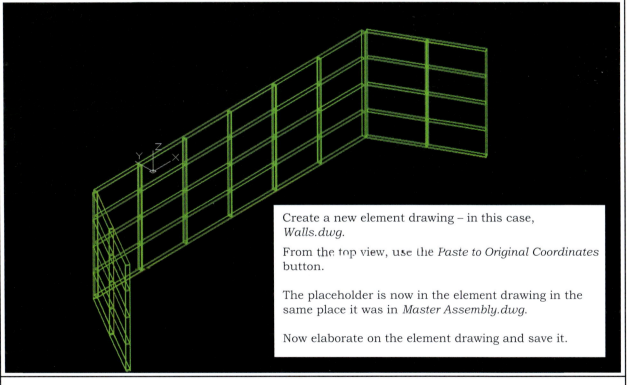

Create a new element drawing – in this case, *Walls.dwg.*

From the top view, use the *Paste to Original Coordinates* button.

The placeholder is now in the element drawing in the same place it was in *Master Assembly.dwg.*

Now elaborate on the element drawing and save it.

FIGURE 4: CREATE AN ELEMENT DRAWING

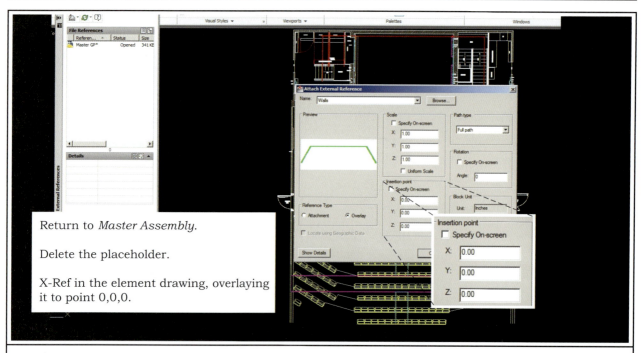

Return to *Master Assembly*.

Delete the placeholder.

X-Ref in the element drawing, overlaying it to point 0,0,0.

FIGURE 5: X-REF THE ELEMENT DRAWING

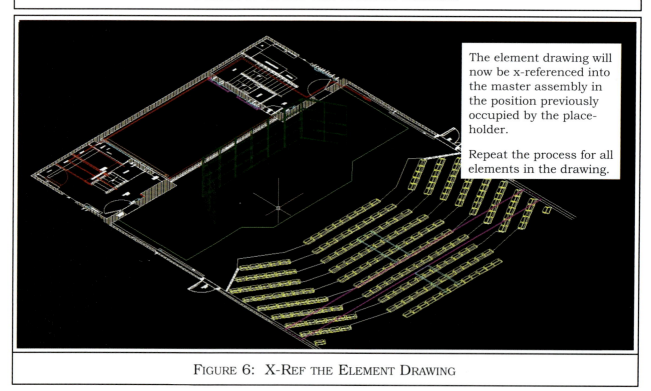

The element drawing will now be x-referenced into the master assembly in the position previously occupied by the place-holder.

Repeat the process for all elements in the drawing.

FIGURE 6: X-REF THE ELEMENT DRAWING

In classical architecture, the shafts of columns may exhibit a slight swelling called entasis. The amount of entasis, as well as the location of the points along the shaft at which it begins and ends, are subject to controversy. There is, however, an easy way to achieve the entasis a designer specifies. The scenic design for TriArts Sharon Playhouse's 2009 production of *A Funny Thing Happened on the Way to the Forum* required several columns with this trait, two of which are shown in Figure 1, and we had no trouble generating the desired look with Sonotube® and dutchman.

These roughly 6'-tall columns were not carrying much weight, and the Sonotube® provided both the needed structure and look. Where the Sonotube® joined the capital and base we cut vertical slits about 18" long into the top and bottom, and then overlapped the edges of the slits, reducing the diameter by about $\frac{1}{2}$". To complete the columns, we sleeved the tapered Sonotube® shafts into decorative capital and base pieces, which we had purchased online.

The exposed portions of the slits were finished with dutchman strips and rotated to face upstage, out of view of the audience. For structural columns, an appropriately sized piece of lumber can be concealed within the hollow assembly.

FIGURE 1: PRODUCTION PHOTO OF *A FUNNY THING HAPPENED ON THE WAY TO THE FORUM* SHOWING CLASSICAL COLUMNS

TECHNICAL BRIEF

Scenery Decks

Doors on Rakes: Avoiding Gaps and Wedging — *Nathan Tomsheck*

The Flip Floor: A Two-Sided Deck Surface — *Bradley Powers*

A Tracking System for Triscuit Decks — *Gregg Carlson*

An Interchangeable Lift-Lid System — *David Calica*

A Low-Profile Sprung Floor — *Erich Bolton*

Two Methods for Planking Floors Quickly — *James Zwicky*

A Sandwich-Style Flip Floor — *Don Harvey*

Comparing Four Standard Stock Platforms: Part I – Weight, Cost, and Strength — *Sean Culligan*

Comparing Four Standard Stock Platforms: Part II – Structural Calculations — *Sean Culligan*

A Simple and Durable Touring Deck — *Joe Stoltman*

A Fast and Inexpensive Grooved Floor — *Hannah Shafran*

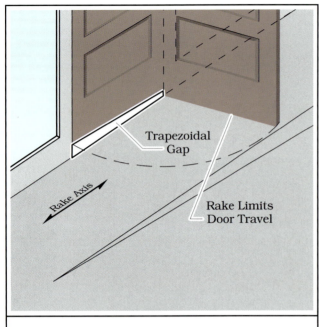

FIGURE 1: DOOR AND RAKE INTERACTION

The door and raked deck in Figure 1 illustrate a problem we've all faced. When the door closes, a triangular or trapezoidal gap appears at the bottom; and the door can only open so far before wedging against the rake. If the door were hinged on its downstage stile, a seemingly quick solution might be to cut the bottom of the door parallel with the rake. This would fix the problem while the door is closed, but then a gap would appear when the door opened.

Moreover, Figure 1 represents only one version of the problem. In addition to the degree of rake, factors such as whether a door is right-handed or left-handed, whether it opens in or out, and whether its casing is parallel to the rake or at an angle to it define the specifics of each case. But combining a rectangular door and a raked floor always produces an unsightly gap and/or the likelihood of wedging. The floating bottom rail shown in Figures 2 and 3 can help solve the problem in almost all cases.

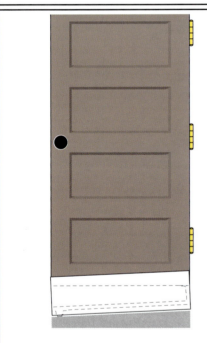

Closed, with the door parallel to the rake axis, the floating rail pivots downward, eliminating the gap.

Opened to the expected full-open position (perpendicular to the rake axis), the floating rail pivots upward, preventing wedging.

In fact, the design of this floating rail would allow the door to open a full 180° without wedging.

FIGURE 2: A FLOATING RAIL IN ACTION

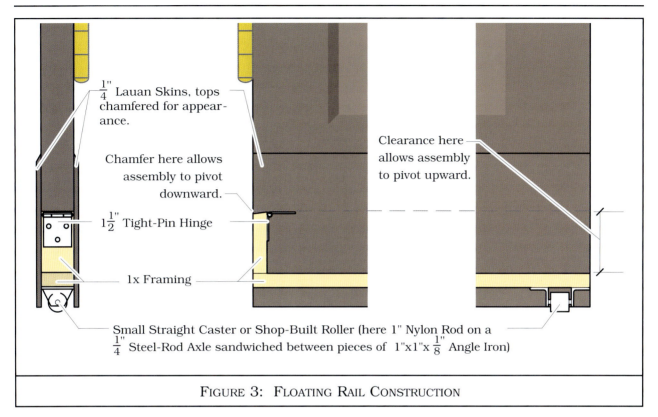

FIGURE 3: FLOATING RAIL CONSTRUCTION

NOTES

The design of a floating rail should take into account the treatment of the door's façade. There's little problem maintaining the clean look of a solid-face door: with a good paint job, the chamfered lip at the top of the lauan skins all but disappears under stage light. But paneled and other types of doors are somewhat more problematic because, except in one position, the lines of a floating rail will be at angles with such doors' other principal lines. Thus, the rail's design should complement the look of a door as it will be seen most clearly by the greatest number of people in the audience.

The door shown in Figures 1 and 2, for instance, hinges on its upstage stile and opens onstage. As illustrated in Figure 3, the lauan skins for that door's floating rail are rectangular and just as wide as the door. Most of the audience will not notice that when the door closes and its rail floats downward, the vertical lines of the door will still be plumb, but those of the floating rail will not; and even those who might notice would be less distracted by the mismatch than they would have been by a gap. Finally, the technical designer should remember that two corners of the rail's skins will protrude beyond the edges of the door, perhaps requiring a bit more than the normally provided casing clearance.

The pair of large doors for the Yale School of Drama's 2002 production of *Alcestis,* offered an interesting twist on the problem: the deck was flat, and the doors played tilted forward about 5° – the equivalent of a 1:12 rake.   The doors played closed most of the time, and the lauan skins of the floating rails we gave them mimicked the lines of the closed doors. The audience seemed not to notice that, when the doors opened, those apparently solid rails floated upward and that there exposed downstage edges were not solid framing but empty voids.

❧❧❧

The University of Cincinnati's "Hot Summer Nights" summer season consisted of three musicals in rotating repertory. The theatre's proscenium-thrust architecture and the rake of the house make the stage floor a very prominent part of any design, and the set designer naturally wanted each of the three shows to have a different floor. Changing over a finished floor of individual $\frac{1}{4}$"-thick 4x8s was judged to be too time consuming for quick turnarounds, especially since making thin sheets lie flat often takes a lot of fasteners.

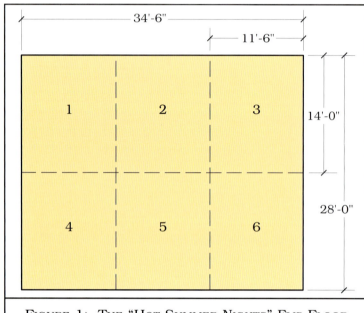

FIGURE 1: THE "HOT SUMMER NIGHTS" FLIP FLOOR

THE FLIP-FLOOR SOLUTION

The solution we devised involved laminating two layers of $\frac{1}{8}$" lauan into a $\frac{1}{4}$" layup that we cut into six lightweight and portable panels measuring 11'-6" x 14'-0" as shown in Figure 1. With this approach, the entire playing space was covered by six panels rather than by 30-plus individual sheets.

We painted one production's floor directly on the stage deck and the other two on either side of the flip-floor panels. At changeover, handling the floor took only three people: one to foot and two to lift each panel, We added a fourth person and a cart when the flip floor needed to be stored to reveal the third floor painted on the stage deck.

PLANNING THE FLIP-FLOOR

To minimize changeover time, we decided to make these productions' panels as large as practicable. We estimated that these particular sections would weigh approximately 125 lbs. each, and, having previously built and used a number of flip floors, we judged that anything larger would be too flimsy and heavy – and, therefore, hard to handle.

Experience had also taught us the importance of wise joint design and grain orientation. Within each layer, we offset the sheets as shown in Figure 2 to leave as few continuous straight-line joints as possible. We also laid the sheets in the two layers at 45° to each other, having learned that sheets laid perpendicular to each other will snap across the grain after only a few weeks of handling. These choices are very important to the longevity of the pieces.

Finally, having used both water-based and alcohol-based contact adhesives in previous flip floors, we had learned that the water-based adhesives leave the sections more flexible. Using alcohol-based adhesives may have other advantages, but since these floors would changeover so many times, we used the water-based contact adhesive.

FABRICATING THE FLIP-FLOOR

Figure 2 illustrates our method for building flip floors. For any laminating process, it is important that the workspace floor be flat (and, preferably, "nail-able") to avoid creating waves in the finished product. Starting with the bottom layer, we lay out enough lauan (good side down) to cover an area

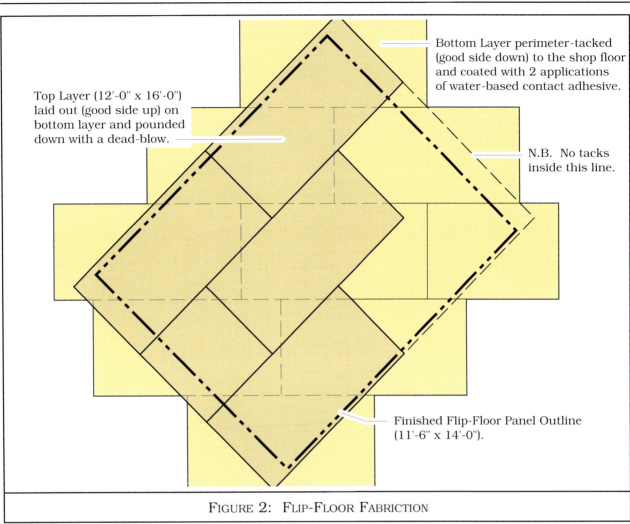

Top Layer (12'-0" x 16'-0") laid out (good side up) on bottom layer and pounded down with a dead-blow.

Bottom Layer perimeter-tacked (good side down) to the shop floor and coated with 2 applications of water-based contact adhesive.

N.B. No tacks inside this line.

Finished Flip-Floor Panel Outline (11'-6" x 14'-0").

FIGURE 2: FLIP-FLOOR FABRICTION

larger than a finished panel. After tacking the outside perimeter down and chalking layout lines for the top layer, we apply two coats of contact adhesive to the layout to assure a good bond.

After the contact adhesive has dried, two people carefully lay out the top layer of lauan within the chalk lines. We take care to minimize gaps between the sheets, because once the pieces touched each other they are stuck for good (or bad). After the top layer has been laid out, we pound the entire surface with a 12" square piece of $\frac{3}{4}$" plywood and a $2\frac{1}{2}$"-pound dead-blow to help ensure a good bond between the layers.

Next, we rough-cut each layup 4" to 6" larger than the final panel size. To cut the panels to their final size, we use a method commonly used in wallpapering: overlapping adjacent panels and then cutting through them at the same time with a utility knife. After we had used this method to join the upstage panels (1, 2, and 3) and the downstage panels (4, 5, and 6) for this production, we overlapped the edges of the upstage and downstage panels and cut the mid-stage seam in one shot.

THE DOS AND DON'TS

This floor works extremely well on an already skinned stage. The design of the layup helps the panels remain very flat, unlike plain sheets of $\frac{1}{4}$" lauan. Like dance floor, a laminated flip-floor tends to hug the floor and is actually a bit difficult to pull up. In fact, this floor stayed down, flat, and smooth with only 1 fastener per corner. On a non-skinned stage, however, a flip floor like this would not work so well. The unevenness inherent in non-skinned stages could cause the seams in a flip floor to lift, creating trip hazards and damaging panel edges. The likeliest solution to this problem – using many more fasteners – would dramatically increase the changeover time.

Flip-floor panels store easily without taking up much depth. We carefully stood ours on edge against the back wall during the season with very little damage to the edges. Tying them to the wall is important to assure safety. Obviously, flip-floor panels can be stored and, if necessary, resized for future use.

Building a flip-floor is a time consuming process, but it can have a great payoff with extended runs. It even helps hide the dreaded seams that designers always see in a floor. Finding the most appropriate sizes and shapes for particular flip-floor panels may take some trial and error, but you'll find this is a quick and lightweight way to changeover flooring.

❧❦❧❦

San Jose Repertory Theatre has developed a tracking system for incorporation in triscuit decks. The system comprises two modified triscuits called the Track Triscuit and Return Triscuit, which have the standard $2\frac{3}{8}$" thickness and nominal 4'x4' footprint of the basic wood-framed triscuit, described in "The Triscuit-Studwall Deck System" in Volume 2 of *Technical Design Solutions for Theatre*. Made of the same materials as those used in the basic triscuit, these modifications differ only in the details of framing and top skin construction.

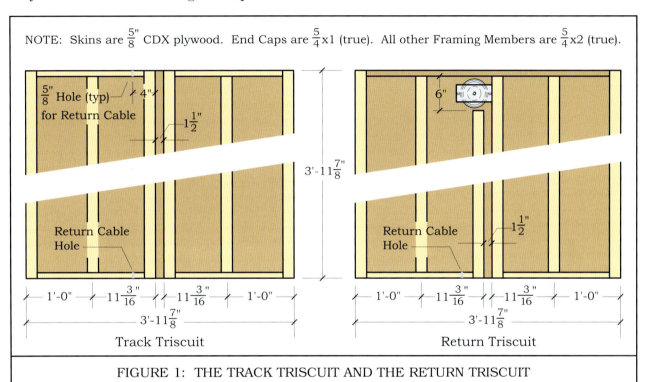

NOTE: Skins are $\frac{5}{8}$" CDX plywood. End Caps are $\frac{5}{4}$x1 (true). All other Framing Members are $\frac{5}{4}$x2 (true).

Track Triscuit   Return Triscuit

FIGURE 1: THE TRACK TRISCUIT AND THE RETURN TRISCUIT

THE TRISCUITS

In place of a single, integral frame, these triscuits essentially have reverse-and-repeat "half frames" separated by a $1\frac{1}{2}$" gap and drilled for return cable as shown in Figure 1. The framing at the return-sheave end of the Return Triscuit (at the right) differs from that of the Track Triscuit in two ways: the half frames are joined by a single end cap, and the inside stile of one of the half frames is cut 6" short to accommodate the return sheave assembly.

Both triscuits' bottom skins – 1'-11$\frac{7}{8}$" x 1'-11$\frac{7}{8}$" squares of $\frac{5}{8}$" CDX plywood – are glued and stapled to the framing as in standard triscuit construction. The top skins (both triscuits) are cut into three panels. The outer panels are glued and stapled in place, but the 11$\frac{11}{16}$" middle panel is drywall screwed into place to allow access to the sheave and cable. Details of the top skin widths are shown in Figure 2.

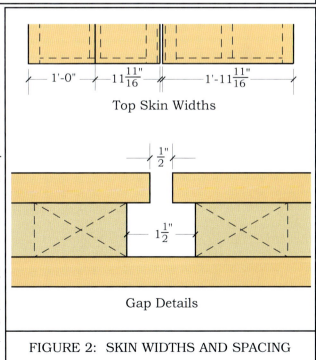

Top Skin Widths

Gap Details

FIGURE 2: SKIN WIDTHS AND SPACING

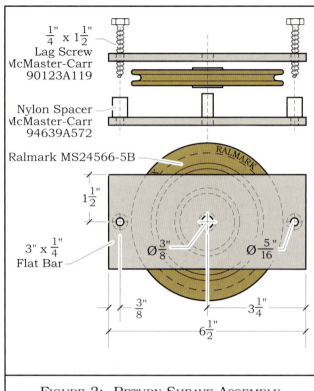

FIGURE 3: RETURN SHEAVE ASSEMBLY

THE RETURN SHEAVE ASSEMBLY

Construction of the return sheave assembly is illustrated in Figure 3. The sheave axle consists of a 1" length of $\frac{3}{8}$" round bar, plug welded into the center hole on the bottom plate. Nylon spacers $\frac{5}{8}$" tall keep the plates from pinching the sheave and act as cable keepers. At installation, the bottom plate is positioned on the triscuit's bottom skin, the sheave and spacers are put in place, the top plate is slid down over the sheave axle, and the assembly is attached to the bottom skin by $\frac{1}{4}$" x $1\frac{1}{2}$" lag screws. Note: clearance for the lag screw heads must be mortised into the underside of the return triscuit's top panels.

THE DRIVE DOG

The drive dog is detailed in Figure 4. Note that the three pieces of flat bar are welded together maintaining a $1\frac{9}{16}$"-wide knife gap before the $\frac{5}{16}$" holes for attaching the UHMW are drilled. After those holes have been drilled, each already chamfered and mortised piece of UHMW is clamped to the assembly and drilled.

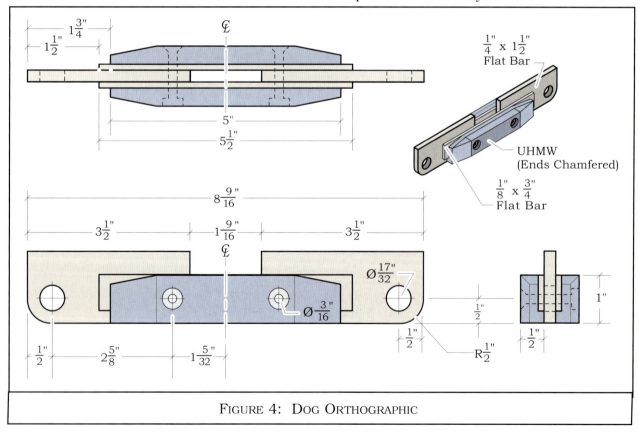

FIGURE 4: DOG ORTHOGRAPHIC

NEXT TIME...

Narrowing the track and return triscuits to allow more flexibility in track placement seems a logical next step. Rotating the sheave plate 90° would permit spacing a pair of 2"-wide stringers only $5\frac{3}{4}$" apart and would result in a $9\frac{3}{4}$"-wide system as shown in Figure 5. The narrow tracks could be placed as close as $5\frac{1}{2}$" apart center to center if the system's components were built reverse and repeat.

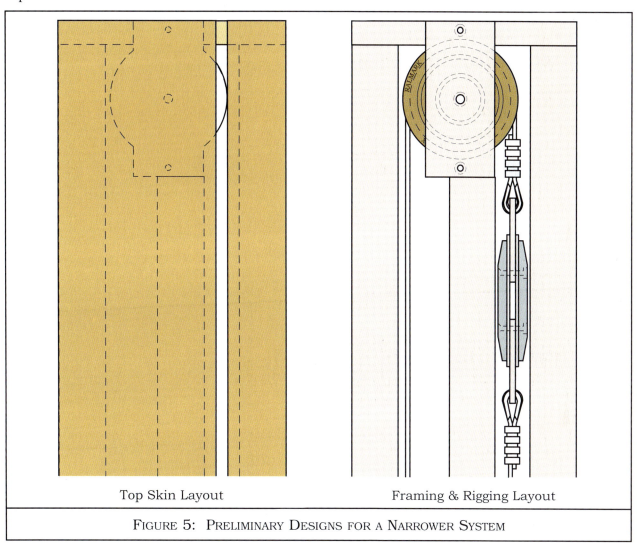

Top Skin Layout   Framing & Rigging Layout

FIGURE 5: PRELIMINARY DESIGNS FOR A NARROWER SYSTEM

To present a variety of locations, Yale Repertory Theatre's 2004 production of *The Intelligent Design of Jenny Chow* required a lift with interchangable lids. The lift lids needed to be able to be changed quickly and quietly. Our solution was the lift bed and storage cart system described here.

LIFT LIDS AND DOGS

The lift lids were 2x4 flat frames covered with plywood. The center cross member in each was off-set to allow a pair of UHMW dogs to track on center (see Figure 1). A notch at the back of each lid contained an eye lag used to pull the lids from the lift bed onto the storage carts with a pull stick. (See Chuck Adomanis' "A Quiet Glide and Unistrut Traveler System" in *Technical Design Solutions for Theatre, Volume 2*, pages 92–93 for lift-lid dog construction details).

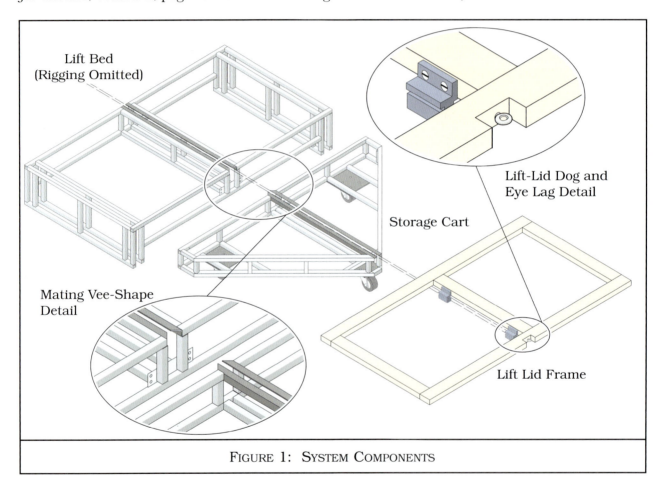

Lift Bed (Rigging Omitted)

Lift-Lid Dog and Eye Lag Detail

Storage Cart

Mating Vee-Shape Detail

Lift Lid Frame

FIGURE 1: SYSTEM COMPONENTS

STORAGE CARTS AND LIFT BED

Both the lift bed and the castered storage carts were made from 1"-square tube steel. As shown in Figure 1, an angle-iron guide track was built into the center of the lift bed and each of the storage carts. The ends of the angle iron track on the lift bed and on the storage carts were cut in mating Vee shapes, allowing the lift bed and the storage carts to self-align when pushed into place. In changing one lid for another, a stagehand aligned the storage cart, footed the back center wheel, and used a pull stick to move the lid straight and evenly onto the storage carts.

More and more theater productions are requiring a floor that can absorb the actions of the performers above. A sprung floor absorbs some amount of the shock caused by jumping or other physical movements. While there currently are a number of commercial solutions, this article presents a method for an inexpensive, build-it-yourself, low-profile sprung floor.

CONSTRUCTION

As seen in Figure 1, this sprung floor consists of rubber $\frac{1}{2}$" x 2"x 2" EFS Springpads® glued to the backs of sheets of $\frac{1}{2}$" CDX plywood that make up the bottom layer of the floor. The floor's top layer is made of sheets of $\frac{1}{2}$" AC plywood installed perpendicular to the lower layer of plywood and with its seams offset by 2' from those in the bottom layer. The construction sequence is simple.

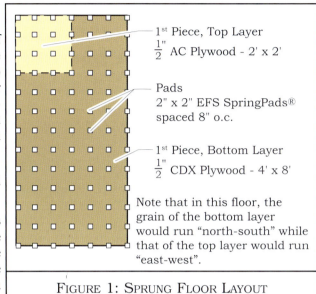

1st Piece, Top Layer
$\frac{1}{2}$" AC Plywood - 2' x 2'

Pads
2" x 2" EFS SpringPads®
spaced 8" o.c.

1st Piece, Bottom Layer
$\frac{1}{2}$" CDX Plywood - 4' x 8'

Note that in this floor, the grain of the bottom layer would run "north-south" while that of the top layer would run "east-west".

FIGURE 1: SPRUNG FLOOR LAYOUT

1. Using a chalk-line, mark out an 8" x 8" grid on the backs of the $\frac{1}{2}$" CDX plywood.

2. Using a flexible glue, attach the rubber pads to the plywood at the intersections of the grid. Figure 1 shows the arrangement of the pads on the 1st sheet to be laid. On the edges next to walls, the pads are set flush with the plywood, but the pads overhang the other two edges. Except along the walls, successive sheets will have overhanging pads on two edges and no pads on the other two. This design allows adjacent plywood sheets to share pads at the edges. EFS recommends doubling up pads at doorways and other "high traffic" areas.

3. During installation, maintain a $\frac{1}{16}$" expansion gap between adjacent sheets. The sheets in the bottom layer are fastened neither to the floor nor to each other, so you may find it helpful to use disposable spacers used in ceramic tile installation to help keep the sheets from shifting out of position before or as the top layer is installed.

4. In installing the top layer, start with a 2' x 2' square of $\frac{1}{2}$" AC plywood, its grain running perpendicular to the grain of the bottom layer. In laying the rest of the top layer, offset the seams from those in the bottom layer as shown in Figure 1. Countersink 1" screws every 18" around the edge of each plywood sheet and every 24" internally throughout the sheet. Be sure to leave a $\frac{1}{16}$" gap for expansion in the top layer as well.

¿▲¿▲¿▲

Covering a deck with planks during load-in is always time-consuming so the production teams for two shows in the Yale Repertory Theatre's 2008–2009 season developed jig-based approaches to build two types of planked floors. Tom Stoppard's *Rough Crossing* called for a floor of planks all of the same width but of various lengths ("Type I" in Figure 1). The floor planks for *Death of a Salesman* were all the same length but of various widths ("Type II" in Figure 1). Both types consisted of planked panels which used 4x8 sheets of $\frac{1}{2}$" plywood as substrates for $\frac{1}{4}$" MDF planks. Both types save load-in time because, once the panels have been finish-nailed to the stage floor, it takes little time to apply finishing touches.

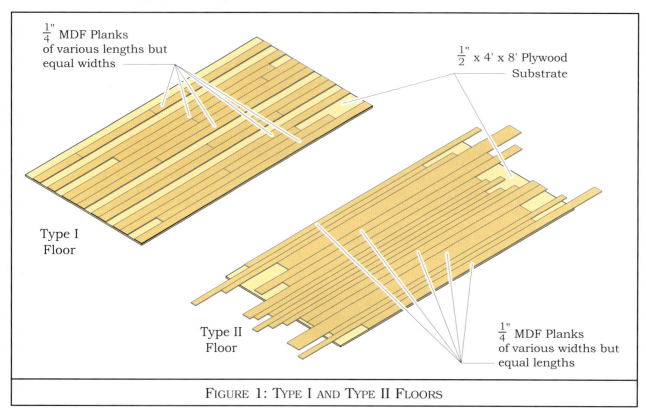

$\frac{1}{4}$" MDF Planks of various lengths but equal widths

$\frac{1}{2}$" x 4' x 8' Plywood Substrate

Type I Floor

Type II Floor

$\frac{1}{4}$" MDF Planks of various widths but equal lengths

FIGURE 1: TYPE I AND TYPE II FLOORS

BUILDING THE TYPE I JIG

Refer to Figure 2. To make a Type I jig, lay out the pattern of planks perpendicular to the long side of a 4'-0" x 6'-0" piece of $\frac{1}{4}$" MDF (the plank guide). Next, after cutting out the MDF plank guide, flip it over and glue and staple $\frac{1}{2}$" plywood guide strips to the bottom to form the Substrate Guide Edges. Make sure to align these strips flush with the inner edge of the jig so that a sheet of $\frac{1}{2}$" plywood fits between them snugly. Leave a 1"-wide release gap between the strips of plywood at the back of the jig to aid in removing completed panels. Flip the now completed jig back over and screw it to a table along its edges. Place another table perpendicular to the first to support the substrate while you work.

BUILDING AND INSTALLING THE FLOOR

Cut enough $\frac{1}{4}$" MDF planks to cover the entire floor. Set half of them aside and cut the others into 2 or 3 lengths, keeping the cut-off for later use. Slide a sheet of $\frac{1}{2}$" plywood substrate into the jig. Glue and staple planks of various lengths to the substrate following the pattern set by the plank guide. Brush or roll glue onto the back of the planks to ensure that the floor will not squeak. Rout off any

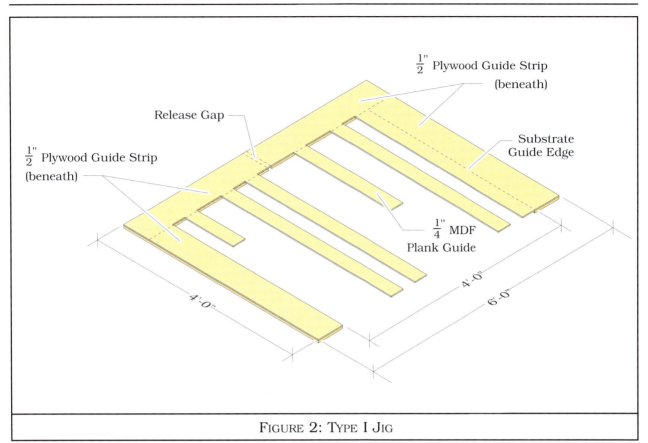

$\frac{1}{2}$" Plywood Guide Strip (beneath)

Release Gap

$\frac{1}{2}$" Plywood Guide Strip (beneath)

Substrate Guide Edge

$\frac{1}{4}$" MDF Plank Guide

4'-0"

4'-0"

6'-0"

FIGURE 2: TYPE I JIG

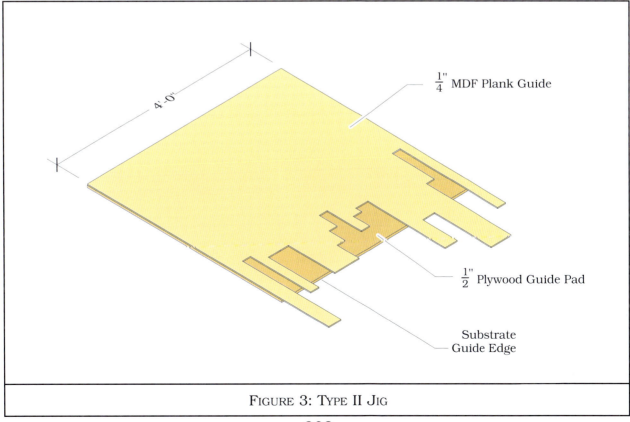

4'-0"

$\frac{1}{4}$" MDF Plank Guide

$\frac{1}{2}$" Plywood Guide Pad

Substrate Guide Edge

FIGURE 3: TYPE II JIG

through the release gap to remove it. Let the sheets dry at least overnight before load-in. At load-in, lay the panels out and finish-nail them to the deck through the voids in the planking. Fill the voids with planks custom-cut from the saved cut-offs and the remaining full length planks. Glue the custom planks thoroughly and staple them to the substrate as before.

BUILDING THE TYPE II JIG

Refer to Figure 3. Like the other jig, the Type II Jig has a $\frac{1}{4}$" MDF plank guide. Instead of using $\frac{1}{2}$" plywood guide strips, however, it uses a 4'-wide guide pad made of $\frac{1}{2}$" plywood. Note that, as shown in Figure 3, the plank guide extends beyond the guide pad at various points in the jig. Cut the guide pad and the plank guide and staple and glue them together.

BUILDING AND LAYING THE FLOOR

In this type of floor, all planks should be 8' long. Each projection in the Type II plank guide represents the width of a plank or group of planks. Consequently, an exact number of planks of the correct size must be used to fill each void. To build the floor, screw the jig to one end of a shop table with the projections facing the other end. Snug a second table up to the end of the first one, and lay a $\frac{1}{2}$" plywood substrate sheet on it, butting the 4' end of the substrate to the pad of the jig. Lay out the planks as indicated by the plank guide, and glue and staple the planks to the substrate. Pull the finished panel out of the jig and let it dry. Be careful not to break the planks that extend past the end of the substrate. At load-in, as with Type I, lay the panels onto the stage floor and finish-nail them down. Take pains to glue the overhanging MDF planks to the substrate of the adjacent panel.

MATERIAL CHOICE AND CONSTRUCTION TIPS

The materials discussed above were chosen for convenience only, for planked-floor panels can be made from various types and thicknesses of sheet goods. Our first Type I floor was built with a $\frac{1}{4}$" plywood substrate and $\frac{1}{4}$" lauan planking; and our first Type II floor, with a $\frac{1}{2}$" CDX substrate and $\frac{1}{4}$" lauan planking. Lauan works well as a planking material, as it is used for cabinet making and already has a wood-grain finish. If durability is a concern, $\frac{1}{2}$" lauan can be substituted for $\frac{1}{4}$" lauan. If wood grain is not required, $\frac{1}{4}$" or thicker MDF would be a good material choice.

Building and loading in a floor takes large amounts of glue and staples. Rolling the glue onto the planks is the easiest method, but painting the glue onto the substrate can work as long as care is taken to ensure that the jig isn't glued to the deck section. If $\frac{1}{4}$" lauan is used, using pneumatically driven $\frac{1}{2}$" fabric staples is an effective way to attach the planks. You can take a marker and color the top of the staples to darken them so that they don't show up as easily. The glue is the real means of attachment, but many staples are required to hold the planks until the glue dries.

≈⋆⋆⋆≈

In its annual Carlotta Festival, Yale School of Drama presents three plays in rotating rep, virtually guaranteeing students an opportunity to explore alternative technical designs for rep. The double-faced floor for the 2010 Festival easily met the basic repertory objectives involving weight and ease of installation. But beyond that, it was an exceptionally "clean" design. It was connected to the stage only at its perimeter and both of its surfaces were completely unmarred by screws, brads or any other fasteners. Because of its construction it was also impressively flat throughout its expanse. Figure 1 shows a photo of the floor laid out and partially loaded in.

FIGURE 1: THE FLIP FLOOR AT LOAD-IN

The 20' x 28' floor consisted of 21 laminated panels – fourteen 4x8s and seven 4x4s – that played directly on the stage floor. The 1"-thick laminates included top and bottom skins of $\frac{1}{4}$" MDF glued to 46" x 94" sheets of $\frac{1}{2}$" blue foam with Wilsonart H2O®. The 1" on all sides of each panel left room for lumber splines that aligned the panels and kept them locked together.

As can be seen in Figure 2, a $\frac{1}{2}$" x 1" x 1" lumber corner block glued into the corners of the panels protected the MDF skins from damage during handling. Each 4x8 panel weighed about 65 lbs. The splines consisted of reasonably clear lengths of 1x stock cut to $\frac{1}{2}$" x 1$\frac{3}{4}$" so that they would fit comfortably in the channels between adjacent panels. All spline edges were generously rounded over to ease assembly and the splines were glued into the panels as shown in Figure 3.

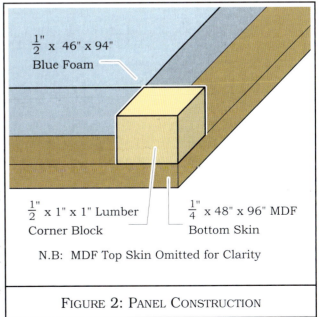

$\frac{1}{2}$" x 46" x 94" Blue Foam

$\frac{1}{2}$" x 1" x 1" Lumber Corner Block

$\frac{1}{4}$" x 48" x 96" MDF Bottom Skin

N.B: MDF Top Skin Omitted for Clarity

FIGURE 2: PANEL CONSTRUCTION

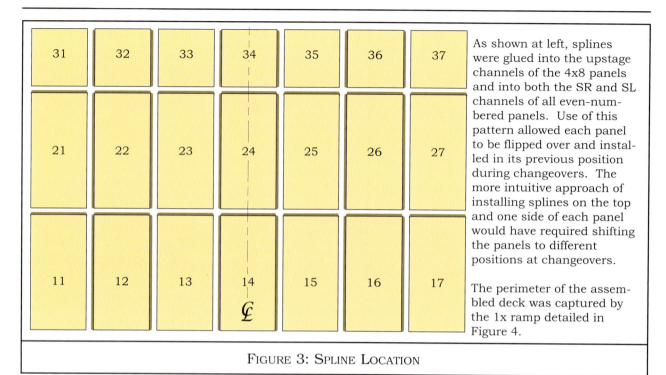

31	32	33	34	35	36	37
21	22	23	24	25	26	27
11	12	13	14	15	16	17

As shown at left, splines were glued into the upstage channels of the 4x8 panels and into both the SR and SL channels of all even-numbered panels. Use of this pattern allowed each panel to be flipped over and installed in its previous position during changeovers. The more intuitive approach of installing splines on the top and one side of each panel would have required shifting the panels to different positions at changeovers.

The perimeter of the assembled deck was captured by the 1x ramp detailed in Figure 4.

FIGURE 3: SPLINE LOCATION

A narrow perimeter ramp cut from $\frac{5}{4}$ lumber ripped to the deck thickness surrounded the assembled floor. In addition to allowing set pieces to roll on and off, it held the panels together and provided the only connection to the stage. The ramp is shown in Figure 4.

CLOSING NOTES

The most difficult aspect of changeover consisted of laying the first row of panels out exactly in position, the splines proving too resilient to provide the backup needed for tapping the panels into place. That need was met by screwing short lengths of angle iron to the stage at the end of each seam. Once all the panels had been laid and tapped firmly into position, the angle iron was pulled up and replaced by the ramp.

For another version, see Bradley Powers' "The Flip Floor: A Two-Sided Deck Surface", pages 194–196.

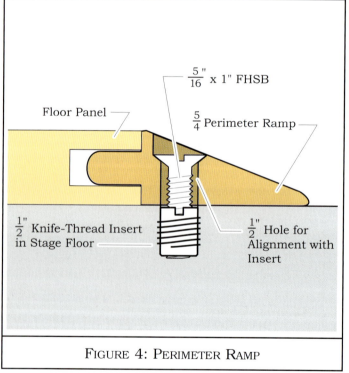

Floor Panel

$\frac{5}{16}$ " x 1" FHSB

$\frac{5}{4}$ Perimeter Ramp

$\frac{1}{2}$" Knife-Thread Insert in Stage Floor

$\frac{1}{2}$" Hole for Alignment with Insert

FIGURE 4: PERIMETER RAMP

Each type of platform has its partisans. Some people stand by 2x4 construction for its low cost and open frame. Others prefer 1x6 construction, which is lighter and uses better quality wood. Then there are the stressed-skin proponents, who prize strength and ease of handling. This article compares 4 standard types of wood platforms in 3 areas: handling weight, cost, and strength. The subsequent article details the calculations behind the comparison.

THE FOUR PLATFORM TYPES COMPARED

1. 2x4 – 2x4 Number 2 SPF (Spruce-Pine-Fir) framing on edge, $\frac{3}{4}$" lid of plywood, MDF, OSB, etc. Two toggles spaced on 32" centers in the 4' orientation.

2. 1x6 – 1x6 Select SPF framing on-edge ripped to $5\frac{1}{4}$" for a total unit height of 6", $\frac{3}{4}$" lid of plywood, MDF, OSB, etc. Three toggles on 24" centers in the 4' orientation. Note that in calculating the bending, shear, and deflection capabilities, the width of the 1x6 is set at $4\frac{1}{2}$" to account for the notching required for the coffin locks: 2 on the 8' side and 1 on the 4' side spaced 2'-0" on center from the corners..

3. 4x8 Slotted Stressed-Skin – $\frac{5}{4}$x4 Number 2 SPF on-face framing recessed $1\frac{3}{4}$" from all edges of $\frac{1}{2}$" AC plywood skins, 2 toggles spaced equally running the length of the unit. Units are splined together by way of the slots with $\frac{5}{4}$x4 FJP (finger-jointed-primed) lumber, as it is slightly thinner than Number 2 – easier to install and less likely to warp.

4. 4x4 Triscuit – $\frac{5}{4}$x2 Number 2 SPF web framing (with the grain) with $\frac{5}{4}$x1 end framing, $\frac{5}{8}$" CDX plywood skins, 5 on-face framing members on 12" centers running with the grain of both skins. Actual dimensions are $3'\text{-}11\frac{7}{8}$" x $3'\text{-}11\frac{7}{8}$" to allow adjustments in alignment, to get 2 pieces out of 1 sheet of plywood, and leave a gap between units to avoid rubbing and squeaking.

CONSTRUCTION OF THE TYPES COMPARED

1. Assembly – The comparison makes no requirement in the use of metal fasteners, but does assume the use of wood glue in all four platform types.

2. Material Grades – The comparison assumes the use of AC Group-1 Interior Plywood for skins. Note that both of the stressed-skin platforms have top and bottom skins. Number 2 Spruce-Pine Fir is assumed for the 2x and $\frac{5}{4}$ stock, and the 1x6 is assumed to be Select Grade.

3. Quality of Construction – There will be differences in the construction quality from one shop to another. This comparison cannot address the impact of such differences, but it does assume that all wood joints have the appropriate amount of adhesive spread over the entirety of the contact surfaces.

4. Material Weights – The weight of a given sample of lumber and plywood can be affected by a variety of factors including the species and grade of the material and atmospheric conditions. The values given here assume the weight of wood to be 35 lbs/ft^3, yielding just under 3 lbs/board-foot (144 in^3). This comparison rounds that value up to 3 lbs. per board-foot.

5. Deflection Criteria – The comparison uses $l/240$ as the basis for comparing deflection, where l is the span.

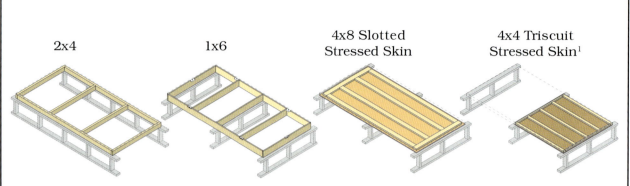

Type	2x4	1x6	4x8 Slotted Stressed-Skin	4x4 Triscuit Stressed-Skin[1]
Cut List	Plywood 1 @ $\frac{3}{4}$" x4x8 AC 2x4 2 @ 7'-9" 2 @ 4'-0" 2 @ 3'-9"	Plywood 1 @ $\frac{3}{4}$" x4x8 AC 1x6 2 @ 7'-10$\frac{1}{2}$" 2 @ 4'-0" 3 @ 3'-10$\frac{1}{2}$"	Plywood 2 @ $\frac{1}{2}$" x4x8 AC $\frac{5}{4}$x4 4 @ 7'-1$\frac{1}{2}$" 2 @ 3'-8$\frac{1}{2}$"	Plywood 2 @ $\frac{5}{8}$" x4x8 CDX $\frac{5}{4}$x2 4 @ 3'-11$\frac{7}{8}$" 6 @ 3'-9$\frac{7}{8}$" 3 @ 3'-10$\frac{1}{2}$" $\frac{5}{4}$x1 4 @ 3'-7$\frac{7}{8}$"
Cost[2]	$44.87	$94.85	$79.88	$73.80
Estimated Weight	113 lbs.	107 lbs.	134 lbs.	72 lbs.
Max Load for Bending (psf)	56.5	80.7	180.8 - 220.3	142.3 - 164.7
Max Load for Shear (psf)	41.3	47.3	279.0	155.0
Max Load, Deflection ℓ/240 (psf)	97.7	234.5	178.9	147.5

[1] *Cut List* and *Cost* reflect the quantities needed to build 32 sq feet of platforming, *i.e.*, one 2x4, 1x6, or 4x8 slotted stressed-skin platform but two 4x4 triscuits. The other values (*Estimated Weight, Bending, Shear*, and *Deflection*) are those of single units. For example, one 2x4 platform weighs 113 lbs, and one 4x4 triscuit weighs 72.7 lbs.

[2] *Cost* calculations are based on prices obtained at the same time from a single vendor.

TABLE 1: COMPARISONS

SUPPORT

All types compared are assumed to be supported on studwalls set 4'-0" apart o.c. and arranged as shown in Table 1 to present the greatest possible tributary area for loading.

THE RESULTS

Whenever cost governs the choice of one platform over another, the 2x4 will win out since, given these prices, it costs only two-thirds as much as its nearest competitor, the 4x4 triscuit. But when cost is weighed against strength a different picture emerges.

Accepted standards for residential construction assume a 40 psf live load for first floors, a 35 psf live load for upper stories, and a combined live-dead load of 50 psf. Keeping that in mind, the shaded cells in the rows labeled Max Load for Bending (psf) and Max Load for Shear (psf) highlight each platform's greatest weakness supported on 4'-0" intervals as shown in Figure 1.

The calculations show that all four platforms are weakest in resisting shear stresses. The 2x4 can withstand a shear load no greater than 41.3 psf and the 1x6 also has a low resistance to failure in shear – only 47.3 psf. It should be clear that if they are to survive as stock platforms both of these platforms should be supported at less than 4'-0" intervals. Reading across the columns, it is clear the stressed-skin platforms are far stronger in all areas than either the inexpensive 2x4 platform or the "Cadillac" 1x6 platform.

Finally, platforms don't fail in deflection, but too much deflection can make a deck feel uncomfortably live. According to the calculations, the 2x4 platform would begin to deflect noticeably and is, therefore the "livest" of the platforms compared here.

ACKNOWLEDGMENTS

The 4x8 slotted stressed-skin platform was developed in 1999 by Stephen E. Rees, Professor Emeritus, SUNY Fredonia. The 4x4 triscuit was developed collaboratively by students in Ben Sammler's Technical Design class. Analysis of the stressed-skin platform's strength was speeded by use of an Excel spreadsheet developed at the Yale School of Drama by an unnamed author. That spreadsheet, as well as the analysis of the lumber-framed platforms described here, was based on procedures outlined in Alys Holden and Bronislaw J. Sammler's *Structural Design for the Stage*, which was also the source of the lumber and plywood design values used.

RESOURCES

Holden, Alys E., and Bronislaw J. Sammler. *Structural Design for the Stage*. Woburn, MA: Focal Press, 1999.

Sammler, Bronislaw J., and Don Harvey. *Technical Design Solutions for Theatre. Vol. 2*. Woburn, MA: Focal Press, 2002.

Part I in this two-part series summarizes the relative merits of four platforms in terms of cost, weight, and strength. This article completes the comparison by documenting, step-by-step, the structural analysis of the four platforms.

For consistency, all four platforms are assumed to be supported at 4'-0" intervals. The analysis follows the procedures described in Alys Holden and Bronislaw J. Sammler's *Structural Design for the Stage*. For non-stressed-skin structures, the procedure comprises these three steps.

1. Determine the platform's ability to withstand bending stresses.
2. Determine its ability to withstand vertical shear stresses.
3. Check to confirm that deflection is within acceptable limits.

The following table presents the relevant values for the 2x4- and 1x6-framed platforms.

	2x4 #2 SPF	1x6 Select SPF
F_b	875 psi	1250 psi
F_v	70 psi	70 psi
E	1,400,000 psi	1,500,000 psi
A	5.250 in.^{2}	3.9375 in.^{2}
S_{x-x}	3.063 in.^{3}	3.445 in.^{3}
I_{x-x}	5.359 in.^{4}	9.004 in.^{4}
ℓ	48.00 in.	48.00 in.
Max Trib Area	10.67 sq. ft.	8.00 sq. ft.

Max Tributary Areas (in Yellow)

2x4 #2 SPF — 2 Toggles 1'-8" o.c. — 10.67 sq. ft.

1x6 Select SPF — 3 Toggles 2'-0" o.c. — 8.00 sq. ft.

THE 2x4-FRAMED PLATFORM'S ABILITY TO WITHSTAND BENDING

This platform's toggles face the greatest potential load. Bending analysis proceeds by (1) finding the adjusted allowable bending stress of the material, (2) finding the maximum resisting moment, and (3) calculating the allowable live load for the toggle based on bending.

1. Find the adjusted allowable bending stress of the material.

$$F'_b = C_D\, C_L\, C_F\, F_b$$

Where F_b = allowable bending stress: *875 psi*
C_D = load duration factor: *0.9*
C_L = beam stability factor: *1.0*
C_F = size factor: *1.5*
F'_b = adjusted allowable bending stress (psi)

$F'_{b'} = (.9)\,(1)\,(1.5)\,(875\ psi) = 1181.25\ psi$

2. Find the maximum resisting moment.

$$M_{resisting} = S\,F'_b$$

$M_{resisting} = (3.063\ in^3)\ (1181.25\ psi) = 3618.1688\ in.\ lbs.$

3. Find the allowable live load for the toggle based on bending.

$$, = \frac{8\, M_{max}}{l^2}$$

$$, = \frac{8\,(2412.11125\ in.\ lbs.)}{(48\ in)^2} = 12.563\ pli\ or\ 150.757\ plf$$

$$, = \frac{150.757\ plf.}{(2.67\ ft)} = 56.5\ psf\ live\ load$$

THE 2x4-FRAMED PLATFORM'S ABILITY TO WITHSTAND VERTICAL SHEAR

Shear analysis proceeds by (1) finding the adjusted allowable shear stress of the material, (2) finding the maximum vertical shear resistance, and (3) calculating the allowable live load for the toggle based on shear.

1. Find the adjusted allowable shear stress of the material.

$$F'_v = C_D\, F_v$$

where $F_v =$ allowable shear stress: 70 psi
$C_D =$ load duration factor: 0.9
$F'_v =$ adjusted allowable shear stress (psi)

$$F'_v = (.9)\,(70\ psi) = 63\ psi$$

2. Find the maximum vertical shear resistance.

$$V_{resisting} = \frac{A\, F'_v}{1.5}$$

$$V_{resisting} = \frac{(5.25\ in^2)\,(63\ psi)}{1.5} = 220.5\#\ at\ each\ end\ of\ the\ toggle$$

3. Calculate the allowable live load based on shear.

$$Live\ Load = \frac{2V_{resisting}}{Tributary\ Area}$$

$$Live\ Load = \frac{2\,(220.5\#)}{10.67\ ft^2} = 41.34\ psf$$

THE 2x4-FRAMED PLATFORM'S DEFLECTION PERFORMANCE

Platforms do not fail in deflection, but they may be unacceptably springy. This comparison assumes an acceptable deflection limit to be $l/240$ of the structural member's length – 0.2 in.

The calculations reveal that the 2x4 #2 SPF framed platform's strength is limited by its ability to resist shear under a live load greater than 41.34 psf.

$$= 0.2\ in = \frac{5\ w\ l^4}{384\ E\ I} \qquad w = \frac{0.2\ in\ (384)\ E\ I}{5\ l^4}$$

$$= \frac{0.2\ in\ (384)\ (1.4x10^6\ psi)\ (5.359\ in^4)}{5\ (48'')^4} = 21.71\ pli\ or\ 260.52\ pl$$

$$= \frac{260.51\ plf}{2.67\ ft} = 97.7\ psf$$

TESTING THE 1x6 SELECT SPF-FRAMED PLATFORM

Performing the same calculations using the values for 1x6 Select SPF reveals that the 1x6 is limited by its ability to resist vertical shear. It can sustain 80.75 psf of bending force and would not deflect unacceptably under a 235 psf loading condition. It can, however, support a shear stress of only 47.3 psf.

STRESSED-SKIN PLATFORM ANALYSIS

The computations to calculate the loads of a stressed-skin platform are much more tedious and would occupy significantly more space than that used by the previous examples. The results listed below were derived from a spreadsheet that has been in use at the Yale School of Drama/Yale Repertory Theatre since 2005.

CONCLUSION

	4x8 Slotted Stressed-Skin	4x4 Triscuit
Overall Deflection	190 psf	240 psf
Top Skin Bending	176 psf	221 psf
Bottom Skin Bending	188 psf	237 psf
Rolling Sear Stress	211 psf	165 psf
Horizontal Shear Stress	167 psf	137 psf

Strength is only one of several criteria on which the choice of a particular stock platform design will be based and, ultimately, such factors as storage space, material availability, shop and run crew experience, and even the designer's personal preference may decide the issue. As this article demonstrates, however, either of the stressed-skins is stronger than the open-frame designs – even though the open-frame designs are much more familiar if not commonly built.

❧❧❧

The entire deck for the 2008 Merry Go Round Theater children's touring production of *Cinderhood* needed to fit in a 15 person cargo van, stand up to outdoor use, and last 10 years. Ideally, its component platforms could be arranged in several different configurations, and it had to be something that the cast of children could set up in roughly half an hour. To satisfy those objectives, Production Manager Shaminda Amarakoon designed the deck system described here, a version of the traditional continental parallel.

CONSTRUCTION

The continental parallel design has two advantages. First, like the more familiar American parallel, its parts break down into only a few pieces – a lid and the lid's supporting gates. That would mean faster set-ups and strikes and fewer chances that pieces would be lost or left behind. Second, unlike the American parallel, the end gates fold in half and inward for storage and transport as shown in Figure 4, taking up the least possible space in the van. Figures 1 through 3 illustrate a 4'x7' parallel.

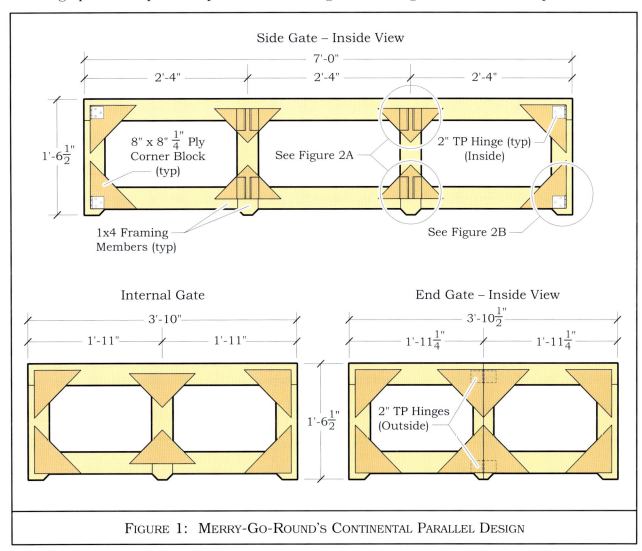

FIGURE 1: MERRY-GO-ROUND'S CONTINENTAL PARALLEL DESIGN

This design's gates are lengths of 1x4 pine pocket-screwed together with the joints reinforced by $\frac{1}{4}$" ply corner blocks. The end and side gates are joined together by four 2" tight-pin hinges, and two more 2" tight-pin hinges mounted on the outside of the end gates allows those gates to fold (see Figure 1).

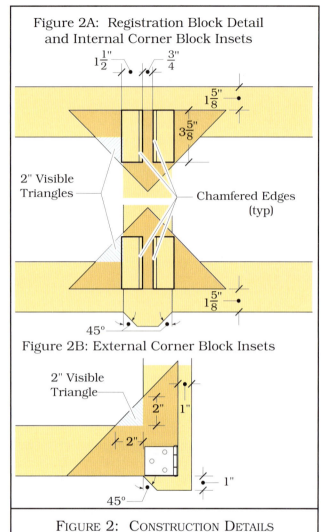

Figure 2A: Registration Block Detail and Internal Corner Block Insets

2" Visible Triangles

Chamfered Edges (typ)

Figure 2B: External Corner Block Insets

2" Visible Triangle

FIGURE 2: CONSTRUCTION DETAILS

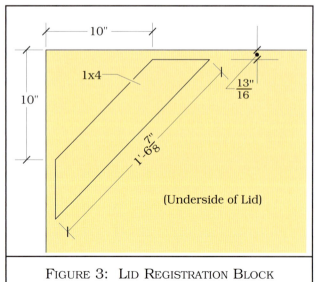

1x4

(Underside of Lid)

FIGURE 3: LID REGISTRATION BLOCK

Pairs of registration blocks centered on the internal uprights and spaced $\frac{3}{4}$" apart speed set-ups: once the perimeter gates have been unfolded, the internal gates are simply dropped into place.

The bottoms of the gates' uprights are chamfered at 45° as shown in Figures 2A and 2B and at the corners of each frame, the corner blocks are inset a full 1" for clearance.

Note in Figure 2 that, on the internal uprights, the corner blocks are inset $1\frac{5}{8}$". This is done purely for aesthetics: to make all the visible triangles of plywood a uniform 2".

The $\frac{3}{4}$" plywood lids of the platforms have registration blocks permanently mounted to the underside in each corner (see Figure 3). The gates are stained and sealed for protection against weather and the lids are painted for traction and then sealed.

SET-UP

The Merry-Go-Round deck comprised 7 parallels: 1 @ 3'x7'; 2 @ 4'x7'; and 4 smaller trapezoidal parallels. It was easily assembled by 4 people in about 20 minutes. The gates were removed from the van and unfolded as shown in Figure 4. Then the internal gates were slid between the registration blocks, which locked them in place and established a solid, stable frame. Finally, the lids were laid in place and kept there by the friction of the corner registration blocks. The completed parallels were clamped together with C-clamps to form the finished decks. (Clamping would be done before lid application in larger decks.)

CONCLUSION

While this article has focused on the construction of rectangular continental parallels, The Merry-Go-Round deck included a number of trapezoidal units whose construction was similar but not identical. One corner of each of the trapezoidal parallels was fastened with loose-pin, rather than tight-pin, hinges to permit folding.

This technique yielded a product that addressed every concern. The deck is suitable for a number of spaces, both outdoors and indoors. It is easily assembled in a minimum amount of time with

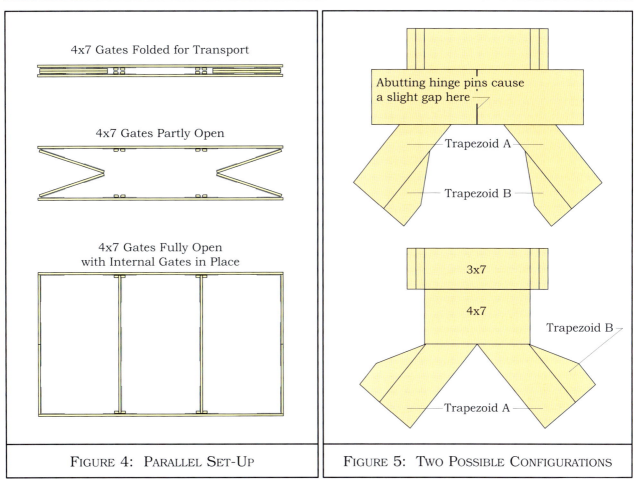

4x7 Gates Folded for Transport

4x7 Gates Partly Open

4x7 Gates Fully Open
with Internal Gates in Place

Abutting hinge pins cause
a slight gap here

Trapezoid A

Trapezoid B

3x7

4x7

Trapezoid B

Trapezoid A

FIGURE 4: PARALLEL SET-UP

FIGURE 5: TWO POSSIBLE CONFIGURATIONS

only 4 people. All the pieces break down flat and thus are easily stored in the cargo van. The use of pocket screws, keystones, corner blocks, stain and sealant during construction produced a deck system that has toured for some years. And finally, using C-clamp connections allows a number of configurations like those shown in Figure 5 without degrading the components.

A production at New York Stage and Film's Powerhouse Theater required that a planked floor be laid out on the theater floor. James Zwicky's article "Two Methods for Planking Floors Quickly" (see pages 202–204) seemed promising, but Technical Director John McCullough and I developed an alternative method of simulating individual lauan planks by grooving sheets of $\frac{1}{4}$" lauan, a process that avoids the cost of building a substrate and yet offers the same advantages in time saved.

OVERVIEW

We cut shallow beveled grooves into one face of the lauan sheets taking care not to cut all the way through. That process established the width of the "planks" and, to avoid ugly 4'-long seams between panels, we cut an interlocking plank pattern into the ends of the panels. To make end seams even less noticeable, we offset the ends of the panels when we fastened them to the floor at load-in.

CREATING THE PLANKED EFFECT

Two guidelines must be observed in using this process. First, the width of the planks must divide evenly into the width of the sheet material being used. If a given plank design cannot be laid out on a 4'-wide sheet of lauan, rip the sheet to a narrower width and treat the cutoff as scrap. Second, to make a symmetrical v-groove, the tablesaw blade must be set to 45° and lowered so that it just protrudes above the tablesaw bed. A $\frac{1}{8}$"-thick blade will protrude just under $\frac{3}{32}$". After the preparations are complete, set the tablesaw fence to the width of a single plank, and, keeping even downward pressure over the blade, cut a groove into a scrap piece of lauan as a test.

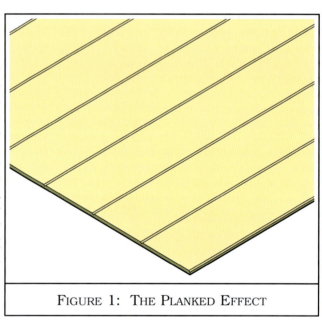

FIGURE 1: THE PLANKED EFFECT

STAGE I: CUTTING THE GROOVES

After making any adjustments suggested by the test, run all the lauan needed for the flooring through the saw. Then, reset the fence to the width of the second plank and run the lauan through the saw again. Repeat this process until all grooves have been cut, and then run each sheet through the tablesaw twice more, with the fence set to the width of the sheet to bevel the outside edges, allowing the seams between sheets to become plank grooves. At this stage, each sheet will appear to be a set of planks as shown in Figure 1. The grooves will have weakened the lauan sheets so, as work progresses, take care to lift material evenly.

STAGE II: CREATING THE TEMPLATE

The layout of the template should be based on the aesthetic of the design, handling and transportation considerations, and the amount of time available. At New York Stage and Film, the sheets would be moved multiple times before installation, so to guard against breakage the individual planks were cut to end on 3" intervals so that no plank extended more than 9" from the main body of the sheet.

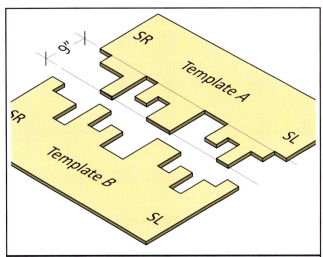

FIGURE 2: TEMPLATES FOR SIXTEEN 3" PLANKS

Two templates that would fit together like those shown in Figure 2 were cut from $\frac{3}{8}$" lauan. The Templates were labeled *A* and *B* as shown, and the stage-left and stage-right sides were noted on the template to avoid confusion in use. The templates were used to trace end-seam patterns onto the lauan sheets and the end seams were cut with a jig saw.

STAGE III: TRIAL ASSEMBLY

During trial assembly the shop corrected the few minor inconsistencies in cutting to ensure a snug fit between sheets and an efficient load-in. The final product was a cleanly planked lauan floor system that installed and struck quickly (see Figure 3).

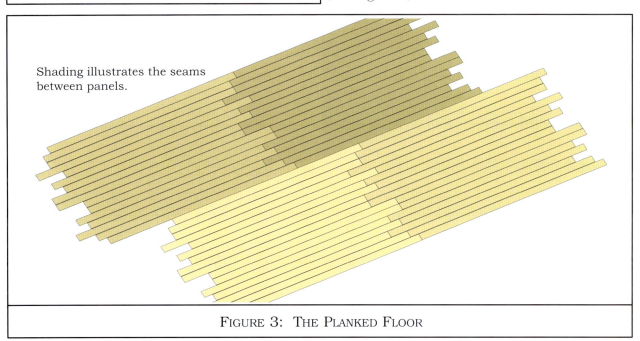

Shading illustrates the seams between panels.

FIGURE 3: THE PLANKED FLOOR

As executed by the Powerhouse Theater scene shop, this planking method requires 2 people, one to run the lauan through the tablesaw and the other to keep consistent downward pressure on the sheets as they passed over the blade by pushing down on them with a stick of lumber. This second person also sped the work by assisting in handling and maneuvering the lauan sheets.

❧❧❧❧❧

TECHNICAL BRIEF

Scenery Hardware

Actor-Friendly Pneumatic Brakes — *Josh Prues*

A Simple Hydraulic Caster Lift System — *Steve Beatty*

A Floating Knife for Tracking Scenery — *Guerry Hood*

A Locking Mechanism for Telescoping Tubing — *Chris Brown*

A Caster Grid — *Justin McDaniel*

Opera-Scale Rotating Walls — *Timothy D. McCormick*

Tracked Scenery Using PVC Glides — *John D. Ervin*

Compact Toggled Tip-Jacks — *Stephen Henson*

Electromagnets as Scenic Connectors — *Mikey Rohrer*

Black Carpeting as a Glide for Narrow Scenic Units — *Don Harvey*

FIGURE 1: THE *GRAND HOTEL* REVOLVING DOOR

The 2001 production of *Grand Hotel* at the University of Cincinnati – College Conservatory of Music required a revolving door platform that was used throughout the show, traveling from one spike to another during scene changes. Our main problem was how to keep the unit securely on spike. Since nearly every part of the 6' x 6' platform was visible to the audience, using cane bolts or toggle clamps was out of the question (see Figure 1). Budgetary and other constraints made tracking in a raised deck impossible; the set designer vetoed the use of lift casters as too clumsy; and the blocking required that one actor be able to move the unit effortlessly and set it on spike reliably.

We solved the problem by reversing the idea of lift casters: instead of lifting the unit $\frac{1}{2}$" to travel, we used pneumatic cylinders fitted with rubber-and-flat-bar "brake pads" to lift the unit a mere $\frac{1}{8}$" when it came to spike. Figure 2 shows the system schematic. Mounted rod-down to the underside of the platform, the cylinders provided just enough lift to take weight off the casters.

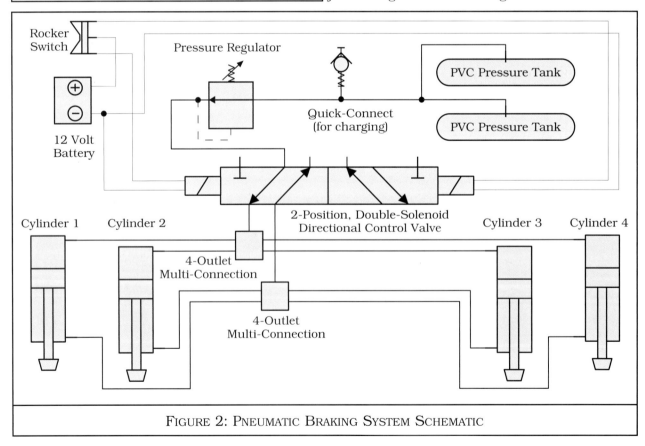

FIGURE 2: PNEUMATIC BRAKING SYSTEM SCHEMATIC

Having only $5\frac{3}{4}$" clearance under the platform, we chose to use 4 compact double-acting air cylinders, mounting one in each corner of the platform. In addition to all the system's tubing, connectors, and valves, the platform also concealed two shop-built 4"-diameter PVC air tanks and a 12-volt battery. The two tanks supplied enough air to actuate the cylinders repeatedly throughout an 8-hour tech rehearsal – certainly more than would be needed for performances. The battery powered the valve that made the system so easy to use: a 2-position, double-solenoid directional control valve. With this valve, we could control the pistons with a double-throw momentary rocker switch discreetly mounted on the door frame at an easy working height for the actor but hidden from the audience.

Designing and building this system was easy and fun! But the best part came when we hit the stage and explained to the actor moving the unit that all he had to do was tip a switch one way to lock the unit on spike and the other way when he needed to move to a new spike. The brakes were nearly instantaneous and could not be detected when set.

PARTS

This chart shows our total cost for the brake system.

Compact Double-Acting Air Cylinder McMaster-Carr: 62245K422	4	$102.36	$409.44
Pneumatic Directional Control Valve McMaster-Carr: 6124K88	1	$82.58	$82.58
12-volt Battery Radio Shack: 23-289	1	$24.99	$24.99
$\frac{1}{4}$" Polyethylene Tubing McMaster-Carr: 50375K11	30	$0.10	$3.00
$\frac{1}{4}$" Acetal Male Straight Adapters McMaster-Carr: 51055K12	10	$1.31	$13.10
$\frac{1}{4}$" 4-Outlet Polybutylene Multi-Connection McMaster-Carr: 5203K55	2	$15.65	$31.30
Double-Throw Momentary Rocker Switch		stock	$0.00
18-AWG Wire		stock	$0.00
Pneumatic Pressure Regulator		stock	$0.00
Air Tanks (4" Schedule-80 PVC Pipe and Caps)	2	shop built from stock	$0.00
		Total	$564.41

A Simple Hydraulic Caster Lift System

Steve Beatty

The deck of a wagon built for a Seattle Pacific University Theatre production was 15' above the stage floor. Since the wagon had a footprint of only 5' x 6', it needed a very heavy base for stability. Further, it had to come onstage during one scene change, spin 180° during the next, and leave the stage before the final scene. In short it needed a retractable-caster system.

After looking at systems developed around Seattle theaters, I settled on hydraulically lifted swivel casters as the key components for a flexible and reusable system. A hybrid of many different caster lifts, the system I developed achieved our goals: it was inexpensive, easy to fabricate and modify, capable of lifting almost any wagon that could fit on our stage, absolutely silent, and quick and simple to operate. The system consists of three parts: a hand-pump/reservoir unit, a valved polyethylene piping system, and several caster-lift units.

OPERATION

To lift the wagon off its frame, a check valve between the pump and the slave cylinders is opened and the hand pump is pumped. The hydraulic fluid flows through the check and overpressure valves, reaches the manifold, and is distributed to the cylinders. The cylinders lift the wagon off its frame and the check valve is closed. After the wagon has moved to spike, the check valve is released, and the weight of the wagon forces the cylinder rods to retract and pushes the fluid back to the reservoir.

OFF-THE-SHELF COMPONENTS

The hand pump is chosen for its reservoir size, as most pumps have more pressure capacity than stage applications need. After determining that Grainger's single-stage 6W462 Enerpac® would work for this application, we found a similar used pump at a local marine surplus yard. Its 43-cubic-inch reservoir offered sufficient volume for several cylinders of the size we used, each of which had an approximate volume of 1 cubic inch.

We also bought the piping system locally. The Weatherhead® push-to-connect fittings sold by Fittings Inc. come in all configurations – tees, unions, and the $\frac{1}{4}$" NPT female adapters our cylinders required – and work well with $\frac{1}{4}$" polyethylene tubing. The Weatherhead® $\frac{1}{4}$" TP16004 tubing we used easily handled our working pressures.

The system also used a check valve (Grainger 1A858) to lock the cylinders in the out position, and an adjustable relief valve we had on hand (similar to Grainger's 2A731) to cycle the fluid back to the reservoir in case an overeager stagehand pumped a little too much.

For this application, we used 1"-bore/1"-throw Sheffer CLH-D4 cylinders that we bought from Columbia Hydraulic Service. Not only did their small volume suit our hand-pump system, they also cost less than $100.00 each.

THE CUSTOM SLEEVES

With the components on hand, the cylinder sleeving setup was the only fabrication required. We mounted the cylinders in a shop-built sleeved tube-steel assembly reminiscent of Telespar®. In fact, we could have used Telespar®, but a very snug fit was not necessary and tube steel is considerably less expensive.

The outer sleeve, 7-gauge $2\frac{1}{2}$"-square tube steel, was cut to the length of the cylinder and rod (with the rod in) plus $\frac{1}{8}$" to allow the cylinder to shift if needed. The outer sleeve also had a mousehole

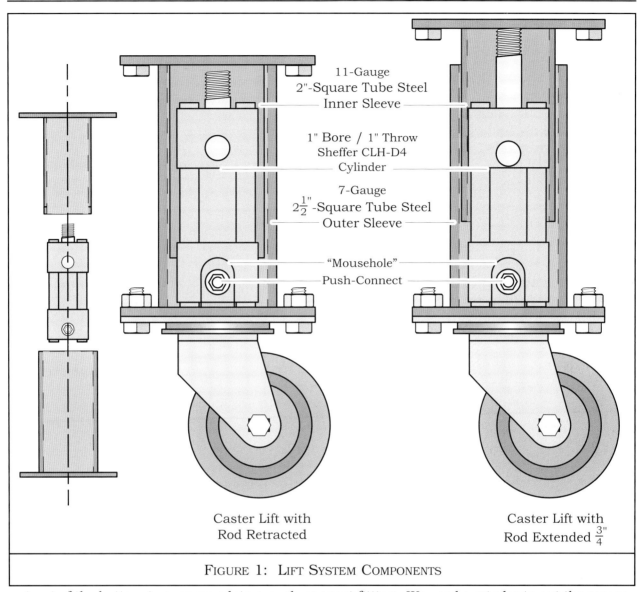

11-Gauge
2"-Square Tube Steel
Inner Sleeve

1" Bore / 1" Throw
Sheffer CLH-D4
Cylinder

7-Gauge
$2\frac{1}{2}$"-Square Tube Steel
Outer Sleeve

"Mousehole"
Push-Connect

Caster Lift with
Rod Retracted

Caster Lift with
Rod Extended $\frac{3}{4}$"

FIGURE 1: LIFT SYSTEM COMPONENTS

cut out of the bottom to accommodate a push-connect fitting. We used a grinder to cut the mouse-hole, but of course a plasma cutter or jigsaw would also work. After cutting the mousehole, we welded $\frac{3}{16}$" flat-bar caster plates for generic 3" swivel casters to the bottom of the outer sleeves.

As Figure 1 shows, the $1\frac{5}{8}$" square body of the cylinders fit (somewhat) snugly inside our 11-gauge 2"-square tube steel inner sleeves, which were capped with $\frac{1}{8}$" flat-bar mounting plates. The inner sleeve was cut to the length of the outer sleeve minus the height of the mousehole, to allow the inner sleeve to bottom out before interfering with the push-connect.

NOTES

In assembling the units, the push-connect is added to the cylinder after the cylinder has been inserted into the outer sleeve. A $\frac{1}{16}$"-aircraft-cable safety (not shown) holds the two sleeves together when the system is pressurized. Running from one bolt hole on the mounting plate to one on the caster plate, the safety keeps the inner sleeve from being over-extended.

No mounting hardware is attached to the end of the cylinder rod. We could have added a swivel foot or a nut, but using it as it was did not damage the rod's threads, so we left it. In fact, nothing attaches the cylinders to the sleeves at all.

Hydraulic fluid is inexpensive to buy, but it is very expensive to dispose of. We found that automobile automatic transmission fluid worked just as well and cost less. Moreover, it was accepted for recycling locally.

This system has allowed us great flexibility over the past few shows. The cylinders, tubing and fittings (though not the check and overpressure valves) work just as well with air as they do with fluid. Using a stock air regulator, a $35.00 air switching valve, and basic air reservoir like those carried by towtrucks to fill up tires, we converted our hydraulic system to a wagon-mounted, pneumatic system for less than $100.00.

RESOURCES

Columbia Hydraulic Service: www.columbiahydraulics.com, 1601 NE Columbia Blvd. Portland, OR 97211. (503) 285-0381

Fittings Inc.: www.fittingsinc.com, PO Box 3647, Seattle, WA 98124. (800) 552-0632

Sheffer Hydraulic and Pneumatic Cylinders: www.sheffercorp.com, 6990 Cornell Road, Cincinnati, OH 45242. (513) 387-2191

❧❧❧❧

The design of Yale Repertory Theatre's 2003 production of *Taming of the Shrew* called for two 20' x 10' flats to travel onstage and meet at center to appear as one 20' x 20' wall. The flats, winch driven simultaneously by aircraft cable secured to the tops, were suspended from a Knight Industries 5300 Series Steel Track. Because the flats needed to meet evenly at center stage and heavy objects hanging on the downstage side of the flats would have forced their bottoms upstage, it was necessary to guide the bottoms of the flats with a knife in a track dadoed into the MDF deck.

The knife system would have to overcome several obstacles. First, stage floor inconsistencies are common, and those in our deck required the knife to be able to constantly adjust vertically as the flats tracked. Second, because the forces at the bottom of the wall were significant, the knives would hold a constant pressure against the upstage edge of the deck track. This pressure would likely cause the knives to creep out of the track, requiring a varying downward force. Third, the movement of the knives in the dado cut track made the MDF corners vulnerable to damage. This vulnerability required us to round over all corners on the knives.

We decided to use the knife system shown in Figure 1. Attached to the framing behind the flats, the system would maintain constant pressure against the deck through the use of a compression spring. In case a quick fix was necessary, a retaining bolt held the compressed system in place.

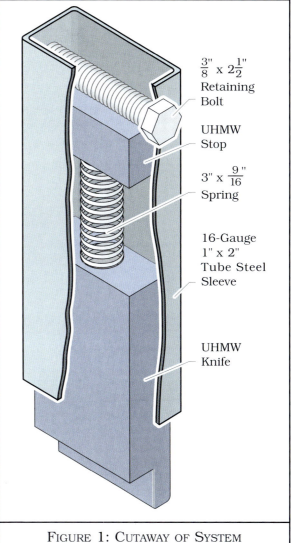

$\frac{3}{8}$" x $2\frac{1}{2}$" Retaining Bolt

UHMW Stop

3" x $\frac{9}{16}$" Spring

16-Gauge 1" x 2" Tube Steel Sleeve

UHMW Knife

FIGURE 1: CUTAWAY OF SYSTEM

COMPONENT LIST

Component	Quan	Material	Cost
Sleeve	1	16-gauge 1" x 2" Tube Steel, $5\frac{1}{4}$" long	(stock)
Retaining Bolt	1	$\frac{3}{8}$" x $2\frac{1}{2}$" Bolt	(stock)
Retaining Nut	1	$\frac{3}{8}$" Nut	(stock)
Knife	1	$\frac{3}{4}$" x 2" UHMW Bar cut to $\frac{3}{4}$" x $1\frac{3}{4}$" x $3\frac{1}{2}$" McMaster-Carr: 8702K114	$4.43 per ft.
Stop	1	UHMW cut to $\frac{3}{4}$" x $1\frac{3}{4}$" x $\frac{3}{4}$" McMaster-Carr: 8702K114	(scrap)
Spring	1	3" x $\frac{9}{16}$" Zinc-Plated Hard-Drawn Steel Spring McMaster-Carr: 9657K174	$4.86 per 6

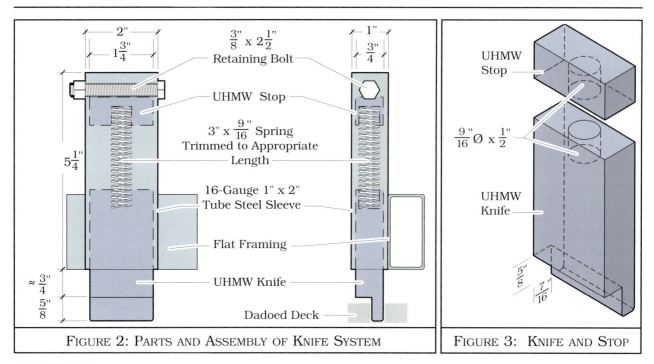

FIGURE 2: PARTS AND ASSEMBLY OF KNIFE SYSTEM

FIGURE 3: KNIFE AND STOP

ASSEMBLY

First, insert the bolt through a $\frac{7}{16}$" hole drilled in the sleeve as seen in Figure 2 and tighten the nut. Slide the spring into the $\frac{9}{16}$" hole in each UHMW piece shown in Figure 3. The friction fit between the UHMW pieces and the spring should hold them all together as one unit. Test fit the pieces and store them until load-in. Our flats were steel framed, so we welded the sleeve directly to the rear of the flats with the sleeve aligned as in Figure 2. It is easiest to hang the flats without the knife, spring, and stop in the sleeve. These pieces can be slid into the sleeve from the top and bolted in place after the flat is hung.

Our carpenter made four knives in under four hours. Guided by only four knives, the walls traveled quietly at around 3' per second and didn't snag during the four weeks they were in use.

OTHER NOTES

1. Attaching the knife system to wood-framed flats may require an angle iron bracket.

2. Initially, the compression in our springs proved too high, resulting in noisy friction between the knife and the track as the walls moved. To quiet the system, we shortened the springs so that maximum extension occurred when the knife touched the dado-cut track's lowest point.

3. Adding a slicker, smoother track liner – a smooth finish tape or an aluminum or plastic channel, for instance – might make the system even quieter.

4. Whatever the choice in track, it is imperative that the track be kept as clean as possible.

❧❧❧❧

Time and time again technicians discover a problem when trying to fit large pieces of scenery into small spaces. During the design of a Yale Repertory Theater production of *Eurydice*, such a problem arose, literally out of our trap room. The design called for two inverted chandeliers to rise from beneath the stage. One needed to rise at an angle of 12° and the other at 6°, as seen in Figure 1. It was decided that a rigid structure would be needed not only to hold the chandelier at an angle, but also keep the unit from spinning. Because our trap room is 8' tall and both chandeliers needed to rise to approximately 18', a telescoping device would be crucial to the design.

FIGURE 1: FULL-STAGE VIEW OF *EURYDICE*

For our production, the chandeliers never had to descend into the floor; they only had to extend upward during the performance. Therefore, it was decided that the telescope did not have to lift the chandelier. The lifting was accomplished by using standard aircraft cable and winches located in the grid. The actors took the picks that had carabiners on the end, and clipped them to the top of the chandeliers. Then the winches lifted the units into place.

THE PRODUCT

Telespar® is steel tube that is manufactured to telescope. When made, it is welded in the corner instead of in the middle of one side. This creates a much tighter tolerance when sleeving sections together eliminating the interference that would be caused by a seam. It is available from local suppliers in a wide range of sizes and lengths, and is most commonly used in street signs. It is also carried by McMaster-Carr, except they call it "Steel Nestable Square Tubing". This is the product that we eventually used for our production, because it's relatively inexpensive, and incredibly easy to get. McMaster-Carr sells perforated and non-perforated tube in sizes ranging from 1" to $2\frac{1}{2}$" square, in increments of $\frac{1}{4}$" and 4', 8', and 12' lengths at good prices. For example, 8' lengths of 1"- to 2"-square tube cost less than $30.00 each. The next thing to think about is how to make each section pick up the subsequent section, so that they actually telescope. In this production we needed to run cable for lights inside the telescope so something low profile was desired. I purchased round-nose spring plungers and coupling nuts, also from McMaster-Carr, and welded them inside each section of tube. For example, a spring plunger, screwed into a coupling nut, was welded inside the $1\frac{3}{4}$" section of tube. The 2" section had a small hole drilled in it to capture the spring plunger, creating the lifting point. The spring plunger engaged as soon as the hole passed over it, lifting the $1\frac{3}{4}$" section of telescope as seen in Figure 2.

PARTS LIST

Part and Part Number	Cost
$\frac{5}{16}$" Steel Round-Nose Spring Plunger with Lock, 3.0 lbs to 15.0 lbs End Force (1226A14)	$2.98
$\frac{1}{2}$" x $1\frac{1}{8}$" Grade-5 Zinc-Plated Steel Coupling Nut (90977A150)	$4.74
Steel Nestable Square Tubing – Solid, Plain Finish, 8' Lengths, one each: $1\frac{3}{4}$" (4931T43), and 2" (4931T44)	$62.82
Total	$70.54

The only drawback to this system was the reset, which took 3 to 4 minutes. You had to let one section down at a time, stop and manually push the spring plunger in, and then continue to let the next section down. It worked wonderfully, given the fact that the chandeliers never needed to reset during the show. If we had needed to reset them, a different option of telescoping would have been needed.

FOR FURTHER INVESTIGATION

In researching Telespar®, I found a few products that could not be tested but seemed promising in our application. At the high end of the spectrum there is the Genie Super Hoist®, a series of alumimum cylinders powered by compressed air. The cylinders, which weigh little and are easy to handle, are used for construction purposes such as lifting sheetrock or air ducts. The

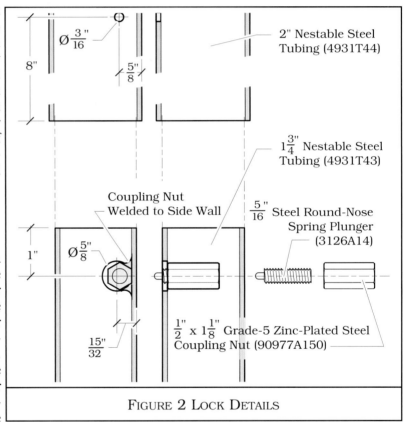

FIGURE 2 LOCK DETAILS

larger of the models I found offered by Material Flow & Conveyor Systems, Inc. collapsed to 54" and extended to 18'-4". This product would do the job but at a cost of $1,600.00, which is quite pricey.

The low end includes the telescoping flagpoles I found online. Described as cost-effective front-yard flagpoles, the most common ones are made from aluminum or fiberglass and extend from around 5' to 20'. When fully extended, the ads say, these flag poles can withstand "years of wind and weather with little or no maintenance" and the average cost is an affordable $200.00.

In assembling stock platforms into a rolling unit, the use of a caster grid can save money and load-in time – especially if the platforms are the $2\frac{3}{8}$"-thick double-sided stressed-skin platforms known as triscuits. A caster grid like that shown in Figure 1 provides 4'-on-center support for stock platforms, with each internal caster holding up one corner of each of four triscuits, minimizing the number of casters needed. The grid consists of two subsystems: the caster plates and the bridging. The caster plates assure correct caster spacing in one direction and transfer the platforms' live and dead loads to the floor. The bridging simply assures caster plate spacing and alignment.

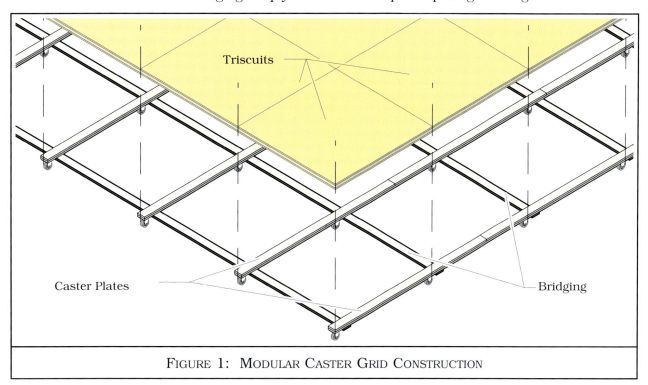

Triscuits

Caster Plates

Bridging

FIGURE 1: MODULAR CASTER GRID CONSTRUCTION

CASTER PLATE CONSTRUCTION

Though 2x4s would work, the caster plates are typically made of 1x4s to make warpage less problematic. In any case, as suggested in Figure 2, the lumber is cut to lengths that assure appropriate offsets between caster plate end joints and platform joints. Further, the casters are bolted to the caster plates with flat-head stove bolts to provide a flat surface for platform installation.

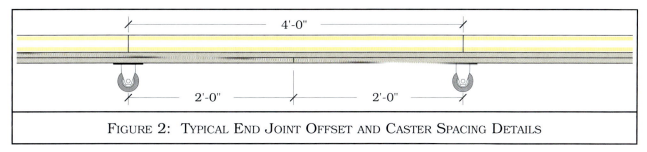

4'-0"

2'-0"   2'-0"

FIGURE 2: TYPICAL END JOINT OFFSET AND CASTER SPACING DETAILS

A NUMBER OF OPTIONS

Figures 1 and 2 show sets of straight casters aligned with their caster plate centerlines, but other orientations can work as well. When using straight casters set in arcs around a pivot point, these caster plates can quickly establish correct caster alignment and placement. After determining the desired wagon moves, designers can layout caster plates which run parallel to the seams in the platforming system and lay out caster placement at an angle to the caster plates.

Further, though designed for use with triscuits. the caster grid is applicable to a variety of platform designs. This system would be applicable to 4x8 stressed-skin platforms or with platforms framed in steel or 2x4s. Clearly, platform-to-casterplate connection details would differ from those described in the following section.

INSTALLING THE PLATFORMING

Before load-in, the bridging and caster plates are cut and the casters are bolted to the plates. At load-in, the caster plates are laid out upside down, correctly spaced and aligned. The bridging is laid out across the bottoms of the caster plates and drywall screwed to them, forming the grid. Once the grid has been flipped over, the $2\frac{3}{8}$"-thick triscuits are attached to the grid's caster plates with 3" drywall screws.

CASTER EFFICIENCY

Using a caster grid, we supported a 20' x 24' wagon with 42 casters carrying worst-case loads of 16 square feet of tributary area. A traditional wagon comprising 4x8 platforms framed with 2x4s and covered with plywood would require 90 casters – more than twice as many. This represents a substantial savings in money, both in casters and hardware, and in time.

On the other hand, though it does represent a significant savings, this system can represent sacrifices in wagon height. A traditional wagon built and castered as described would have a height of only 1" plus caster height, while this system is more than 4" over caster height. As with most construction decisions the pros and cons must be weighed to determine the most efficient course of action for any piece of scenery.

❧❧❧

For a 2005 Wolf Trap Opera Company production of *Don Giovanni*, Set Designer Cameron Anderson specified three walls that could rotate 360° to establish various settings, which are shown in Figure 1. Measuring 22' long, 10' high, and 1' thick each, the larger two walls offered sizeable challenges, not the least of which was that they had to rotate freely above a 2'-tall raked show deck. Each wall had three parts: the wall panels, the wall supports, and the knee wall masking. Figure 2 shows their construction.

THE WALL PANELS

The 1"-thick wall panels were framed in 16-gauge 1"-square tube steel and covered front, back, and sides, with $\frac{1}{4}$" lauan. Each of the larger two walls comprised three sections that were bolted together in load-in. The center section of each wall contained a 12'-long, $1\frac{1}{2}$" schedule-40 black pipe welded into its center and protruding 2' from the bottom as a pivot. These pipes sleeved into pillow blocks in the wall supports.

THE WALL SUPPORTS AND THE KNEE WALLS

Constructed almost entirely of $\frac{1}{4}$" steel plate, the supports may have been larger than necessary but they did function well. Each consisted of one piece 1'-9" x 10'-0" and one piece 2'-0" x 10'-0" tack-welded into an "L" and braced by steel-plate gussets. Steel-plate tabs welded on top of the gussets allowed for attachment to the knee walls. On the front of each support, two Browning® 2" ball bearing pillow blocks were bolted one above the other along the centerline, one flush to the top and the other $5\frac{1}{2}$" from the bottom. According to the manufacturer, once the pillow blocks' set screws had been tightened on the pipe pivots, the pillow blocks would carry the weight of the wall panels and the pivots would never slip down and touch the stage floor. As a precaution, however, we welded a 5" x 1'-0" plate-steel "safety tab" to the bottom of the front of each support to catch the bottom of the pipe pivot in case the set screws failed. In the center of the safety tab, we welded a 2"-tall piece of 2" schedule-40 black pipe, the "grease cup", which we filled with gear grease to avoid noise and friction in case the pivots did slip. They never did.

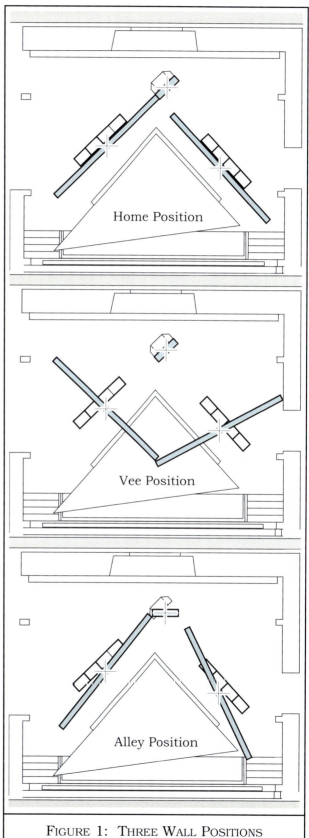

FIGURE 1: THREE WALL POSITIONS

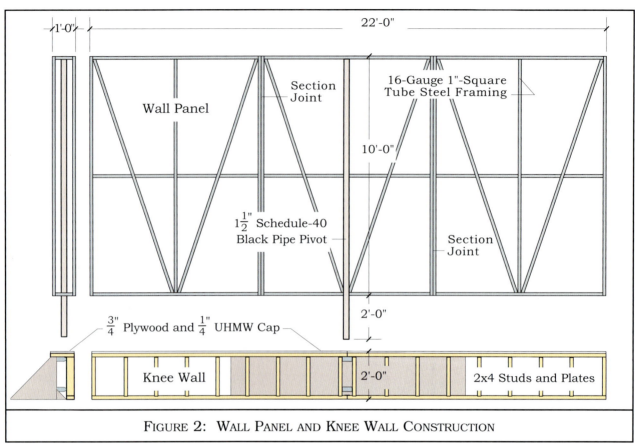

FIGURE 2: WALL PANEL AND KNEE WALL CONSTRUCTION

The 2'-0"-tall knee walls hid the wall supports and continued the paintable surface of the walls. The knee walls were 2x4 stud walls capped with a 12"-wide plywood return and $\frac{1}{4}$" UHMW to minimize the potential for unwanted friction during rotation. Figure 4 illustrates the walls' versatility.

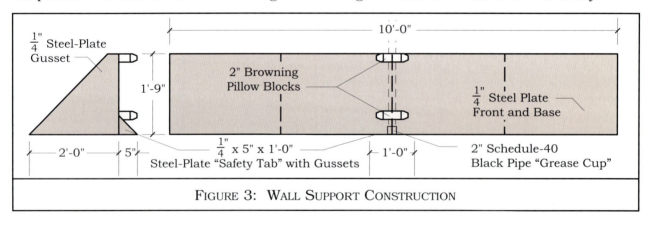

FIGURE 3: WALL SUPPORT CONSTRUCTION

ABOUT CAMERON ANDERSON

Cameron Anderson designs for the opera and theater throughout the United States and abroad. Career highlights include designing *West Side Story* in Norway at the Kilden Performing Arts Center and at the Vancouver Opera, *Simon Boccanegra* at the Teatro Colon in Buenos Aires, *Maria Padilla* for The Minnesota Opera, and *Il Barbieri di Siviglia* for Opera Theater of Saint Louis. Visit her website at www.cameronanderson.net to see her full portfolio.

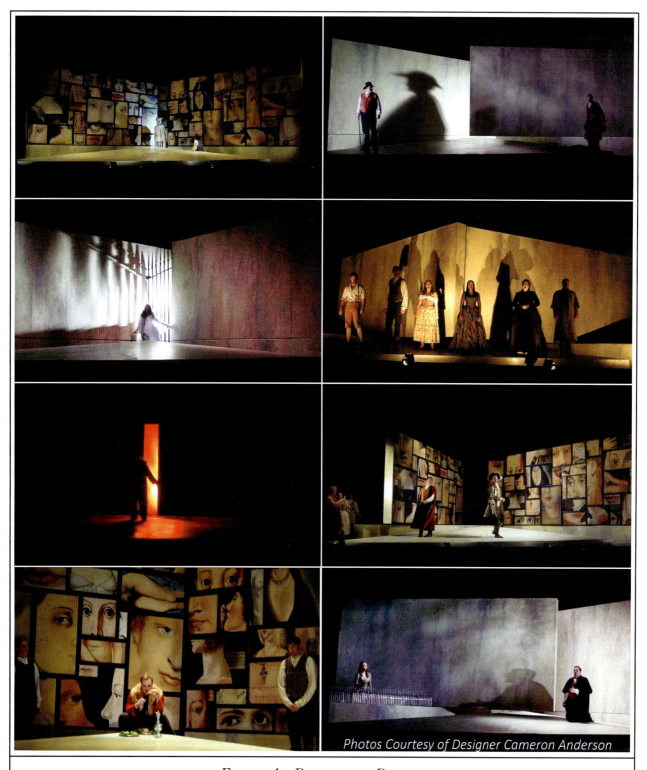

Photos Courtesy of Designer Cameron Anderson

FIGURE 4: PRODUCTION PHOTOS

For our production of Tirso de Molina's *The Last Days of Don Juan*, the designer specified a Hell-mouth trap opening made from a pair of sliding covers, opening and closing in guillotine fashion. He also requested that we avoid the use of traditional neoprene casters due to their inherent similarities of an approaching subway. Furthermore, casters have a tendency to allow the scenery to drift slightly off course over repeated use. Audience proximity and aesthetic values of the design required that the seam between the sliding traps and the rest of the set have a near-invisible gap of $\frac{1}{8}$" or less, which encouraged us to explore alternative methods of tracking the scenery. Another concern was that most hell mouths function only once during the play's climax, but this one also saw action during Don Juan's debaucheries throughout the evening. For those unfamiliar with the story, this means we used it a lot. We considered several options of silent, low friction, skid materials for our tracks, such as Teflon and nylon, but finances, product availability, and the general lack thereof led us to a rather unique and effective solution: PVC pipe.

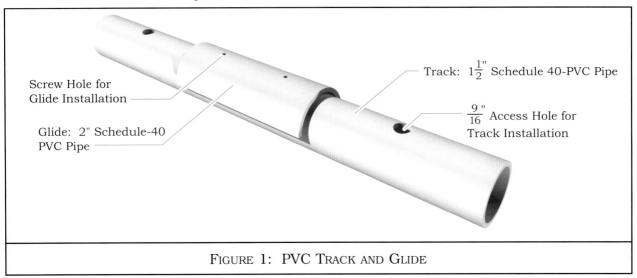

Screw Hole for
Glide Installation

Glide: 2" Schedule-40
PVC Pipe

Track: $1\frac{1}{2}$" Schedule 40-PVC Pipe

$\frac{9}{16}$" Access Hole for
Track Installation

FIGURE 1: PVC TRACK AND GLIDE

Figure 1 illustrates the system's components. We used $1\frac{1}{2}$" schedule-40 PVC pipe as our tracks and short pieces of 2" schedule-40 PVC pipe, halved lengthwise, as glides on the under-side of the scenery. The tracks were held to the floor with drywall screws every 12" on center. To keep the screws from deforming the cylindrical cross-section of the tracks, they were only inserted through the part of the tube wall which was in direct contact with the stage floor. We simplified the installation process, by using a $\frac{9}{16}$" paddle bit to drill through the top surface of the tubing and allowing the momentum of the carpenter's downward force to cause the tip of the paddle bit to make a small nick in the inner wall of the tubing. This conveniently served as a starter hole for the mounting screws. The diameter of the paddle bit was chosen to provide an access hole large enough for an extended driver-drill tip, such as the Makita "Stubby".

Our glides were cut 6" long and spaced as far apart as beam spans of the framing would normally allow. To prevent scraping as the glides moved along the track, we countersunk the holes on the underside of the glides to accommodate the heads of the mounting screws (see Figure 2). We used two screws per glide to prevent them from rotating.

In the spirit of education, and simply out of curiosity, we decided to test and compare the friction of our PVC tracks to similar materials using the method described in the *Technical Design Solutions* articles "Comparing Four Plastics as Scenery Glides" by Edmund B. Fisher and "Plastic Glides: A Second Look" by Karl Ruling and Scott Werbin. The only divergence we made from these methods was the use of a larger diameter pulley (a 6"-loft block) to further remove unwanted drag resulting from a low ratio between the rope and block diameters.

We tested the PVC with and without lubrication and discovered that a light spray of WD40® on the tracks made for easier platform movement, especially in the initial "shove" to overcome static friction. Our test sled weighed 9.25 lbs. (4.196 kg). We tested each method 10 consecutive times. The results are shown in Table 1.

	Range	Average
Without Lubricant	.270 - .324	.290
With Lubricant	.189 - .243	.220

TABLE 1: COEFFICIENTS OF KINETIC FRICTION

PERFORMANCE ASSESSMENT

We paid about $0.10 per foot for the PVC, making this an incredibly affordable solution. When fully loaded, each sliding platform weighed approximately 600 lbs. but could easily be pushed by a lone stagehand. The PVC track and glide system was impressively silent and provided a satisfyingly slick move (it appeared to be gliding on ice as opposed to bumping along our rugged stage floor). Further, it allowed the moves to be so accurate as to leave an immeasurably small gap between adjacent, stationary platforms. We were unable to wedge a piece of paper in the seam. It was so successful, in fact, that we would gladly use it again – even in a gently curved track. PVC is so flexible that it could produce gradually curved tracking. The only design change needed would be to make the glides swivel around a single, centered attachment.

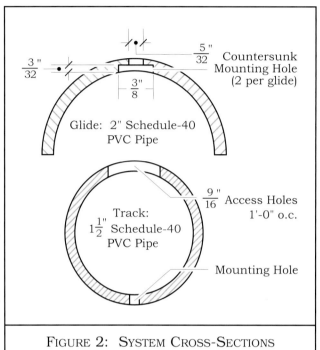

FIGURE 2: SYSTEM CROSS-SECTIONS

REFERENCES

Fisher, Edmund B. "Comparing Four Plastics as Scenery Glides". *Technical Design Solutions for Theatre, Vol. 1*, ed. Bronislaw J. Sammler and Don Harvey. Boston: Focal Press, 2002.

Ruling, Karl G., and Scott Werbin. "Plastic Glides: A Second Look". *Technical Design Solutions for Theatre, Vol. 1*, ed. Bronislaw J. Sammler and Don Harvey. Boston: Focal Press, 2002.

The scenic design of *Ragtime* at PCPA Theaterfest in 2008 required a number of castered units that could be rolled easily into a number of locations and locked on spike. The units ranged in size from 3' x 3' x 4' to 3' x 10' x 8' and in weight from 100 lbs. to 550 lbs. As the design required all exterior surfaces to be solid and flat, all parts of the positioning/locking mechanism had to be hidden inside the units. The number of units involved made hydraulics unaffordable, and the number of moves made using stock air tanks and pneumatics impossible even if tanks were swapped during intermission. The solution was to use toggle-clamp actuated tip-jacks.

EXECUTION

These tip-jacks consisted of primary and secondary caster plates hinged to the frame with casters mounted approximately 4" in from the ends, As Figures 1A and 1B illustrate, the primary caster plate consisted of two pieces of $\frac{3}{4}$" plywood screwed together with the upper piece overhanging the lower. The overhanging piece overlapped but was not connected to the secondary caster plate, a single piece of $\frac{3}{4}$" plywood. A length of $\frac{3}{16}$" aircraft cable terminating in a stop sleeve was reeved downward through the primary caster plate. The aircraft cable then passed around a muling sheave and extended upward, where it was connected to a manually operated toggle clamp bolted to the frame within easy reach. When the toggle clamp was activated, the aircraft cable pulled the caster plates downward, lifting the unit onto its casters with $\frac{1}{2}$" clearance. When the clamp was deactivated, the unit's weight let the unit settle securely into place.

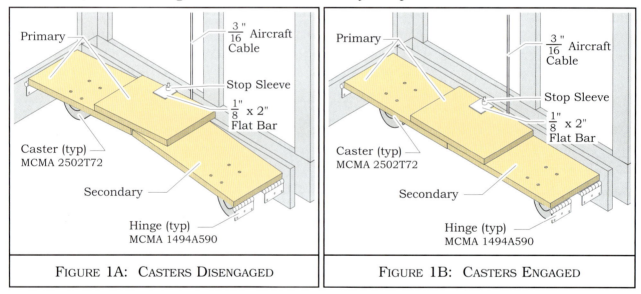

FIGURE 1A: CASTERS DISENGAGED	FIGURE 1B: CASTERS ENGAGED

HARDWARE DETAILS

As can be seen in Figures 1A, 1B, and 2, a 2"-long piece of $\frac{1}{8}$" x 2" flat bar drilled for use as a washer for the aircraft cable kept the stop sleeve from being pulled into the plywood. Figure 2 also shows how two pieces of $\frac{3}{16}$" x $2\frac{1}{2}$" flat bar were welded into an angled mount to the muling sheave at an approximately 14° tilt that allowed the aircraft cable to run down beside the primary caster plate but then come up through it. Figure 3 illustrates how two more pieces of $\frac{3}{16}$" x $2\frac{1}{2}$" flat bar were welded together to pad the toggle clamp out from the unit's frame to allow the lever to pull completely back to its retracted position. Wooden mounts for the sheave and toggle clamp would work equally well. As a final touch, adjusting the eyebolt in and out of the toggle clamp and securing it with a jam nut allowed for fine tuning the tension on the aircraft cable.

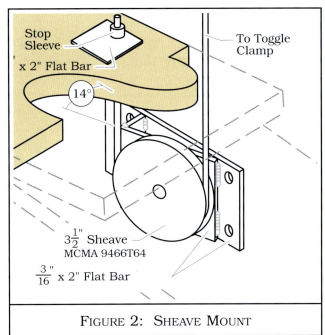

FIGURE 2: SHEAVE MOUNT

PRACTICE

The toggle clamp handles were accessed through rectangular holes large enough for a hand to reach through comfortably. Mortising a $\frac{1}{4}$" deep lip around the holes and cutting $\frac{1}{4}$" MDF panels to sit snugly on the mortised ledges covered the holes completely. 1"-diameter finger holes were drilled into the panels. Since the lever delivers a significant mechanical advantage (approx. 6:1), which multiplied the leverage provided by the tip-jack (approx 3:1 in this case), a stagehand can engage the system on a unit weighing as much as a few hundred pounds with relative ease.

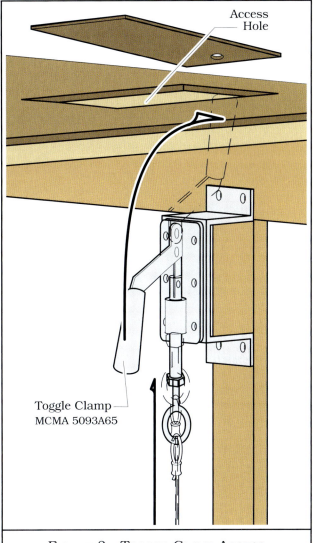

FIGURE 3: TOGGLE CLAMP ACCESS

ACKNOWLEDGMENTS

Special thanks to Mari Cataldo and Kevin Loeffler for their patience and creativity in taking this concept from napkin sketches and long winded explanations to functioning scenery.

❧❧❧

During the 2010 season at The Chautauqua Theatre Company a familiar problem arose: how to connect two scenic elements quickly. The specific element for this production of *Macbeth* was a large stair unit that split into two pieces and rolled about the stage on air casters. Production Manager Joe Stoltman devised a solution using electromagnets that allowed the actors to move both units separately into place and flip a toggle switch to lock them together.

In choosing components, they were guided primarily by considerations of simplicity, reliability, and availability. Knowing that they wanted all of the components contained within the unit, the staff decided to power the magnets with a 12-volt DieHard® Marine Deep-Cycle/RV Battery (Group Size 29HM), purchased locally. Arbitrarily judging that 300 lbs. of force would be enough to hold the units together, they purchased two McMaster-Carr magnets (5698K312) that are rated at 160 lbs. of pull apiece. Each magnet cost $70.35.

It seemed intuitively obvious that the battery would power the system satisfactorily but, to make sure, they used the following approach to calculate how long the battery would work before having

W = V x A
20 = 12 x A
A = 20 ÷ 12
A = 1.7 AMPS

FIGURE 1: EQUATION

to be recharged. The chosen magnets draw 10 watts each – a total of 20 watts – and the battery supplies 12 volts. Plugging those values into the *W=VxA* formula at the left reveals that the magnets will draw 1.7 amps. The battery is rated at 115 amp-hours when discharged over 20 hours, so the current flow during this time would be 115/20 = 5.75 amps. Theoretically, since the magnets draw only 1.7 amps, the system should operate 68 hours (115/1.7) between charges. The electromagnets were wired in parallel with the positive lead running to an on/off toggle switch.

While the magnets held with enough force, they could easily be sheared apart if one of the units were pushed from the side. To avoid that problem the electromagnets were mounted and the units' framing modified as indicated in Figure 2 to key the units together.

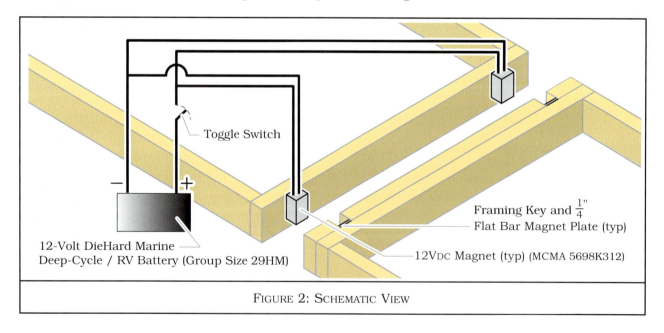

Toggle Switch

Framing Key and $\frac{1}{4}$"
Flat Bar Magnet Plate (typ)

12-Volt DieHard Marine
Deep-Cycle / RV Battery (Group Size 29HM)

12VDC Magnet (typ) (MCMA 5698K312)

FIGURE 2: SCHEMATIC VIEW

Space on and offstage was at a premium for the Yale Repertory Theatre's 2010 world-premiere musical *We Have Always Lived in the Castle*. Each unit that tracked onto the stage had to be built with severely narrowed profiles and, even with those reductions, upstage/downstage clearances were limited to as little as $\frac{3}{4}$". The kitchen counter discussed here provides a case in point.

FIGURE 1: THE COUNTER AND THE WALL

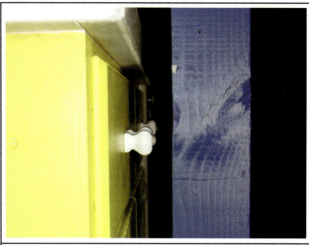

FIGURE 2: THE COUNTER AND THE COLUMN

FIGURE 3: THE CARPETING GLIDE

The counter was a standard 36" tall, but it played in front of the lattice-like wall that flew in behind it (also visible in Figure 1), and on its way on and offstage it had to track past a column downstage (see Figure 2). This logistical geometry limited the counter's depth to a scant $11\frac{1}{4}$", threatening to make the unit prone to tipping over as it traveled across the stage.

Adding casters to the unit would have aggravated the problem for hiding them inside the unit's frame would have made its footprint even narrower. So, instead, the technical team used a type of glide that is too often overlooked: black carpeting.

The carpeting is visible in Figure 3 – just visible – and that is one of its other advantages. Black carpeting tacked upside down to the bottom of a unit often goes completely unnoticed. Additionally, it is quiet, inexpensive, and widely available, and it requires very little troubleshooting while providing the widest possible base.

TECHNICAL BRIEF

Scenery Mechanics

Guiding Scenery with Linear Bearings — *HaeWon Yang*

A Curved Track and V-Groove Caster Guide — *Nathan Wells*

Tripping Casters with Pneumatics: System Basics — *Kimberly Corbett*

A Stabilizer Sleeve for Pneumatic Lift Jacks — *Steven Green*

Building Portable Pneumatic Systems:
  An Overview — *Lily Twining*

Using an Endless-Loop Winch as a One-Way Drive — *Jonathan Pellow*

A 20'-0"-tall palm tree in The Yale Repertory Theatre's 2003 Latin-culture-based production of William Shakespeare's *Taming of the Shrew* had to track upstage and downstage about 6'-0" to accommodate scene changes. The tree was supported and tracked solely from the bottom, and technical director, Chris Hourcle, used open linear bearings on a triangular carriage as shown in Figure 1 to guide it smoothly and quietly.

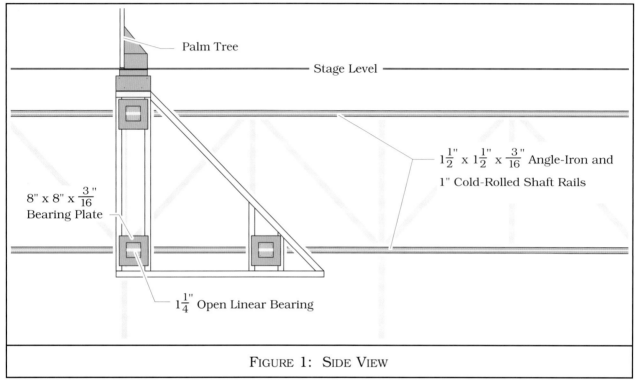

Palm Tree

Stage Level

$1\frac{1}{2}$" x $1\frac{1}{2}$" x $\frac{3}{16}$" Angle-Iron and 1" Cold-Rolled Shaft Rails

8" x 8" x $\frac{3}{16}$" Bearing Plate

$1\frac{1}{4}$" Open Linear Bearing

FIGURE 1: SIDE VIEW

THE BEARINGS AND RAILS

Linear bearings like that shown in Figure 2 have no moving parts. They are designed to slide over smooth cylindrical rails and are not easily damaged by dirt or water. The biggest advantage of the Frelon-lined bearings we used, however, is that they stabilized the palm tree and let it move silently.

As shown in Figure 2, we built our rails by welding together 12'-0"-long pieces of $1\frac{1}{4}$" cold-rolled shaft and $1\frac{1}{2}$" x $1\frac{1}{2}$" x $\frac{3}{16}$" angle iron. We took great pains to maintain precise alignment between the shaft and the angle. To avoid heat distortion in either the shaft or the angle we alternated welds first on one side of the angle, then on the other.

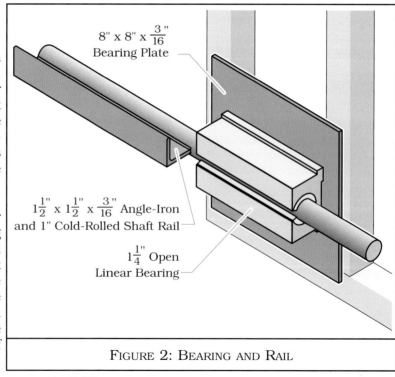

8" x 8" x $\frac{3}{16}$" Bearing Plate

$1\frac{1}{2}$" x $1\frac{1}{2}$" x $\frac{3}{16}$" Angle-Iron and 1" Cold-Rolled Shaft Rail

$1\frac{1}{4}$" Open Linear Bearing

FIGURE 2: BEARING AND RAIL

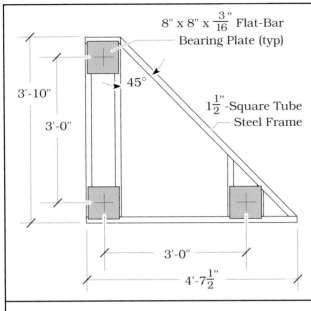

8" x 8" x $\frac{3}{16}$" Flat-Bar
Bearing Plate (typ)

45°

$1\frac{1}{2}$"-Square Tube
Steel Frame

3'-10"

3'-0"

3'-0"

4'-$7\frac{1}{2}$"

FIGURE 3: THE *SHREW* UNDER-STAGE CARRIAGE

THE CARRIAGE

The *Shrew* palm tree was essentially a cut-out: painted $\frac{1}{4}$" MDF on a 1"-square tube steel frame. But because it was 20'-0" tall, we supported and guided it with a fairly large under-stage carriage as shown in Figure 3. The dimensions given in the figure are, of course, design-specific and can be adapted as necessary. In fact, the only essential feature of any version is provision for a 3-point bearing-plate arrangement. With its three bearing plates 36" apart on center, the carriage was tall and long enough to provide ample support for the palm tree.

We used $1\frac{1}{2}$"-square tube steel in our carriage to minimize weight and maximize stability, but other materials could work equally well, as long as the material choices and joining methods keep the bearings correctly spaced and properly aligned.

RESOURCES

The double-length Frelon-lined open linear bearings (part number 6374K31) used in this application were purchased from McMaster-Carr.

❧❧❧❧

A Curved Track and V-Groove Caster Guide

Nathan Wells

The Royal Shakespeare Company's production of *Servant of Two Masters* in New Haven, Connecticut's 2001 International Festival of Arts and Ideas had two triangular wagons that tracked onstage along a curved line while just clearing other closely spaced scenic elements. The wagons, measuring about 8'-0" on each side, had neither motors nor any of the limit switches, electric eyes, or other position-sensing-and-feedback devices commonly used to control scenery movement. Instead, they were pushed by actors and guided into position by a pair of V-groove fixed casters running on a curved black-pipe and flat-bar track as shown in Figure 1.

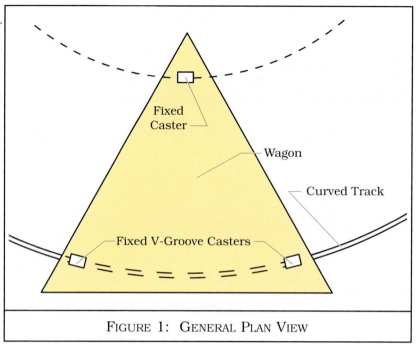

FIGURE 1: GENERAL PLAN VIEW

TRACK CONSTRUCTION

As Figure 2 illustrates, the track consisted of two parts: a rail made of $\frac{3}{4}$" schedule-40 black pipe, and a rail bed made of 2" x 2" x $\frac{1}{4}$" flat bar bent "the hard way" to a uniform radius at a steel yard. A 3" joining pin of $\frac{13}{16}$"-diameter round bar was plug-welded into one end of each section to assure proper alignment between sections (see Figure 3). Holes were drilled and tapped in the other end of each pipe for set screws, which securely joined the sections together at load-in. After the sections had been joined, carpenters screwed the whole assembly to the floor through countersunk holes

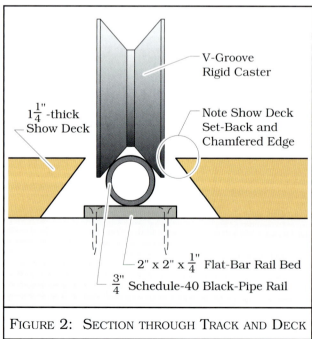

FIGURE 2: SECTION THROUGH TRACK AND DECK

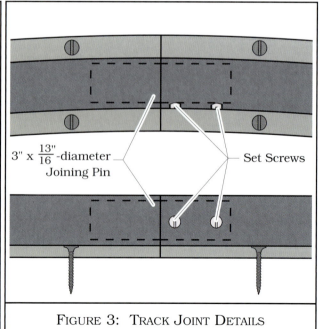

FIGURE 3: TRACK JOINT DETAILS

drilled about 1'-0" apart along both sides of the rail bed as shown in Figure 3 and then loaded in the show deck. At a thickness of $1\frac{1}{4}$", the show deck was almost exactly as thick as the track was tall. Each deck section was chamfered as shown in Figure 2 to provide space for the collection of dirt and debris and set back slightly from the track to minimize the width of the track gap.

OBSERVATIONS

Bolted to the downstage edge of the wagon frames with their axles aligned with the track's radii, the V-groove casters rode low and as quietly as possible on the track. The weight of the wagon kept the casters seated on the pipe regardless of where and how forcefully the actors pushed and, despite the mere $\frac{1}{4}$" clearance between the wagons and other scenic elements, no collisions occurred.

This system worked well on all solid and level stage floors. The company also had on hand a second show deck – one with the track and deck built into a 6"-deep metal frame that could be leveled and adjusted for use on uneven stage floors. Any further refinement of the system might involve replacing the wagon's upstage fixed caster with a zero-throw caster. Using a zero-throw caster would eliminate any alignment issues, prevent any caster marks, and reduce the effort needed to push the wagon.

It's a common problem in theatre – a piece of furniture needs to roll easily onstage and off for shifts but stay fixed on spike during the action of the play. In many cases, perhaps the most appropriate solution is a self-contained system of castered pancake cylinders. Although such systems can represent costly initial investments, they are versatile enough that a small collection of stock parts offers great flexibility over years of use. At the Yale School of Drama, we have re-arranged parts to move everything from beds to kitchen sinks with a minimum of noise and crew effort.

Figure 1 shows how a typical four-castered unit works. A switch controls the passage of pressurized air from the tank to the cylinders. When the switch is open, the entire system is activated to a constant pressure. When it is closed, the system is deactivated as the pressure is released. In the system shown in Figure 1, air pressure extends the casters; in others, it retracts them. But the result is the same in either case: changes in air pressure alternately lift the unit onto its casters and set it back on the floor.

SYSTEM COMPONENTS

The Tank. A 2- or 3-gallon portable air tank mounted to the unit in such a way that it can be charged easily should be sufficient for any system. The bigger the tank, the more operating cycles it will support, but the tanks must be reasonably small for concealment within furniture, McMaster-Carr lists several compact models, all with a maximum pressure of 200 psi.

Fabco-Air Pancake® Cylinders. Figure 2 shows the 1"-stroke, $2\frac{1}{2}$"-bore Fabco-Air C-521-X Pancake® Cylinder. Compact enough for most applications, the $3\frac{3}{4}$"-diameter C-521-X has a maximum operating pressure of 250 psi. Bored and tapped to accept a $\frac{1}{2}$" bolt, its piston rod provides a convenient caster mount.

In simple cylinder systems, only one of the ports is used and the other remains open. In such a set-up, air drives the piston in one direction; gravity and the weight of the unit, in the other. More advanced designs use air pressure to drive the piston in both directions.

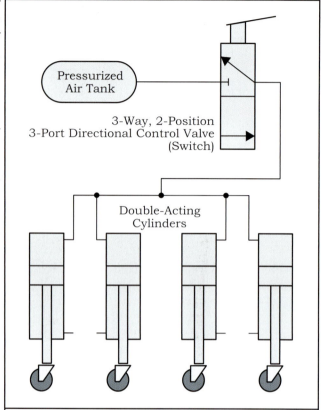

FIGURE 1: FLOW DIAGRAM A FOUR-CASTER LIFT

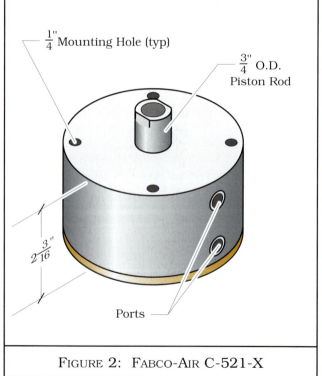

FIGURE 2: FABCO-AIR C-521-X

The Switch. A pneumatic switch controls cylinder actuation. When using air pressure to lift the unit onto its casters and gravity to set it on the floor, a 3-way, 2-position, 3-port directional control valve is a sufficient switch. Such valves are available in finger-operated and pedal-operated designs, and the choice of one over another depends on how the crew will move the unit.

Miscellaneous Components. $\frac{1}{8}$" or $\frac{1}{4}$" pneumatic tubing, available in clear, black, and other colors, carries air between devices. Ideally, the path between the switch and each cylinder should be the same length so that the pressurized air reaches each at the same time. Instant (push-to-connect) fittings connect components easily and allow speedy troubleshooting and modifications. In these fittings, the hose is directly inserted and "locked" in place. They are available for both tube-tube and tube-thread connections.

Regulators indicate how much pressure is in a given part of the system and are indispensable on the tank. Another worthwhile addition to any system is a leg off the air tank that connects to a male air hose quick-disconnect fitting through a cut-off valve. This simplifies recharging. More complicated systems incorporate flow control valves to refine the movement of each cylinder. All parts are obtainable from McMaster-Carr, Grainger, or specialty vendors.

ASSEMBLING THE PARTS

Perhaps the only challenging aspect of designing these systems is deciding how to mount the various components to the unit. In the simplest systems, pressurizing the system may either extend or retract the piston, and configuring the parts depends upon the available mounting space.

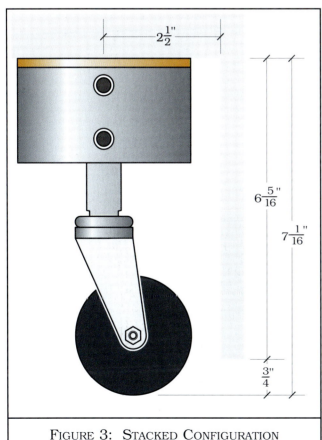

Figure 3 shows a C-521-X in a "stacked" configuration and plumbed to extend the piston rod and lift a skirted piece of furniture off its $2\frac{1}{2}$" Colson Series 2 caster. The cylinder is bolted to a framing member installed $6\frac{5}{16}$" above the base of the skirt to allow $\frac{3}{4}$" clearance at full piston rod extension. The $2\frac{1}{2}$" offset between the inside of the skirt and the center of the cylinder accommodates the caster's $2\frac{13}{32}$" swivel radius.

Should there be too little clearance for a stacked configuration, the limited-height configuration shown in Figure 4 may be useful. Using the same caster, this system, plumbed to lift the unit by retracting the rod, needs almost $\frac{3}{4}$" less headroom; and the use of a shorter caster could reduce the needed headroom to less than 5".

NOTES

Loads and Loading. At a mere 50 psi, a single Pancake® can lift a 223 lbs. load when retracting and a 245 lbs. load when extending, and caster loading capacity is likely to be the limiting factor: the $2\frac{1}{2}$" Colson Series 2 used in this discussion, for instance, has a limit of 200 lbs.

FIGURE 3: STACKED CONFIGURATION

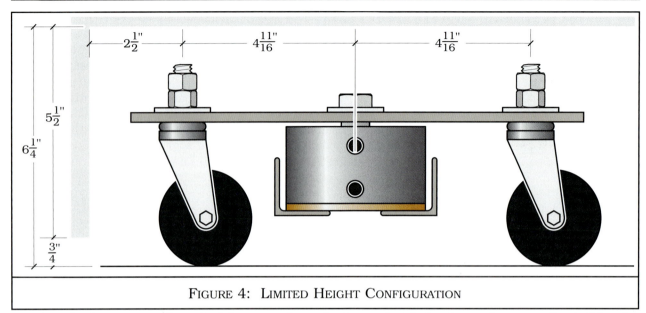

FIGURE 4: LIMITED HEIGHT CONFIGURATION

Further, both systems described here involve cylinder-rod side loads, and in any limited-height system design the distance between the piston rod bolt and the caster stem should be kept to the minimum allowed by the caster's swivel radius – $4\frac{11}{16}$" in this case. The pairing of casters as shown in Figure 4 minimizes side loading. Steel is the best medium for the mounting plates, as the hole patterns must have very tight tolerances in order to fit the manufactured components properly and the plates must be rigid enough to not deflect under the piston's force. Some set-ups may require that each cylinder-caster pair act separately so as to not snag each other should one activate more easily. Although the plates take precision and forethought, the results are worth the effort.

Noise. These systems do not create excessive noise when actuated, but depressurizing them to set units on spike sends out a high-pressure spurt of air. A commercially available muffler attached to the system's exhaust will reduce or eliminate the noise, as will running a hose from the exhaust to a bottle of sand or crumpled burlap.

Leaks. Leaks can sometimes reduce a system's effectiveness to the point of non-operation. Using Teflon® tape and firmly tightening all connections can prevent most leaks. To find non-obvious leaks, apply soapy water to the tubing and connections; it will bubble anywhere air escapes. Repair or replace bad components.

Unit Balance. For systems partially driven by gravity, flow control valves within the system are particularly useful. In addition to being heavy enough to exhaust the system, the weight of units using these systems needs to be more-or-less balanced or the units will rock when rising and descending. Flow control for each cylinder can compensate for uneven loading.

RESOURCES

Colson, colsoncaster.com
Fabco-Air, fabco-air.com
McMaster-Carr, mcmaster-carr.com

❧❧❧❧

The scene design for a production of *Taming of the Screw* at the Long Island Shakespeare Festival included 5 large wagons that had to be locked in 15 to 22 different locations to indicate changes of scene. All sides of each wagon were in view of the audience at one time or another, and the scene designer was keen on hiding the position-locking mechanisms from audience view. The stabilized lift jacks described here were designed to fit within the confines of 2x4 framing, lock the platforms on spike with the flip of a hidden switch, and stabilize the platforms for the actors' use.

Each platform was fitted with a pair of pneumatic lift jacks that, when actuated, partially lift it off its casters. The key parts of each jack are an angle-iron mounting bracket, a compact double-acting pneumatic cylinder, a black-pipe stabilizing sleeve, and a flat-bar and industrial felt presser pad as shown in Figure 1. The stabilizing sleeve protects the extended cylinder rod from the threat of being bent as the platform is jostled by the movement of the actors.

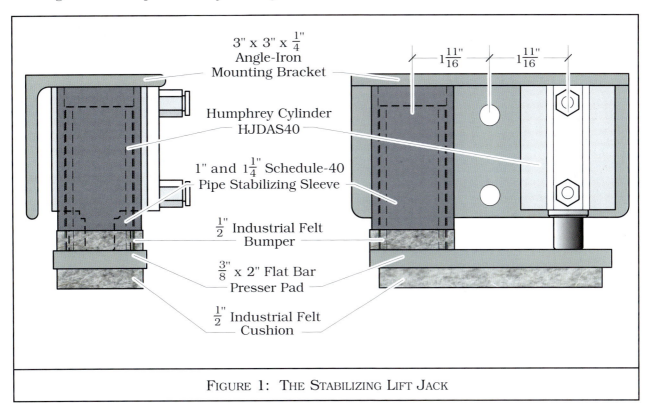

3" x 3" x $\frac{1}{4}$"
Angle-Iron
Mounting Bracket

$1\frac{11}{16}$" $1\frac{11}{16}$"

Humphrey Cylinder
HJDAS40

1" and $1\frac{1}{4}$" Schedule-40
Pipe Stabilizing Sleeve

$\frac{1}{2}$" Industrial Felt
Bumper

$\frac{3}{8}$" x 2" Flat Bar
Presser Pad

$\frac{1}{2}$" Industrial Felt
Cushion

FIGURE 1: THE STABILIZING LIFT JACK

COMPONENTS

The mounting bracket is a piece of 3" x 3" x $\frac{1}{4}$" angle iron cut to a 6" length and drilled with six holes: two $\frac{7}{16}$" holes for the $\frac{3}{8}$" bolts that connect the bracket to platform framing, and four $\frac{5}{16}$" holes (not shown) for the $\frac{1}{4}$" bolts that join the cylinder to the bracket. This design uses a Humphrey HJDAS40 cylinder with an $1\frac{1}{4}$" throw and an $1\frac{1}{2}$" bore because, with a maximim cross-sectional dimesnion of just over $2\frac{1}{4}$", it comfortably fits the leg of the bracket. With modifications to the bracket design, any other short-throw, double-acting cylinder with a 1" to 2" bore would work. Conveniently, the end of this cylinder's rod is threaded for a $\frac{5}{16}$" bolt.

The stabilizing sleeve consists of two short lengths of schedule-40 black pipe. The 3"-long outer sleeve of $1\frac{1}{4}$" schedule-40 black pipe is welded to the bracket; the $2\frac{3}{4}$"-long inner sleeve of 1" sched-ule-40 black pipe, to the presser pad. The presser pad is a $5\frac{1}{4}$" length of $\frac{3}{8}$" x 2" flat bar, drilled and countersunk for the cylinder-rod bolt. Before the presser pad is bolted to the cylinder rod, a washer-like bumper is cut from $\frac{1}{2}$" industrial felt and slipped over the inner sleeve to prevent any metal-on-metal "clank" when the pad retracts. A cushion of $\frac{1}{2}$" industrial felt glued to the bottom of the presser pad reduces noise when the rod is extended.

CONTROL

For this installation, the presser pads were controlled by solenoid-actuated, 4-way, 2-position, spring-return directional control valves, plumbed with the cylinders normally extended to save battery life. The solenoids were powered by sealed lead-acid batteries that were trickle-charged overnight between performances, and an on/off toggle switch was hidden in scenery on each wagon. Pressurized air was supplied from pairs of 60 cubic-inch tanks plumbed in series for a total volume of 120 cubic inches. To accomplish the large number of moves required for most of the wagons, I hid an additional 7-gallon tank in scenery on the wagons. Pressurized at 80 psi, the combination provided enough air for roughly 15 cycles of presser pad movement. The schematic for the electrical connections is shown in Figure 2.

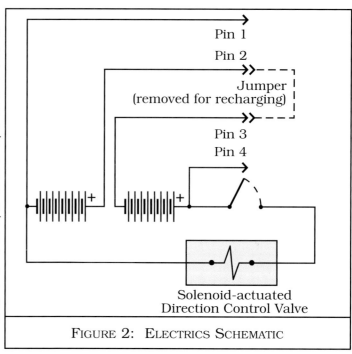

FIGURE 2: ELECTRICS SCHEMATIC

CONCLUSION

This system solved the problem of how to lock a wagon in place without any visible mechanism. Because the system fits a standard 2x4-framed platform, it is fairly simple to bolt 2 jacks and the controls to the platforms after the casters have been attached. The parts are not hard to find and no special equipment or tools are necessary for fabrication.

RESOURCES

Surplus Center: www.surpluscenter.com
Humphrey Products Company: www.humphrey-products.com

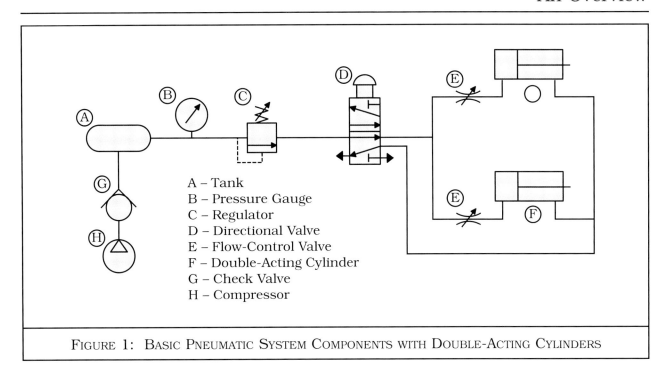

FIGURE 1: BASIC PNEUMATIC SYSTEM COMPONENTS WITH DOUBLE-ACTING CYLINDERS

Several previous articles have explained how to put together one type of pneumatic system or another. This overview explains how to build a system customized for any purpose. The basic components of a pneumatic system are shown in the schematic above.

TANKS

The air tank holds all of the air the system needs. Tanks are rated with a maximum pressure in lbs./in^2 (psi). An air tank's rating is based on the tank's material and the process used in its manufacture. Maximum tank pressures range from 100 psi to 600 psi, and tank capaciiies between 0.3 gallons and 240 gallons. For most small pneumatic systems, a 30-gallon tank with a maximum pressure of 100 psi is appropriate. In portable systems, the size of the tank is an important consideration. Smaller tanks can more easily be tucked into a scenic element or a backstage corner, and 4"-diameter tanks are available. An air tank's cost depends on its maximum pressure, capacity, and dimensions. Portable tanks for most applications cost between $100.00 and $1,000.00.

PRESSURE GAUGES

Pneumatic system gauges serve two purposes: they ensure that tanks are never overfilled and they monitor system pressure, offering a way to check for leaks. Gauges typically cost around $25.00, and the choice of one over another depends on the system's operating pressure range.

REGULATORS

Regulators control the amount of air pressure released from the air tank. If a regulator is used to limit a system's pressure to a required 45 psi, the system's air tank might be filled to 100 psi to make the air supply last longer. Regulators cost between $30.00 and $100.00 depending on style and capacity.

DIRECTIONAL VALVES

Directional valves direct the flow of air through the system. Directional-control valve specifications include five key terms:

Way	the number of ways (directions) air can move
Position	the number of locations a valve operator has
Ports	the number of holes the valve casing has
Valve Operator	the type of device that drives the valve, e.g., toggle switch, push button, etc.
Return	the means by which a valve is returned to its normal position

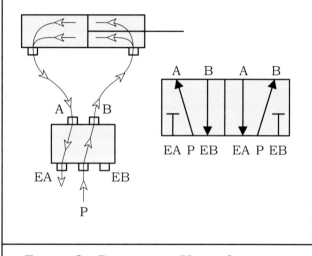

FIGURE 2: DIRECTIONAL VALVE OPERATION

The type of cylinder(s) a system uses will dictate the required number of ways, positions, and ports, while the type of valve operator and return (handles and springs, for instance), as well as the size of the valve, are determined by how it will be handled and where it will be mounted. Three-way, 2-position control valves are generally used with single-acting cylinders; and 4-way, 2-position control valves, with double-acting cylinders. Figure 2 shows how air flows through a 4-way, 2-position valve and into a double-acting cylinder. Helpful schematics like that shown at the right in Figure 2 often accompany directional valves' catalog descriptions. These valves typically cost between $15.00 and $100.00.

FLOW CONTROL VALVES

Flow control valves, also known as cylinder-speed controls, limit the speed with which air passes through the system. Thus, they can speed up or slow down the extension or retraction of a cylinder rod, change how fast an action occurs, or synchronize the operation of several cylinders. Manufactured as single or bi-directionals, they can control the speed of the air as it passes through the system in one or both directions. Flow control valves cost from $15.00 to $35.00.

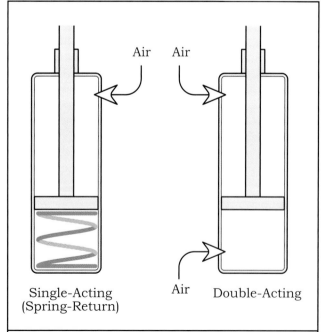

Single-Acting
(Spring-Return)

Double-Acting

FIGURE 3: TWO CYLINDER TYPES

CYLINDERS

Cylinders can be used to raise and lower scenic elements, to hold or release dropping objects, or to lock elements in place; and use determines the type of cylinder needed. Cylinders come in a wide range of shapes and sizes, but all cylinders are of one of two basic types: single-acting and double-acting. As Figure 3 illustrates, single-acting (spring-return) cylinders have one port through which compressed air can push the rod. Keeping the rod extended requires constant pressurization. Once pressure is released, the spring (sometimes assisted by gravity) will retract the rod. Consequently, single-acting cylinders are best used, for instance, to push a unit up when gravity and the spring will be enough to retract the rod fully.

As Figure 3 also shows, double-acting cylinders have two air compartments: pressurizing one compartment extends the rod; pressurizing the other retracts it. In some applications, the spring of a single-acting cylinder is not strong enough to retract the cylinder rod, and a double-acting cylinder is required. Double-acting cylinders are also used when controlling rod travel in both directions is important. Cylinder costs range from $10.00 to $100.00 depending on the materials used, the mounting hardware provided, and on stroke length – the distance the rod can extend.

CHECK VALVES

Check valves allow air to flow in one direction only. Unlike many other pneumatic system components, check valves are general service devices that can be used with air, water, oil, or gas. They range in price from $8.00 to $300.00, depending on the type of valve, the material used, and the maximum pressure they can resist. They are best used at the input of the air tank, allowing the tank to be filled while keeping the air from escaping.

TUBING AND MISCELLANEOUS COMPONENTS

The discussion of compressors is beyond the scope of this article. Any pneumatic system consists of a series of pipe-to-tube adapters, elbow fittings, tee-fittings, and connection adapters. The quality of construction, materials used, and the maximum system pressures determine the costs of these components, and the type to be used is specific to individual applications.

RESOURCES

Alan Hendrickson
Grainger: www.grainger.com
McMaster-Carr: www.mcmaster.com

❧❧❧❧

Using an Endless-Loop Winch as a One-Way Drive

Jonathan Pellow

A heavy wagon needed to move upstage once during each performance of a 2011 production of *Touch(ed)* at the Williamstown Theatre Festival. Since the crew could push the wagon downstage for reset, plans were made to move it by a cable attached to a spiral-grooved-drum hand winch without a return-cable track built into the deck. When a winch with a spiral drum was not available, we devised a way to use an endless-loop grommet-drive hand winch instead.

ADAPTING THE GROMMET-DRIVE

A grommet-drive winch is designed to pull a continuous loop of cable. Normally, the drive side of the cable loop enters the winch, wraps over a series of drive sheaves and idler sheaves, and runs back into the track as a return cable. Grommet-drive winches rely on friction between the sheaves and the cable to move the load, and that friction is normally developed by tensioning the closed cable loop.

Since this production had no return-cable track, the Williamstown team provided the required friction by connecting the return cable to a length of handline that ran straight up, over a spot block on the grid, and back down to a 100 lb sandbag as shown in Figure 1. As the winch pulled the wagon upstage, the sandbag descended, keeping constant tension on the cable.

A FEW NOTES

- This solution requires the same amount of vertical travel for the sandbag as the wagon covers in its travel.

- The weight of the sandbag reduced the effort required of the winch operator.

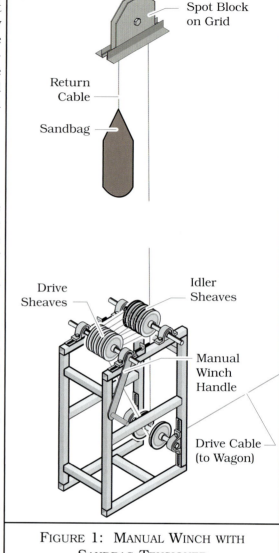

FIGURE 1: MANUAL WINCH WITH SANDBAG TENSIONER

- The more pulling force the winch needs to supply, the heavier the sandbag will have to be to provide enough traction. In this case, the winch was estimated to be supplying around 300 lbs of pulling force. A more detailed analysis of the cable tensions in a typical grommet drive system can be found on pages 360 to 363 of Alan Hendrickson's *Mechanical Design for the Stage*.

❧❧❧

TECHNICAL BRIEF

Scenery Tools

Two Useful Shop Tools — F. Chase Rozelle III

An Affordable Steel Roller — Chris Brown

Handy Tip Carts — Steven Neuenschwander

A Shop-Built Ladder Standoff — Rich Desilets

A Shop-Built Rotisserie for Welding Large Units — Brian Dambacher

A Winch-Driven Bench-Mount Panel Saw — Jeff Smejdir

A Shop-Built Sliding-Head Hold-Down — Eric Casanova

A LEVER-ARM RETRACTABLE CASTER

The uses for a retractable caster in both the scene shop and onstage are many. There are many designs for this bit of hardware, but few are as easy to manufacture as that illustrated in Figure 1. The caster's vertical movement is executed with the now familiar lever-arm toggle clamp. Some of these clamps, such as McMaster-Carr's 5093A58, feature plungers with internal threads, and some stem casters, such as McMaster-Carr's 2834T61, have perfectly matching external threads. Epoxy or thread-locking compound will keep the two pieces mated, and at under $25.00 a set, they make a very cost-effective addition to any theatre's stock.

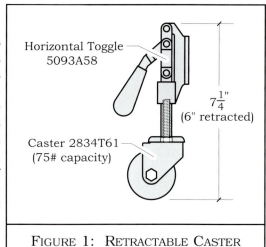

FIGURE 1: RETRACTABLE CASTER

A COUNTERSINK LAYOUT JIG

Striking thin sheet goods such as MDF or Masonite for reuse in future productions is often a tenuous proposition. Inevitably, one or two screws are overlooked in the haste of strike, and the goods crack or tear in a way that makes entire 4x8s worthless. The problem is locating the original screws in the less-than-ideal lighting conditions of strike – especailly when the material has a variegated paint treatment. If the screws are randomly located, the problem becomes even greater. One solution to this problem is to locate the screws on perfect 16" centers. A jig such as that pictured in Figure 2 allows for just such precision. Made out of a used piece of MDF, the jig can be laid out on sheets of new goods. A countersink-equipped screw gun can, even with less-than-skilled labor, create sheet after sheet of perfectly countersunk, ready-for-installation sheets of MDF. Not only will all sheets be installed with evenly spaced screws, these screws will be easy to find at strike.

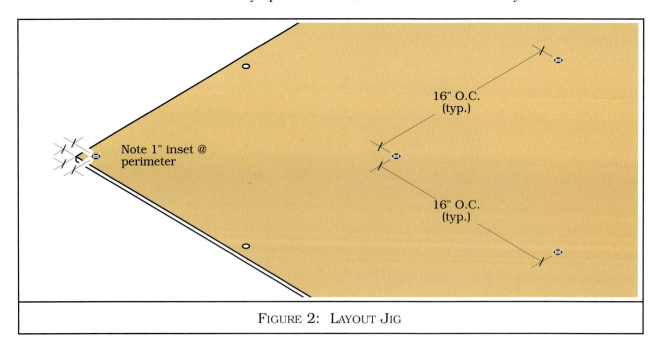

FIGURE 2: LAYOUT JIG

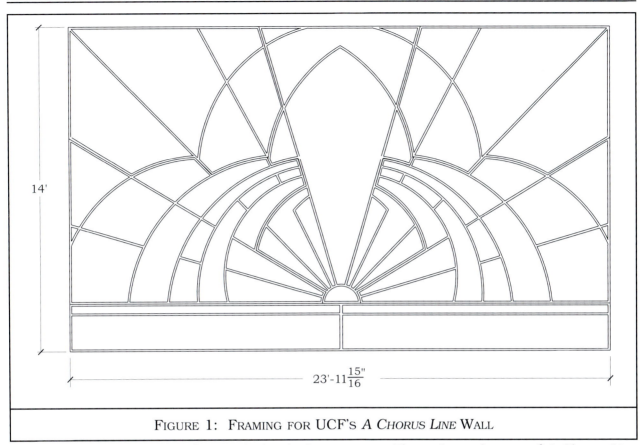

FIGURE 1: FRAMING FOR UCF'S *A CHORUS LINE* WALL

Designs for the University of Central Florida Conservatory Theatre's production of *A Chorus Line* included the 14'x24' flown wall shown in Figure 1, a tracery of thin arcs of different sizes strong enough to support panes of Plexiglas® some mirrored and others translucent. Square-tube steel was the obvious framing material, and the need for an inexpensive, efficient method of bending consistent arcs led us to build an affordable steel roller.

This roller comprises the 3 independent roller stations shown in Figure 2: two identical end stations and a mid-station. The height of the mid-station's wheel can be changed by turning the threaded rod on which the wheel is mounted. Achieving a desired arc is a trial-and-error process in which gross adjustments are made by moving the end stations closer to or farther from the mid-station and/or by blocking them up. The stock is then pushed back and forth through the roller, and the arc is formed by tightening the mid-station screw between passes. For use, the stations are temporarily bolted to a table or the floor, but bolts were not used in setting up for the photo in Figure 2.

FIGURE 2: BENDER SETUP

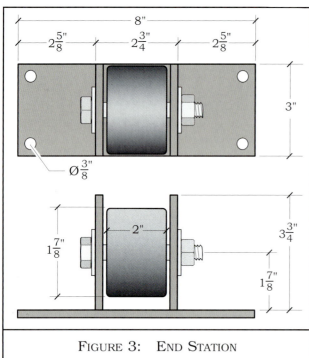

FIGURE 3: END STATION

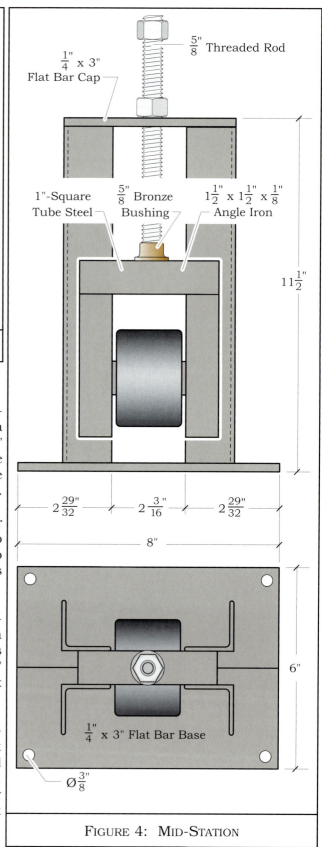

CONSTRUCTION NOTES

In addition to the wheels and connecting hardware, construction of this roller required only a few short lengths of $\frac{1}{4}$" x 3" flat bar and $1\frac{1}{2}$" x $1\frac{1}{2}$" x $\frac{1}{8}$" angle iron as shown in Figures 3 and 4. The dimensions were chosen to suit the no-name casters we found at a local building supply store.

The end stations were made of $\frac{1}{4}$" x 3" flat bar welded together, and the only important detail to note is that the flat bar uprights were cut to extend above the tops of the end-station wheels to help guide the tube steel as it was rolled.

The mid-station was somewhat more complicated. Here, the wheel rode on an axle carried by a U-shaped frame made of 1"-square tube steel as shown in Figure 4. Four pieces of $1\frac{1}{2}$" x $1\frac{1}{2}$" x $\frac{1}{8}$" angle iron welded to a base and cap made of $\frac{1}{4}$" x 3" flat bar guided the "U" up and down.

The bushing welded to the "U" received and prevented damage to the $\frac{5}{8}$" threaded-rod screw that drove the wheel up and down. The rod passed through a $\frac{5}{8}$" nut welded in the center of the cap. The rolling force was applied to the wheel by turning the threaded rod at a second $\frac{5}{8}$" nut welded to its top end.

FIGURE 4: MID-STATION

FINAL COMMENTS

Operating this roller was even easier than building it. We rough-cut our $\frac{1}{2}$"-square tube steel stock overlong to account for the waste we knew would occur at the ends. But then, once the three stations had been aligned with each other and bolted down, two carpenters quickly formed the square-tube steel into the elegant arcs that framed the wall shown in Figure 5.

FIGURE 5: PRODUCTION PHOTO OF UCF'S *A CHORUS LINE*

Shop-built tip carts are simple but effective tools for moving pieces of scenery or other awkward items around the stage or shop. Moreover, they take only about 30 minutes to build and can be tucked away in any convenient corner.

Construction is simple. Cut two scraps of $\frac{3}{4}$" plywood into rectangles measuring 9" x 18" and glue them together. Use a round-over bit to ease the edges and sand the top and bottom surfaces of the layup. Mark the centerline of the long side of the rectangle. Center a pair of 3" straight casters on this line, perpendicular to the line and 1" in from each edge. After marking and drilling the caster plate holes, countersink them to keep the top of the tip cart flat. Bolt the casters to the plywood with flat-head bolts and nylocks.

FIGURE 1: A TYPICAL TIP CART

Carpeting the tops of the carts can help protect the painted surfaces of any items they carry, and it may also add a useful amount of friction between the cart and the items. On the other hand, if your shop typically builds $3\frac{3}{4}$"-wide flats, you can rout a 4"-wide slot down the 18" length to hold the base of the flat, improving its stability as you move flats around.

❧❧❧

The crown molding was the last scenic item to go up on the set for *Wait Until Dark* at The Raven Theater in Healdsburg, California, in February, 2007. With the appliances and a stair unit already in place, I decided to make an extension ladder accessory to hold the ladder away from the flats.

FIGURE 1: THE STANDOFF IN USE

FIGURE 2: STANDOFF CONSTRUCTION

None of the connecting hardware in this device penetrates the stiles of the ladder. Like commercially available ladder stabilizers, this attachment gave one of our extension ladders a wider top bearing, distributing whatever weight was on the ladder across the surface of the flats, and the 10" standoff distance it provided made attaching the crown molding very easy. As a plus the lx4s made a temporary shelf to rest the molding on while starting the 3" screws.

ﻗﺒﻗﺒﻗﺒ

A Shop-Built Rotisserie for Welding Large Units

Brian Dambacher

In April 2006, the shop staff at the Meadow Brook Theatre in Michigan was presented with a project an example of which is shown in Figure 1: ten identical butterfly wings measuring 11' wide x 18' tall, framed in $\frac{3}{4}$"-square 6061-T6 aluminum box with interior veins of $\frac{3}{8}$" 6061-T6511 aluminum round stock.

Normally, welding pieces this large would take several hours, even with the aid of jig blocks. To save time and make the process a little less physically taxing, ATD/Shop Foreman, Jeff Camp, built a sort of rotisserie, consisting of a steel frame and a pair of armatures mounted on boom bases.

FIGURE 1: BUTTERFLY WING ON THE BENCH

COMPONENTS

The custom-built steel frame carried a number of stock flats secured together and stiffened as necessary. The frame rotated horizontally on two shop-built armatures (one at each end of the frame) made from swivel Cheseboros, forged C-clamps and short scraps of 16-gauge 1" x 3" tube steel and $1\frac{1}{2}$" schedule-40 black pipe. The two armatures were held up on stock boom bases and $1\frac{1}{2}$" schedule-40 black pipe. In Figure 2, the frame has been rotated to be perpendicular to the stage floor. The frame and base need no further discussion. See Figure 3 for detail of the armatures.

CONSTRUCTION AND USE

The first wing was welded on a conventional template bench. It was then moved to the rotating template bench, where it was used to place jig blocks that were subsequently screwed down.

FIGURE 2: FRAME, ARMATURE, AND BASE

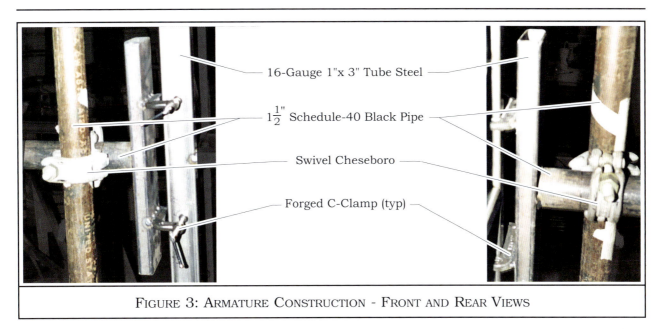

16-Gauge 1"x 3" Tube Steel

$1\frac{1}{2}$" Schedule-40 Black Pipe

Swivel Cheseboro

Forged C-Clamp (typ)

FIGURE 3: ARMATURE CONSTRUCTION - FRONT AND REAR VIEWS

As they welded, the carpenters rotated the bench into whatever position seemed most convenient for the moment. Consequently, the rotating template bench and its jigs allowed them to save time and avoid fatigue.

&a &a &a

A Winch-Driven Bench-Mount Panel Saw

Jeff Smejdir

One element of the scenic design for the Denver Center Theatre Company's production of *Crowns* was a sizeable deck of tapered planks, the longest of which measured 64'. To cut the tapers, Master Carpenter Eric Moore, designed and built a winch-driven bench-mount panel saw that could make cuts 40' long. This article describes a re-creation of that tool, which consists of three sub-assemblies: the saw and carriage; the track and saw bed, and the winch and control system. Figure 1 describes how the tool works. The winch-driven cable pulls the saw to make one continuous cut.

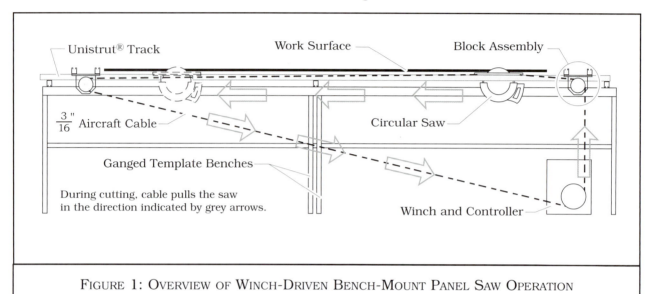

FIGURE 1: OVERVIEW OF WINCH-DRIVEN BENCH-MOUNT PANEL SAW OPERATION

TRACK AND SAW BED

First things first, note that bench-mount panel saws must be set up in such a way that they cut as they move away from the operator. In the setup shown in Figures 3 and 4, the operator's station is next to the winch at the bottom of the picture, and the saw cut begins at that end of the track.

Figures 3 and 4 show our bench-mount saw at two stages of assembly and testing. To begin its assembly, we clamped two template benches together and screwed scrap lengths of P1000 slotted Unistrut® to their tops. The shorter scrap, visible in Figure 3 only, extended about 2" beyond the template bench and supported only the closer track. The other – the cantilevers – extended 12" farther and supported both tracks.

The tracks were made from two 14' lengths of Unistrut® that we bolted to the cantilevers. Before tightening the carriage in place, we slid it back and forth manually with the saw unplugged to tweak the track alignment. Finally, we bolted two previously made-up assemblies of stock 6" loft blocks and scrap Unistrut® to the ends of the

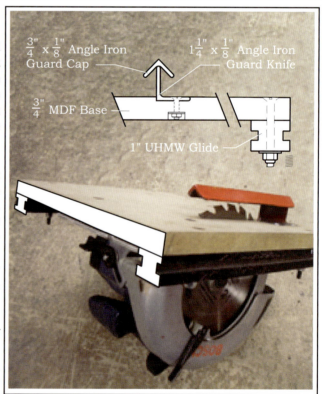

FIGURE 2: THE SAW AND CARRIAGE

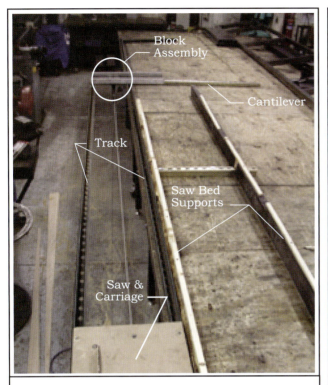

FIGURE 3: SETUP VIEW 1

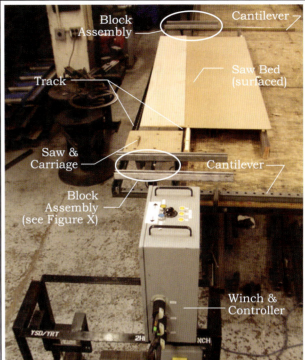

FIGURE 4: SETUP VIEW 2

tracks. A close-up of a typical block assembly is shown bolted to a pair of tracks in Figure 5. We spaced our block assemblies far enough apart to give the saw blade 10' of clear travel. To provide the bench-mount panel saw with a work surface, we screwed scrap-lumber saw-bed supports to the tops of the benches as shown in Figure 3 and topped these supports with a work surface of $\frac{1}{4}"$ MDF as shown in Figures 4 and 6. Note that as the saw glided along the tracks in its first pass under power, it trimmed the edge of the MDF work surface. The newly cut edge served as a materials-alignment reference while we used the saw. As indicated in Figure 6, narrow materials to be tapered can be held in place by screws driven up through the work surface. Wider materials can be clamped to the work surface instead.

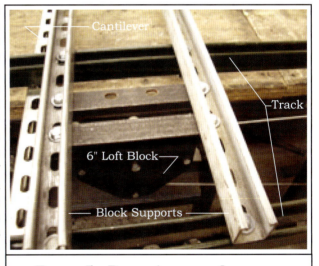

FIGURE 5: BLOCK ASSEMBLY INSTALLED

WINCH AND CONTROL SYSTEM

This set-up used a stock winch assembly, (2 HP gear motor, 10" drum,) to pull $\frac{3}{16}"$ aircraft cable through the block assemblies. Winch control was supplied by a jog box: forward/reverse buttons, and a speed pot. A power-strip on/off switch supplied AC to the circular saw. Aircraft cable was secured to the carriage by pinching the cable between the saw shoe and a nut.

CHECK-OUT AND OPERATION

Before each use, the operator must check all mechanical connections – those on the saw and carriage as well as those on the track. Next, the operator must assure that the saw and its on/off switch are working properly and that the blade guard is in place and secure. Finally, the operator must run the carriage up and down the track under winch power but with the saw off, checking that the saw's power cable is well managed and that the carriage travels smoothly.

❧❧❧

A Screw Holding Material in Place on the Work Surface

MDF Work Surface

Scrap-Lumber Bed Support

FIGURE 6: CLOSE-UP AT START OF CUT

This shop-built sliding-head hold down is designed to secure projects to wooden working surfaces. The #56-K "Pony" Deep Reach clamp can be purchased for less than $20.00 and, when not used as a hold down, it can be used as intended in a bar clamp, while the pipe and base store away.

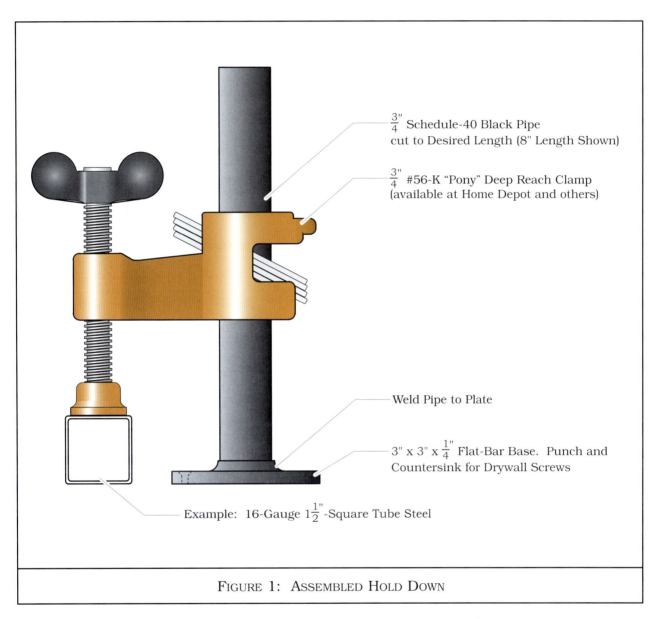

$\frac{3"}{4}$ Schedule-40 Black Pipe
cut to Desired Length (8" Length Shown)

$\frac{3"}{4}$ #56-K "Pony" Deep Reach Clamp
(available at Home Depot and others)

Weld Pipe to Plate

3" x 3" x $\frac{1"}{4}$ Flat-Bar Base. Punch and
Countersink for Drywall Screws

Example: 16-Gauge $1\frac{1}{2}"$-Square Tube Steel

FIGURE 1: ASSEMBLED HOLD DOWN

The base of the hold down illustrated in Figure 1 is a 3" x 3" square of $\frac{1}{4}"$ flat bar that, because of its size, gives the hold down more leverage than an ordinary pipe flange would.

❧❧❧❧❧

Combined Topical Index: Volumes I through III

Costumes

Collaborating in Metal Costume Construction	*Deanna Jane Stuart*	II:2
Building Authentic Elizabethan Ruffs	*Robin Hirsch*	II:5
A Milliner's Approach to Maskmaking: Part I	*Jon Cardone*	II:8
A Milliner's Approach to Maskmaking: Part II	*Laura G. Brown*	II:10
Collapsible Change Booths	*Cheng-Heng Lee*	II:13
Taking a Pattern from an 18th-Century Clothing Piece	*Linda Kelley-Dodd*	III:2
Deriving a Pattern for 18th-Century American Men's Fall-Front Breeches	*Linda Kelley-Dodd*	III:5

Lighting

Hanging Cardboards	*Eugene Leitermann*	I:2
A System to Facilitate Hanging Lights	*Jerry Limoncelli*	I:4
Another System to Facilitate Hanging Lights	*Jack D. Sutton*	I:5
Computer-Assisted Lighting Design	*Larry Schwartz*	I:6
Acid-Cut Gobos	*Jaylene Graham*	I:9
An Improved Boom-Base Sandbag	*Jon Lagerquist*	I:11
Easily Concealed, Low-Profile Lighting Fixtures	*Jon Carlson*	I:12
Low-Cost ACL Fixtures	*John Holloway*	I:14
Two Devices to Simplify Cable Tracing	*Steven A. Balk*	I:16
Organizing Electrical Cable in a Smaller Production Department	*Jonet Buchanan*	II:16
Extending the Life of Strip-Light Color Media	*Barbara Mangrum*	II:18
Inexpensive MR16 Lamp Holders	*William C. Harrison Jr.*	II:19
Calculating LED Circuit Requirements	*Daniel T. Lisowski*	III:10
Magnetic Color Flipper for a Source Four® 10° Follow Spot	*Kathryn Krier*	III:13
Focus Track and Chair	*Jonathan A. Reed*	III:15
The Panhandler: Pillow-Block Assist for ERS Panning	*Brian Swanson*	III:17
Modular Stor-Mor Solution	*Joel Furmanek*	III:18
The Cadillac of Rolling Booms	*Matt Welander*	III:20
Dimmable Fluorescents	*Alan Hendrickson*	III:22
Guidelines for Using Neon on Steel Structures	*Chris Swetcky*	III:25
Using Black Screening Material As Inexpensive "Black Scrim" Panels	*Barbara Tun-Tionyco*	III:27

Lighting Effects

Simple Smoke	*Michael D. Fain*	I:20
A Fog Machine Silencer	*Kenneth Sanders*	I:21
A Fog Manifold	*Andy Sharp*	I:22
Ground Row/Fog Disperser	*Tim Clinton*	I:24

Pyro Stand	*Michael D. Fain*	I:26
A Photographic Aid in the Preparation of Scenic Projections	*Jon Farley*	I:28
A Fiber Optic Star Drop	*Billy Woods*	I:30
A Television Lighting Effect	*Michael Van Dyke*	I:32
Dancing Light	*Martin Gwinup*	I:34
A Schmitt-Trigger Practical Switch	*Alan Hendrickson and Patrick Seeley*	II:22
Moving Leaves by the Power of Spring	*Mark R. Weaver*	II:23
A Ground-Fog Generating System	*Erik Walstad*	II:24
A Phase-Changing Moon Box	*Christopher Jensen*	II:26
The World's Brightest Glowing Thing	*Stuart Wheaton*	II:29
Disappearing Footlights	*Scott L. Silver*	II:31
Modifying Kodak's Fun-Flash® for Theatrical Effects	*James S. Hill*	II:33
Simultaneous Realtime Control of Sound and Light with MIDI	*Lee Faulkner*	II:34
A Sure-Shot Fireball Effect	*Dave King*	II:36
A Motorized, Mirrored Rain Effect	*Adriane Levy*	II:39
Theatrically Safe Outdoor Bonfires	*Ashley Elder*	II:42
A Free-Falling Ball of Light	*Donald W. Titus*	II:44
A Motion-Controlled Practical	*Pablo Souki*	III:30
Overlooking-the-Town Light Box	*Christopher Jensen*	III:32
A Light-Beam Box	*Michael Kraczek*	III:34
Safe Chimney Smoke Generators	*Maura LaRiviere*	III:36
An Inexpensive Fog Chiller	*Steven Hood*	III:39
Constructing a Battery-Powered Candle	*Eric Lin*	III:41
Simulating Neon with Rope Light	*Chris Russo*	III:42
A Liquid Lamp	*Karen Walcott*	III:43

PAINTING

Theatrical Applications of Analine Dye	*Theodore G. Ohl*	I:36
Metallic Painting Process	*Judy Zanotti*	I:37
Frosting Plexiglass Windows with Beer and Epsom Salts	*Curtis Hardison*	I:38
Texture Techniques Using Paper and Flexible Glue	*Martin Gwinup*	I:39
Photo-Murals for the Stage	*Christopher H. Barreca*	I:41
Painting Photographic Scenery Using Friskets	*Charles Grammer*	I:44
Photocopy Transfers	*David A. Stach*	I:46
Two Periscopes for Full-Scale Cartooning	*Max Leventhal*	I:47
Easy Stenciling Technique	*Tom LeTourneau*	I:50
Using Embossed Wallpaper for Low Relief	*Kelly Dean Allison*	II:48
Dyeing Marble Patterns into Fabric	*Priscilla Putnam*	II:49
A Durable, Rough Texture Coating for Scenery and Props	*Pater Liao*	II:51

Shop-Made Naugahyde	*April Busch*	II:53
Simple and Inexpensive Stained Glass	*Michael Broh*	II:55
Creating an Antique Mirror Effect	*Michael Broh*	II:57
A Durable Plaster Texture Revisited	*Owen M. Collins*	III:46
An Affordable Gold Leaf Finish	*Ben Stark*	III:47
A More User-Friendly Lining Stick	*Don Harvey*	III:49
Large-Scale Crackle Paint Effect	*Ben Stark*	III:52
A Clean Solution for Colored Dirt	*Nora Hyland*	III:53
Using Alum to De-Wrinkle Drops	*Nicole L. Bromley*	III:55

PROJECTIONS

Melded Technologies: Video Projections and Moving Mirrors	*M. Barrett Cleveland*	III:58
Low-Memory, High-Quality Digital Images for the Stage	*David B. Carter*	III:61
A Servo-Controlled Projector Dowser	*Lung-Kuei Lin*	III:64
Low-Cost RP Screens for the Stage	*Daniel J. Anteau*	III:66
A Stock Batten-Mounted Projector Bracket	*Pierre-André Salim*	III:68

PROPS

Snowballs for the Stage	*Theodore G. Ohl*	I:52
Artificial Canapes	*Sharon Braunstein*	I:53
Stage Blood	*Randy Fullerton*	I:54
A Remote-Controlled Portable Water Source	*Cosmo Catalano, Jr.*	I:56
Circuitry for a Remotely Dimmable, Portable Lighting Practical	*Donald R. Youngberg*	I:58
Remote-Controlled Live Fire	*Chris P. Jaehnig*	I:59
High-Volume Low-Cost Modelling Clay	*Jon Lagerquist*	I:61
Gelatin Molds	*Mark Shanda*	I:62
A Remote-Controlled Flash Effect	*Steven A. Balk*	I:63
Growing Flowers Onstage	*Scott Servheen*	I:65
Break-Away Glass: Formula and Process	*Bill Ellis*	I:67
A Butane Torch for Use Onstage	*Rod Hickey*	I:69
A Safe Lamp-Oil Torch	*Alan Hendrickson*	I:71
A Light-Sensitive Portable Practical	*Tim Fricker*	I:73
Faking Waterproof Beer Can Labels	*Chris Higgins*	I:74
Quick Casts in Under Two Hours	*Christopher Sibilia*	I:75
Liquefied Auto Body Putty	*Dr. Ronald Naverson*	I:77
A Very Useful Snow Machine	*Richard Gold*	I:78
More Stage Blood	*Ben Thoron*	II:60
Low-Tech Ghost Effects: Moving Furniture	*Scott Werbin*	II:61
Latchless Rotating Shelving	*Kevin Hines*	II:63
Rat Trap Stage Trick	*Robert C. Cotnoir*	II:64

A Flashing Cane for Casting Spells	*Rich Desilets*	II:65
Building Distorting Mirrors	*Colin Young*	II:66
Pneumatic Debris Cannons	*Robin M. MacDuffie*	II:67
A Recycled-Bike Rig for a "Zinging" Puppet	*Chris Knasiak*	II:69
A Simple Approach to Complicated Theatrical Sculpture	*Chris Van Alstyne*	II:70
Ornate Chandeliers Made Simple	*Neil Mulligan*	II:72
Maskmaking 101	*Kathryn Goodman and Ray Kent*	II:75
Creating a Glass Block Effect	*Jim Bazewicz*	II:78
The Cheap, Easy, and Effective Snow Machine	*Parris Bradley*	II:79
Making a Severed Head	*Michael Banta*	III:72
Replicating Bones, Part I: Molds	*Julia Powell*	III:75
Replicating Bones, Part II: Casting	*Julia Powell*	III:78
Realistic Stage Stun Gun	*Mike Vandercook and Joe Huppert*	III:80
CO_2 Gunshot Wound	*Brian Smallwood*	III:82
Three Favorite Blood Recipies	*Jennifer McClure*	III:85
Three Techniques for Applying Stage Blood	*Sandra Jervey and Jennifer McClure*	III:87
Urinal Head Wax Mold Casting Process	*Andrew Hagan*	III:90
A Device to Simulate Urination Onstage	*Ryan C. Hales*	III:93
Bas-Relief Sculptures in Durham's Rock Hard Water Putty®	*Greg Blakey and Samantha Porter*	III:94
A Cremora®-Fueled Pyrotechnic Alternative	*Adam J. Dahl*	III:96
A Remotely Extinguished Cremora®-Fueled Flame Effect	*Chris Peterson*	III:99
A Mechanism for a Battery-Operated Torch	*Katherine Gloria Tharp*	III:102
A Safe Glass Mirror Breaking Effect	*John McCullough*	III:104
1970s' Period Pull-Tab Beverage Cans	*Jeff Smejdir*	III:105
An Affordable Chair for *Sweeney Todd*	*Colin Buckhurst*	III:108
Using a Trolling Reel to Move Small Furniture and Props	*Steve Schmidt*	III:110
Hand-Held Dancing Fireflies	*Andrew V. Wallace*	III:111

RIGGING HARDWARE

A Hinge Device to Facilitate Hanging Vertical Booms	*William R., Jr. Wyatt*	I:82
Sandwich Batten Clamps	*Jon Lagerquist*	I:84
Spider-Cable Clamps	*Tom Neville*	I:86
PVC and Steel Pipe Traveller System	*David Sword*	I:88
The Internal Expansion Pipe Splice	*Richard Mone*	I:89
A "Bulldog Clip" Quick Release Rig	*Scott Robertson*	I:91
Phenolic Resin Pulleys: Out of the Skies and Into the Future	*Corky Boyd*	I:92
A Mini-Pinrail for Counterweight Rails	*Steve Nelson*	II:82
Shop-Built Scenery Bumpers and Rollers	*Tracy K. Lewis*	II:83

A Quick-Release for Drops	*Shuen-Cheng Shih*	II:85
A Pneumatically Tripped, Circular Curtain	*Kraig Blythe*	II:87
A Modular Aluminum Drop Rig	*Mario Tooch*	II:89
A Quiet Glide and Unistrut Traveler System	*Chuck Adomanis*	II:92
Pneumatic Drop Boxes	*Andrew Plumer*	II:94
A Quick-Load Floor Pulley Design	*Joanne Chang*	II:97
An Adjustable Flat Hanger	*Moshe H. Peterson*	III:114
A Versatile Flat-and-Track System	*Rich Desilets*	III:115
A Convenient Shop-Built Mini-Arbor	*Joe Hamlin*	III:116
A Sleeve for Increasing Arbor Capacity	*Drew Becker*	III:118
Positioning Catches for Traveler Track	*Justin Elie*	III:119
Plans for a Double Kabuki Drop	*Kate Wicker*	III:120
An Inexpensive Quiet Shop-Built Track System	*Shaminda Amarakoon*	III:122
A Simple Drop Rig for Small Payloads	*Andrew V. Wallace*	III:124

RIGGING TECHNIQUES

Flying Drops in Limited Fly Space	*Bruce W. Bacon*	I:96
A Quick and Simple Rigging System	*Darryl S. Waskow*	I:99
A Quick and Simple Rigging System: Addendum	*Jon Lagerquist and Jamie C. Anderson*	I:101
A Simultaneous Travel-Fly Rig	*Don Holder*	I:102
A Travel-Fly Rig Modified	*Paul Carter*	I:104
A Quiet Wire-Rope Curtain Track	*Kieran Kelly*	I:105
Automatic Drop Tripping	*John C. Howard*	I:106
Rotating Flats While Flying	*Jon Lagerquist*	I:107
Offset Flying	*John C. Howard*	I:110
A Tracked System for Flying Actors	*Delbert L. Hall*	I:111
A Safe and Sag-Free Cable Curtain Track	*Ann Johnson*	I:113
A Parallel-Guide Rig	*Magi Oman*	I:115
A Simple Approach to Stretching Drops	*Ray Inkel*	II:100
Panel-Tipping Rig	*Eric Weston*	II:103
Quiet, Heavy-Duty Traveler Track	*Richard Gold*	II:105
Self-Trimming Flown Units	*Michael Patterson*	II:108
A Flying Rig for Low Ceiling Theaters	*James Lile*	II:111
Adjustable Scenery Picks of Unistrut	*Christopher L. Morris*	II:113
An Irising Portal	*Chuck Adomanis*	II:115
Flying an Actor with a Ghost-Load Rig	*Mark Prey*	III:126
Hardware for a Ghost-Load Rig	*Michael Madravazakis*	III:128
An Inexpensive Controllable Drip System	*Stuart Little*	III:131
Fabric Swag Scene Changes Made Easy	*Aaron Bollinger*	III:133
Tilting a Wall	*Greg Winkler*	III:135

Pick Length Calculator: A Quick Reference	*Andrew James Gitchel*	III:137
Rocking a Batten for *Pirates of Penzance*	*Brian Frank*	III:139
A Tricking Batten System for Stretched Panels	*Aaron Verdery*	III:141
Falling Leaves Effect for the Stage	*Kellen C. McNally*	III:143
A Temporary Lineset for Lightweight Objects	*Amanda J. Haley*	III:145
Automating a Snow Bag	*Ryan Retartha*	III:146
Soaker-Hose Rain Effect	*Thomas R. Delgado*	III:147
A Fan Powered Confetti Drop	*Alex Bergeron*	III:148
A Device for Dropping Sand from Above	*Mike Backhaus*	III:150
Four Continuous-Beam Formulas for Stage Battens	*Dan Perez*	III:151

SAFETY

General Specifications for Stairs and Ladders	*Theodore G. Ohl*	I:118
Compliance with Fire Safety	*George Lindsay*	I:119
Determining Tension in Bridling Lines	*Paul Carter*	I:121
Allowable Loads on Lumber-Nail Joints	*John Marean*	I:122
A Comparison of Rope-Braking Devices	*Jon Lagerquist*	I:125
Fire Safety Handbook	*DWPhineas Perkins*	I:128
A Stock Safety Rail System	*Mark Stevens*	II:118
CO2 Fire Suppression System for Theatrical Fire Effects	*Jens McVoy*	II:120
An LED and SPST Safety Feedback	*Jim Siebels*	III:154
Introducing a Live Animal to the Stage	*Kristan Falkowski*	III:155
Comparison of Safety Wrap Techniques for Counterweight Linesets	*John Starmer*	III:157

SCENERY

Sawdust Street Bricks	*Douglas L. Rusk*	I:132
Decision Trees	*Walter Williams*	I:133
Improved Soft-Covered Stock Masking Units	*James Hull Miller*	I:136
Mass-Producing Styrofoam Balusters	*James Brewczynski*	I:138
Laying Out Odd-Shaped Raked Decks	*M. Craig McKenzie*	I:141
Free-Standing Curved Staircase	*Phillip Grayson*	I:144
I-Beam Tracking System	*Edmund B. Fisher and Thomas P. Sullivan*	I:146
A Measured Approach to Kerfing	*Daniel J. Culhane*	I:148
Alternate Spike Marks	*Andrew Mudd*	I:149
Lightweight Acting Cubes	*Fritz Schwentker*	II:124
Step Modules for Stock 6:12 or 8:10 Stairs	*John D. Ervin*	II:127
Flexi-Pitch Escape Stairs	*Kevin Hines*	II:129
A No-Weld Spiral Staircase	*David A. Griffith*	II:132
Pinless (and Painless) Pipe Pockets	*Elisa R. Griego*	II:134
Spot-Welding Scrim with Sobo	*Robert Coleman*	II:137

Handrail Armatures for a Grand Staircase	Stephen Lars Klein	II:140
Tube Steel Perimeter Framing for Flats	Robert Duggan	II:143
Triscuit Cart	Scott Braudt	II:145
A Pre-Cambered Overhanging Ceiling	Jason Davis	II:147
Whalers – Low-Profile Stiffeners for Steel-Framed Flats	Rob Kovarik	II:149
A Space-Saving Rain Wall	Eugene Yang	II:151
Fabric Hinges for Space-Frame Flats	Richard Gold	II:154
PVC Framing for Non-Weight-Bearing Scenery	Owen M. Collins	II:156
A Modified Parallel Platform Unit for Audience Risers	Owen M. Collins	II:158
Pneumatically Actuated Caster Planks	Drew Monahan	III:162
Making Oversized Cove Moulding on the Table Saw	Nick Bria	III:165
Using 18-Gauge $1\frac{1}{2}$"-Square Tube Steel to Build Taller and Longer	Annie Jacobs	III:167
Compound Miters Simplified	Peter Malbuisson	III:169
Kerfing Steel for Larger Arcs	Andrew Farrow	III:172
"Pacing" Groundrow Elements	Kevin Hines	III:174
Building Stairs from Scrap Plywood	David A. Griffith and Gerald Kawaoka	III:176
Isolating Door Vibration in Flats	Sam Michael	III:177
Changing Portraits with Ganged Sunroofs	Andrew F. Southard and Don Harvey	III:179
Eleven Quick Tips	Craig Martin	III:181
Flexi-Pitch Handrail	Dorian James Robison	III:182
Fauxberglass: An Inexpensive Alternative to Fiberglass	Kalen Larsen	III:184
Setting Up an X-Ref Master File	Ted Griffith	III:186
Providing a Column Shaft with Entasis	Dan Perez	III:189

SCENERY DECKS

Stressed-Skin Platform Units	Bronislaw J. Sammler	I:152
Modular Platform Legging	Tony Forman	I:153
Open Corner Platforms	Keith Bangs	I:155
Lap-Joint Decks	William Buck	I:157
A Platform System	Bronislaw Sammler	I:159
Two Methods of Constructing Terrain Decks	David Cunningham	I:162
A Non-Skid Ground Cloth	Philip E. Hacker	I:164
A Laminated Plywood Turntable	Thomas P. Sullivan	I:166
A Plasticene/Styrofoam Deck Plug	David C. Perlman	I:168
The "Perfect" Soft Floor	Neil Gluckman	I:169
Bondo® Floor Repairs	John E. Wainwright	II:160
The Triscuit-Studwall Deck System	Don Harvey	II:161
Using Medium-Density Fiberboard as a Deck Lid	Eric Weston	II:164
The Steel-Framed Texas Triscuit	Tim Francis	II:166

A Frameless Turntable	*Alys Holden*	II:168
Sand on Stage: Minimum Weight, Maximum Effect	*Jody Kovalik*	II:171
Doors on Rakes: Avoiding Gaps and Wedging	*Nathan Tomsheck*	III:192
The Flip Floor: A Two-Sided Deck Surface	*Bradley Powers*	III:194
A Tracking System for Tricsuit Decks	*Gegg Carlson*	III:197
An Interchangeable Lift-Lid System	*David Calica*	III:200
A Low-Profile Spung Floor	*Erich Bolton*	III:201
Two Methods for Planking Floors Quickly	*James Zwicky*	III:202
A Sandwich-Style Flip Floor	*Don Harvey*	III:205
Comparing Four Standard Stock Platforms: Part I - Weight, Cost, and Strength	*Sean Culligan*	III:207
Comparing Four Standard Stock Platforms: Part II - Structural Calculations	*Sean Culligan*	III:210
A Simple and Durable Touring Deck	*Joe Stoltman*	III:213
A Fast and Inexpensive Grooved Floor	*Hannah Shafran*	III:216

SCENERY ELECTRONICS

Sliding Electrical Contacts	*Arthur Oliner*	I:172
A Low-Voltage Remote Controller for Special Effects	*Kenneth J. Lewis*	I:174
Two Simple LED Circuits	*Tom Neville*	I:176
A Touch-Tone Relay Controller for Special Effects	*Steven E. Monsey*	I:179
Programmable Logic Controllers	*John Huntington III*	I:181
A Miniature Chase Controller	*Chih-Lung Liu*	II:174
A Low-Voltage Cue-Light System	*Geoff Zink*	II:176
Focusable Cue Lights	*O-Jin Kwon*	II:179

SCENERY HARDWARE

Floor-Mount Curved Track Using Polyethylene Pipe	*Mark Sullivan*	I:186
Underhung Hinge	*William Buck*	I:188
Nylon Rollers	*Ray Forton*	I:190
Nylon Rollers Modified	*Thomas G. Bliese*	I:192
Zero-Throw Casters	*James Bender*	I:193
A Simple Flush-Mount Hinge	*Kerro Knox 3*	I:195
An Elevator Door Hinge	*Victoria Peterson*	I:197
Toggle-Clamp Locks	*Richard Gold*	I:198
A Quick-Locking Jack	*C. Ken Cole*	I:201
A Second Drive for Elevator Drive Movement	*Don Harvey*	II:182
A Telescoping Fire Pole	*Chris Weida*	II:184
A Self-Paging Cable Tray	*Loren Schreiber*	II:186
Nylon Rollers Revisited	*James Ryan*	II:188
A Pipe and Ball-Bearing Pivot	*Vicky Peterson*	II:190
Weld-On Holes	*Randy Steffen*	II:193

A Wheel-less Revolve	*Jim Ryan*	II:194
A Tensioning Sheave for a Deck Winch System	*Andrew Lanzarotta*	II:197
A Spectacular Electrified Fence	*Ben Sumner*	II:199
Actor-Friendly Pneumatic Brakes	*Josh Prues*	III:220
A Simple Hydraulic Caster Lift System	*Steve Beatty*	III:222
A Floating Knife for Tracking Scenery	*Guerry Hood*	III:225
A Locking Mechanism for Telescoping Tubing	*Chris Brown*	III:227
A Caster Grid	*Justin McDaniel*	III:229
Opera-Scale Rotating Walls	*Timothy D. McCormick*	III:231
Tracked Scenery Using PVC Glides	*John D. Ervin*	III:234
Compact Toggled Tip-Jacks	*Stephen Henson*	III:236
Electromagnets as Scenic Connectors	*Mikey Rohrer*	III:238
Black Carpeting as a Glide for Narrow Scenic Units	*Don Harvey*	III:239

SCENERY MATERIALS

Corrugated (Kraft) Cardboard As a Scenic Material	*John Robert Hood*	I:204
Scenic Uses for Double-Stick Tape	*Anne LaCourt*	I:205
A Curved Handrail of WEP	*Michael E. Boyle and Raymond P. Forton*	I:207
Comparing Four Plastics as Scenery Glides	*Edmund B. Fisher*	I:210
Plastic Glides: A Second Look	*Karl Ruling and Scott Werbin*	I:213
Structural Fiberglass and its Applications	*Andi Lyons*	I:215

SCENERY MECHANICS

Basic Hydraulics	*Alan Hendrickson*	I:218
Low Pressure Air Casters	*David Kriebs*	I:221
Shop-Built Pneumatic Cylinders	*Michael Bianco*	I:224
Pneumatic Door Stabilizer	*Jeff Dennstaedt*	I:226
A Simple Lift Jack	*Mark Stevens*	I:229
A Pneumatic Floor Lock System	*Delbert L. Hall, Ph.D.*	II:202
Tap-Water Hydraulic Power	*Gregory Bell*	II:204
A System for Rotating Linked Periaktoi	*F. Leonard Darby*	II:207
A Telescope-Stabilized Lift Rig	*Corin Gutteridge*	II:210
A Spring-Driven Revolve	*Daniel J. Culhane*	II:213
Single-Orientation Curved Tracking	*A. D. Carson*	II:216
Rotating Doors	*Jim Kempf*	II:218
A Pneumatic Tab Turner	*Michael Patterson*	II:221
Roller Chain Turntable Drives	*Alan Hendrickson*	II:224
A Hand-Driven Endless-Loop Turntable Drive	*Alan Hendrickson*	II:227
A Plausible, Practical Raft	*Fred Ramage*	II:230
Flipping Trap Unit	*Robert Duggan*	II:233

A Control Rig for a Down-Opening Trapdoor	*Randy Steffen*	II:236
Mini-Paint-Roller Piston	*Loren Schreiber*	II:238
Guiding Scenery With Linear Bearings	*HaeWon Yang*	III:242
A Curved Track and V-Groove Caster Guide	*Nathan Wells*	III:244
Tripping Casters With Pneumatics: System Basics	*Kimberly Corbett*	III:246
Stabilizing Pneumatic Lift Jacks	*Steven Green*	III:249
Building Portable Pneumatic Systems: An Overview	*Lily Twining*	III:251
Using an Endless-Loop Winch as a One-Way Drive	*Jonathan Pellow*	III:254

SCENERY TOOLS

Styrofoam Molding Cutter	*Rob Chase*	I:232
A Jig for Installing Roto-Locks in Platform Decks	*Patrick Markle*	I:235
Homasote "Brick" Facings for the Stage	*Don Harvey*	I:237
A Pantograph Molding Jig	*Jeff Dennstaedt*	I:238
A System for Duplicating Steel Tube Frames	*Geoffrey Webb*	I:240
Door Vises for Edge Mortising	*Victoria Peterson*	I:241
A Simple Cut-off Jig	*Karl Ruling*	I:243
An Inexpensive Pipe-Clamp Bench Vise	*Patricia Bennett*	I:244
An Ethafoam Rod Splitter	*Mark Shanda*	I:245
A Swivel Caster Bolt-Hole Jig	*Bonnie McDonald*	II:240
A Shop-Built Adjustable Router Fence	*David Boevers*	II:241
A Tool for Mass-Producing Homasote Brickface	*Kevin Hines*	II:243
A Hot-Wire Bow for Cutting Blue Foam	*Doug Harvey*	II:245
A Shop-Built Circle Guide for Torch-Cutting	*Jim Larkin*	II:247
Scene Shop Tuffets	*Stephen Lars Klein*	II:249
Improved Scene Shop Tuffets	*Michael Immerwahr*	II:250
A 4-sided Steel-Marking Gauge	*Barbara J. Wohlsen*	II:251
A Jig for Cutting Ellipses	*Michael Parrella*	II:252
Two Useful Shop Tools	*F. Chase Rozelle III*	III:256
An Affordable Steel Roller	*Chris Brown*	III:257
Handy Tip Carts	*Steven Neuenschwander*	III:260
A Shop-Built Ladder Standoff	*Rich Desilets*	III:261
A Shop-Built Rotisserie for Welding Large Units	*Brian Dambacher*	III:262
A Winch-Driven Bench-Mount Panel Saw	*Jeff Smejdir*	III:264
A Shop-Built Sliding-Head Hold Down	*Eric Casanova*	III:267

SOUND

Using a Piano to Create a Reverberation Effect	*Serge Ossorguine*	I:248
A Versatile Audio Power Meter	*Steven E. Monsey*	I:250
Notes on Designing and Building a Concussion Mortar	*David C. Bell*	I:253
An Inexpensive Monitor Microphone	*Karl Ruling*	I:255
A Simple Audio Compressor/Limiter	*Jamie C. Anderson*	I:256

Horn-Hat Mics for Sound Reinforcement	*Tien-Tsung Ma*	I:258
An Audio Test-Tone Generator	*Jim van Bergen*	I:260
How to Use Your Headset as a Page Mic	*Darren Clark*	II:256
Amplified–to–Line Signal Converter	*Mark D. Dingley*	II:257
Two Head Attachment Methods for Wireless Microphones	*Rob Zoland*	II:258
A Device to Determine Sound System Polarity	*Chris Cronin*	II:259
Making a Prop Tape Player Cue-able	*Jon Cardone*	II:262
A Bench-Built XLR Tester	*Patrick Barrett*	II:265
Inexpensive Digital Noise Reduction	*Shane Rettig*	II:268
Two-Scene Sound Control	*Brian MacQueen*	II:270
Recreating an Acoustic Space with Discrete-6 Recording	*Brian MacQueen*	II:272